Unity 5.x Game Development Blueprints

A project-based guide to help you create amazing games with Unity 5.x

John P. Doran

[PACKT]
PUBLISHING

BIRMINGHAM - MUMBAI

Unity 5.x Game Development Blueprints

First published: May 2016

Production reference: 1190516

Published by Packt Publishing Ltd.
Livery Place
35 Livery Street
Birmingham B3 2PB, UK.

ISBN 978-1-78588-311-8

www.packtpub.com

Credits

Author
John P. Doran

Reviewer
Sebastian T. Koenig, Ph.D.

Commissioning Editor
Amarabha Banerjee

Acquisition Editor
Larissa Pinto

Content Development Editor
Prashanth G Rao

Technical Editor
Mohit Hassija

Copy Editor
Dipti Mankame

Project Coordinator
Bijal Patel

Proofreader
Safis Editing

Indexer
Rekha Nair

Production Coordinator
Arvindkumar Gupta

Cover Work
Arvindkumar Gupta

About the Author

John P. Doran is a technical game designer who has been creating games for over 10 years. He has worked on an assortment of games in teams consisting of just himself to over 70 people in student, mod, and professional projects in different roles, from game designer to lead UI programmer. He previously worked at LucasArts on *Star Wars: 1313* as a game designer. He later graduated from DigiPen Institute of Technology in Redmond, WA, with a Bachelor of Science in game design.

John is currently a part of DigiPen's Research and Development branch in Singapore in addition to DigiPen Game Studios. He is also the lead instructor of the DigiPen-Ubisoft Campus Game Programming Program, instructing graduate-level students in an intensive, advanced-level game programming curriculum. In addition to that, he also tutors and assists students in various subjects and gives lectures on C#, C++, Unreal, Unity, game design, and more.

He is the author of *Unreal Engine Game Development Cookbook, Building an FPS Game in Unity, Unity Game Development Blueprints, Getting Started with UDK, UDK Game Development, Mastering UDK Game Development,* and he cowrote *UDK iOS Game Development Beginner's Guide,* all available from Packt Publishing. More information about him can be found at http://johnpdoran.com.

Acknowledgments

A big thanks goes to my brother Chris and my wife Hien for being supportive and patient with me as I spent my free time and weekends away from them to finish the book.

On that same note, I also want to thank Samir Abou Samra and Elie Hosry for their support and encouragement while working on this book, as well as the rest of the DigiPen Singapore staff.

Having the opportunity to create an updated version of one of my favorite books was such a pleasure. With that in mind, I want to thank Nadeem Bagban for approaching me, Joel Ulahanna and Prashanth G for keeping me on track, and everyone else at Packt for being great as always.

Last but not least, I'd like to thank my family as well as my parents Joseph and Sandra Doran, who took me seriously when I told them I wanted to make games for a living.

About the Reviewer

Sebastian T. Koenig, Ph.D., received his doctorate in human interface technology from the University of Canterbury, New Zealand, developing a framework for individualized virtual reality cognitive rehabilitation. He obtained his diploma in psychology from the University of Regensburg, Germany, in the areas of clinical neuropsychology and virtual reality rehabilitation.

Dr. Koenig is the founder and CEO of Katana Simulations, where he oversees the design, development, and evaluation of cognitive assessment and training simulations. His professional experience spans over 10 years of clinical work in cognitive rehabilitation and virtual reality research, development, and user testing. Dr. Koenig has extensive experience as a speaker at international conferences and as a reviewer of scientific publications in the areas of rehabilitation, cognitive psychology, neuropsychology, software engineering, game development, game user research, and virtual reality.

Dr. Koenig has developed numerous software applications for cognitive assessment and training. For his work on the Virtual Memory Task, he was awarded the prestigious Laval Virtual Award in 2011 in the Medicine and Health category. Other applications of his include the virtual reality executive function assessment in collaboration with the Kessler Foundation, NJ, USA, and the patent-pending Microsoft Kinect-based motor and cognitive training JewelMine/Mystic Isle software at the USC Institute for Creative Technologies, CA, USA.

Dr. Koenig maintains the website http://www.virtualgamelab.com about his research and software development projects. His website also contains a comprehensive list of tutorials for the Unity game engine.

www.PacktPub.com

eBooks, discount offers, and more

Did you know that Packt offers eBook versions of every book published, with PDF and ePub files available? You can upgrade to the eBook version at www.PacktPub.com and as a print book customer, you are entitled to a discount on the eBook copy. Get in touch with us at customercare@packtpub.com for more details.

At www.PacktPub.com, you can also read a collection of free technical articles, sign up for a range of free newsletters and receive exclusive discounts and offers on Packt books and eBooks.

https://www2.packtpub.com/books/subscription/packtlib

Do you need instant solutions to your IT questions? PacktLib is Packt's online digital book library. Here, you can search, access, and read Packt's entire library of books.

Why subscribe?

- Fully searchable across every book published by Packt
- Copy and paste, print, and bookmark content
- On demand and accessible via a web browser

Table of Contents

Preface

Unity, available in free and pro versions, is one of the most popular third-party game engines available. It is a cross-platform game engine, making it easy to write your game once and then port it to PC, consoles, and even the Web, which makes it a great choice for both indie and AAA developers.

Unity 5.x Game Development Blueprints will takes you on an exploration of using Unity to the fullest extent, working on 3D and 2D titles, exploring how to create GUIs, and publishing the game for the world to see. Getting the opportunity to make a second edition of this book, I've updated each of the projects from the previous book to the latest version of Unity, making use of the latest features while also adding in three entirely new game projects for this book.

Using this book, you will be able to create a 2D twin-stick shooter, a clicker title, an endless runner, a shooting gallery, a side-scrolling platformer with an in-game level editor, a first-person survival horror shooter game, and a GUI menu system to use in all your future titles. In addition, you will learn how to publish your game with an installer to make your title look really polished and stand out from the crowd.

Each chapter either pushes your skills in Unity into new areas or pushes them to the very limits of what they can be used for.

What this book covers

Chapter 1, 2D Twin-stick Shooter, shows you how to create a 2D multidirectional shooter game. In this game, the player controls a ship that can move around the screen using the keyboard and shoot projectiles in the direction the mouse is pointing at. Enemies and obstacles will spawn towards the player, and the player will avoid/shoot them. This chapter also serves as a refresher for a lot of the concepts of working in Unity and gives an overview of Unity's native 2D tools.

Chapter 2, Creating GUIs, expands on our twin-stick shooter game, adding additional UI elements, including a main menu as well as a pause menu and options menu, and it gives us the ability to restart our project.

Chapter 3, GUIs Part 2 – Clicker Game, expands on our GUI knowledge with the implementation of a clicker game. Over the course of the chapter, you learn how to create and animate buttons, how to work with accessors (get/set functions), and how to build a simple shop for your projects dealing with UI assets such as Scrollviews and Masks.

Chapter 4, Mobile Endless Game – Procedural Content, has us building a game similar in gameplay to the popular mobile title *Flappy Bird* while learning how to create endless levels by creating content at runtime. In addition, we go over topics such as creating a repeating background, using sorting layers.

Chapter 5, Shooting Gallery – Working with Animations and Tweens, has you build a simple shooting gallery game in which players can shoot at targets before the time is up. In the meantime, you learn the various ways of animating things such as using Unity's built in animations or a tweening library such as iTween. Finally, we will use PlayerPrefs to set a new high score.

Chapter 6, Side-scrolling Platformer, shows you how to create a side-scrolling platformer. You learn the similarities between working in 2D and 3D and the differences, in particular, when it comes to physics.

Chapter 7, First Person Shooter Part 1 – Creating Exterior Environments, discusses the role of an environment artist who has been tasked to create an outdoor environment while learning about mesh placement. In addition, we will also learn some beginner-level design.

Chapter 8, First Person Shooter Part 2 – Creating Interior Environments, discusses the role of a level designer who has been tasked to create an interior environment using assets already provided to them by the environment artist.

Chapter 9, First Person Shooter Part 3 – Implementing Gameplay and AI, shows how we are going to be adding interactivity in the form of adding in enemies, shooting behaviors, and the gameplay to make our game truly shine. In addition, we'll also learn how to use an Xbox 360 controller to send input to our game.

Chapter 10, Building an In-Game Level Editor, talks about how we can add in functionality to our previously created side-scrolling platformer game in the form of an in-game level editor, which can be used for future projects. In addition, we'll also look at the Immediate Mode GUI System (IMGUI) to see how we can create GUI elements directly through code.

Chapter 11, Finishing Touches, talks about exporting our game from Unity and then creating an installer so that we can give it to all of our friends, family, and prospective customers!

What you need for this book

Throughout this book, we will work within the Unity 3D game engine, which you can download from http://unity3d.com/unity/download/. The projects have been created using version 5.3.4f1 but should work with minimal changes for future versions.

For the sake of simplicity, we will assume that you are working on a Windows-powered computer. Although Unity allows you to code in either C#, Boo, or UnityScript, for this book, we will be using C#.

Who this book is for

This book is best suited for C# developers who have some basic knowledge of the Unity game development platform. If you are looking to create exciting and interactive games with Unity and get a practical understanding of how to leverage key Unity features, then this book is your one-stop solution.

Conventions

In this book, you will find a number of text styles that distinguish between different kinds of information. Here are some examples of these styles and an explanation of their meaning.

Code words in text, database table names, folder names, filenames, file extensions, pathnames, dummy URLs, user input, and Twitter handles are shown as follows: " From the Project tab, double-click on the Sprites folder."

A block of code is set as follows:

```
public void ButtonClicked()
{
    controller.Cash -= cost;
    switch (itemType)
    {
        case ItemType.ClickPower:
            controller.cashPerClick += increaseAmount;
            break;
        case ItemType.PerSecondIncrease:
            controller.CashPerSecond += increaseAmount;
            break;
    }

    qty++;
    qtyText.text = qty.ToString();
}
```

When we wish to draw your attention to a particular part of a code block, the relevant lines or items are set in bold:

```
public void ButtonClicked()
{
    controller.Cash -= cost;
    switch (itemType)
    {
        case ItemType.ClickPower:
            controller.cashPerClick += increaseAmount;
            break;
        case ItemType.PerSecondIncrease:
            controller.CashPerSecond += increaseAmount;
            break;
    }

    qty++;
    qtyText.text = qty.ToString();
}
```

New terms and **important words** are shown in bold. Words that you see on the screen, for example, in menus or dialog boxes, appear in the text like this: "With Unity started and the launcher, select **New**. Select a **Name** and a **Project Location** of your choice somewhere on your hard drive, and ensure that you have **2D** set. Once completed, select **Create project**."

 Warnings or important notes appear in a box like this.

Tips and tricks appear like this.

Reader feedback

Feedback from our readers is always welcome. Let us know what you think about this book—what you liked or disliked. Reader feedback is important for us as it helps us develop titles that you will really get the most out of.

To send us general feedback, simply e-mail feedback@packtpub.com, and mention the book's title in the subject of your message.

If there is a topic that you have expertise in and you are interested in either writing or contributing to a book, see our author guide at www.packtpub.com/authors.

Customer support

Now that you are the proud owner of a Packt book, we have a number of things to help you to get the most from your purchase.

Downloading the example code

You can download the example code files for this book from your account at http://www.packtpub.com. If you purchased this book elsewhere, you can visit http://www.packtpub.com/support and register to have the files e-mailed directly to you.

You can download the code files by following these steps:

1. Log in or register to our website using your e-mail address and password.
2. Hover the mouse pointer on the **SUPPORT** tab at the top.
3. Click on **Code Downloads & Errata**.
4. Enter the name of the book in the **Search** box.
5. Select the book for which you're looking to download the code files.
6. Choose from the drop-down menu where you purchased this book from.
7. Click on **Code Download**.

Once the file is downloaded, please make sure that you unzip or extract the folder using the latest version of:

- WinRAR / 7-Zip for Windows
- Zipeg / iZip / UnRarX for Mac
- 7-Zip / PeaZip for Linux

The code bundle for the book is also hosted on GitHub at `https://github.com/PacktPublishing/Unity-5.x-Game-Development-Blueprints`. We also have other code bundles from our rich catalog of books and videos available at `https://github.com/PacktPublishing/`. Check them out!

Downloading the color images of this book

We also provide you with a PDF file that has color images of the screenshots/diagrams used in this book. The color images will help you better understand the changes in the output. You can download this file from `https://www.packtpub.com/sites/default/files/downloads/Unity5xGameDevelopmentBlueprints_ColorImages.pdf`.

Errata

Although we have taken every care to ensure the accuracy of our content, mistakes do happen. If you find a mistake in one of our books—maybe a mistake in the text or the code—we would be grateful if you could report this to us. By doing so, you can save other readers from frustration and help us improve subsequent versions of this book. If you find any errata, please report them by visiting http://www.packtpub. com/submit-errata, selecting your book, clicking on the **Errata Submission Form** link, and entering the details of your errata. Once your errata are verified, your submission will be accepted and the errata will be uploaded to our website or added to any list of existing errata under the Errata section of that title.

To view the previously submitted errata, go to https://www.packtpub.com/books/content/support and enter the name of the book in the search field. The required information will appear under the **Errata** section.

Piracy

Piracy of copyrighted material on the Internet is an ongoing problem across all media. At Packt, we take the protection of our copyright and licenses very seriously. If you come across any illegal copies of our works in any form on the Internet, please provide us with the location address or website name immediately so that we can pursue a remedy.

Please contact us at copyright@packtpub.com with a link to the suspected pirated material.

We appreciate your help in protecting our authors and our ability to bring you valuable content.

Questions

If you have a problem with any aspect of this book, you can contact us at questions@packtpub.com, and we will do our best to address the problem.

1
2D Twin-stick Shooter

The *shoot 'em up* genre of games is one of the earliest kinds of game. In a shoot 'em up, the player character is a single entity fighting a large number of enemies. They are typically played using a top-down or side-scrolling perspective, which is perfect for 2D games. Shoot 'em up games also exist within many other categories, based upon their design elements.

Elements of a shoot 'em up were first seen in the 1961 Spacewar! game. However, the concept wasn't popularized until 1978 with Space Invaders. The genre was quite popular throughout the 1980s and 1990s and went in many different directions, including *bullet hell* games, such as the titles of the Touhou Project. The genre has gone through a resurgence in recent years with games such as Bizarre Creations' *Geometry Wars: Retro Evolved*, which is more popularly known as a twin-stick shooter.

Project overview

Over the course of this chapter, we will be creating a 2D multidirectional shooter game similar to Geometry Wars.

In this game, the player controls a ship. This ship can move around the screen using the keyboard and shoot projectiles in the direction that the mouse is pointing. Enemies and obstacles will spawn toward the player, and the player will avoid/shoot them. This chapter will also serve as a refresher for a lot of the concepts of working in Unity and give an overview of the native 2D tools in Unity.

Your objectives

This project will be split into a number of tasks. It will be a simple step-by-step process from beginning to end. Here is the outline of our tasks:

- Setting up the project

- Creating our scene
- Adding player movement
- Adding shooting functionality
- Creating enemies
- Adding GameController to spawn enemy waves
- Particle systems
- Adding audio
- Adding points, score, and wave numbers
- Publishing the game

Prerequisites

Before we start, we will need to get the latest Unity version, which you can always get by going to `http://unity3d.com/unity/download/` and downloading it there:

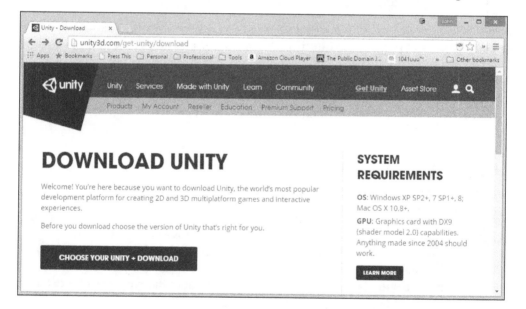

From here, you'll want to select the **Choose your Unity + Download** button and from the following menu select the edition of Unity you'd like to use and then download the Launcher.

Everything that we will be covering will work in the Personal Edition, unless I mention specifically otherwise. At the time of writing, the latest version is 5.3.4, but the project should work with minimal changes in future versions.

We will also need some graphical assets for use in our project. These can be downloaded from the example code provided for this book on Packt Publishing's website (`http://www.PacktPub.com`).

Navigate to the preceding URL, download the `Chapter1.zip` package, and unzip it. Inside the `Chapter1` folder, there are a number of things, including an `Art Assets` folder, which will have the art, sound, and font files you'll need for the project as well as the Twinstick Shooter folder which contains the finished project for you to take a look at.

Setting up the project

At this point, I assume that you have Unity freshly installed and have started it up.

1. With Unity started and the launcher, select **New**. Select a **Name** and a **Project Location** of your choice somewhere on your hard drive, and ensure that you have **2D** set. Once completed, select **Create project**. At this point, we will not need to import any packages, as we'll be making everything from scratch. Have a look at the following screenshot:

2. From there, if you see the **Welcome to Unity** popup, feel free to close it out as we won't be using it. At this point, you will be brought to the general Unity layout, as follows:

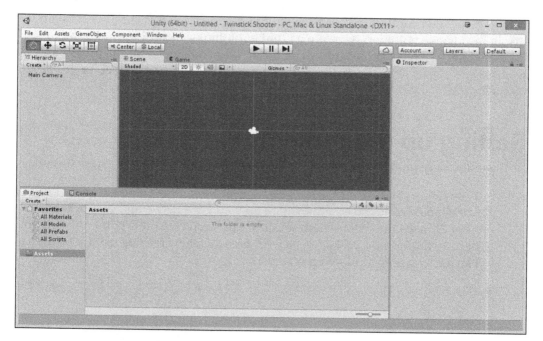

 Again, I'm assuming you have some familiarity with Unity before reading this book; if you would like more information on the interface, please visit http://docs.unity3d.com/ Documentation/Manual/LearningtheInterface.html.

Keeping your Unity project organized is incredibly important. As your project moves from a small prototype to a full game, more and more files will be introduced to your project. If you don't start organizing from the beginning, you'll keep planning to tidy it up later on, but as deadlines keep coming, things may get quite out of hand.

This organization becomes even more vital when you're working as part of a team, especially if your team is telecommuting. Differing project structures across different coders/artists/designers is an awful mess to find yourself in.

Setting up a project structure at the start and sticking to it will save you countless minutes in the long run and only takes a few seconds, which we'll be doing now. Perform the following steps:

1. Click on the **Create** drop-down menu below the **Project** tab in the bottom-left corner of the screen.

2. From there, click on **Folder,** and you'll notice that a new folder has been created inside your **Assets** folder.

3. After the folder is created, you can type in the name for your folder. Once done, press *Enter* for the folder to be created. We need to create folders for the following directories:

    ◦   Prefabs

    ◦   Scenes

    ◦   Scripts

    ◦   Sprites

If you happen to create a folder inside another folder, you can simply drag and drop it from the left-hand side toolbar. If you need to rename a folder, simply click on it once and wait, and you'll be able to edit it again.

You can also use *Ctrl + D* to duplicate a folder if it is selected.

4. Once you're done with the aforementioned steps, your project should look something like this:

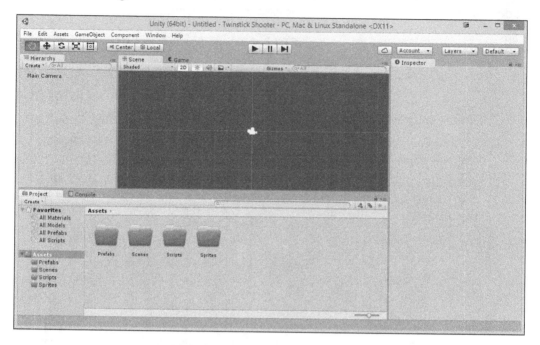

Creating our scene

Now that we have our project set up, let's get started with creating our player:

1. From the **Project** tab, double-click on the Sprites folder. Once inside, right-click within the Sprites folder and select **Import New Asset** to select the playerShip.png file from the Chapter 1/Art Assets folder from our example code to bring it in. Once added, confirm that the image's texture type is **Sprite** by clicking on it and from the Inspector tab, confirm that the **Texture Type** property is Sprite (2D and UI). If it isn't, simply change it to that, and then click on the **Apply** button. Have a look at the following screenshot:

If you do not want to drag and drop the files, you can also right-click within the `Sprites` folder in **Project Browser** (bottom-left corner) and select **Import New Asset** to select a file from the `Chapter 1/ Art Assets` folder to bring it in.

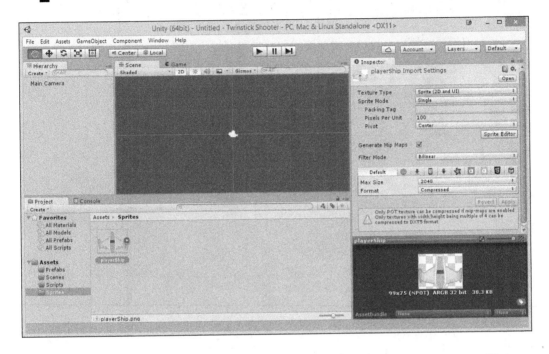

 The art assets used for this tutorial were provided by Kenney. To see more of their work, please check out www.kenney.nl.

2. Next, drag and drop the ship into the scene (the center part that's currently dark gray). Once completed, set the position of the sprite to the center of the screen (0, 0) by right-clicking on the **Transform** component and then selecting **Reset Position**. Have a look at the following screenshot:

Now, with the player in the world, let's add in a background. However, instead of creating a huge image or copying and pasting a similar image over and over, we will learn how we can use a material with a repeating texture.

3. From the **Project** tab, bring the background sprite into the project and then select it and change the **Texture Type** in the **Inspector** tab to **Texture**, and click on **Apply**.

4. Now, let's create a 3D cube by selecting **Game Object | Create Other | Cube** from the top toolbar. Change the object's name from **Cube** to Background. In the **Transform** component, change **Position** to (0, 0, 1) and the scale to (100, 100, 1).

Since our camera is at 0, 0, -10 and the player is at 0, 0, 0, putting the object at position 0, 0, 1 will put it behind all of our sprites. By creating a 3D object and scaling it, we are making it really large, much larger than the player's monitor. If we scaled a sprite, it would be one really large image with pixilation, which would look really bad. By using a 3D object, the texture that is applied to the faces of the 3D object is repeated, and since the image is tileable, it looks like one big continuous image.

5. As we won't be using it (and we're a 2D game), remove the BoxCollider component by right clicking on it from the Inspector tab and then selecting Remove Component.

6. Next, we will need to create a material for our background to use. To do so, under the **Project** tab, select **Create | Material**, and name the material `BackgroundMaterial`. We can create a new folder called `Materials` to store this, but since this project will only use one it is OK to stay in **Sprites**. Under the **Shader** property, click on the drop-down menu and select **Unlit | Texture**. Click on the **Texture** box on the right-hand side and select the background texture. Once completed, set the **Tiling** property's **x** and **y** to `25`. Have a look at the following screenshot:

> In addition to just selecting from the menu, you can also drag and drop the background texture directly onto the **Texture** box and it will set the property.
>
> Tiling tells Unity how many times the image should repeat in the **x** and **y** positions, respectively.

7. Finally, go back to the Background object in Hierarchy. Under the **Mesh Renderer** component, open up **Materials** by left-clicking on the arrow, and change **Element 0** to our **BackgroundMaterial** material. Consider the following screenshot:

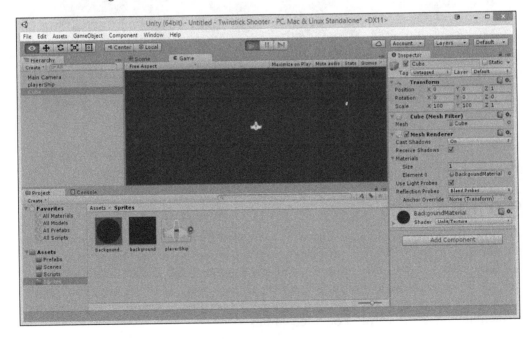

You can also add a material to an object by dragging and dropping the material onto the object in the **Scene** tab.

Well, at this point we have a color, but we don't have the stars from our image repeating.. This is due to how the **Wrap Mode** property is set. In Unity 5.2, the default mode is Clamp, which means that the edges of the image will be extended out rather than repeat. Let's fix that now.

8. From the **Project** tab, select the background texture object. Once selected, go to the **Inspector** tab, change the **Wrap Mode** to **Repeat**, and then click on **Apply**. Finally, select the Cube object from **Hierarchy** and then in the **Inspector** tab at the top, rename the object to Background.

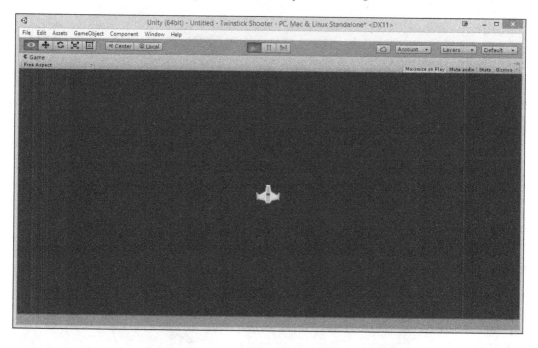

Now, when we play the game, you'll see that we now have a complete background that tiles properly.

Scripting 101

In Unity, the behavior of game objects is controlled by the different components that are attached to them in a form of association called composition. These components are things that we can add and remove at any time to create much more complex objects. If you want to do anything that isn't already provided by Unity, you'll have to write it on your own through a process we call **scripting**. Scripting is an essential element in all but the simplest of video games.

Unity allows you to code in either C#, Boo, or UnityScript, a language designed specifically for use with Unity and modeled after JavaScript. For this book, we will use C#.

C# is an object-oriented programming language – an industry-standard language similar to Java or C++. The majority of plugins from Asset Store are written in C#, and code written in C# can port to other platforms, such as mobile, with very minimal code changes. C# is also a strongly typed language, which means that if there is any issue with the code, it will be identified within Unity and will stop you from running the game until it's fixed. This may seem like a hindrance, but when working with code, I very much prefer to write correct code and solve problems before they escalate to something much worse.

Implementing player movement

Now, at this point, we have a great-looking game, but nothing at all happens. Let's change that now using our player. Perform the following steps:

1. Right-click on the **Scripts** folder you created earlier, click on **Create**, and select the **C# Script** label. Once you click on it, a script will appear in the **Scripts** folder, and it should already have focus and be asking you to type a name for the script – call it `PlayerBehaviour`.

> Note that I'm using Behaviour instead of Behavior. Either is fine to use as long as you're consistent, but since Unity's base script is called MonoBehaviour, I use the same spelling to avoid confusion.

2. Double-click on the script in Unity, and it will open **MonoDevelop** or **Visual Studio Community 2015** depending on how you installed Unity and what OS your computer is running.

> While code can be written in any program that can support text (such as Notepad), both of these pieces of software are integrated development environments (IDEs) that are created to make software development easier and more convenient to work with giving users access to useful features. MonoDevelop is open source, multi-platform, and is included with your Unity installation, but Visual Studio is a very popular tool with programmers and has some nice features that are exclusive to it. However, it can only be used for free by individual developers or for education and open source projects. For this book, we will not be doing anything specific to either IDE, so it's up to you which you'd like to use.

If you'd like to change which piece of software to use to open script files in Unity, you can go to the **Edit | Preferences** menu and then go to **External Tools** and under **External Script Editor**, click on the drop-down menu and select whichever you'd like to use.

After your IDE has loaded, you will be presented with the C# stub code that was created automatically for you by Unity when you created the C# script.

Let's break down what's currently there before we replace some of it with new code. At the top, you will see two lines:

```
using UnityEngine;
using System.Collections;
```

Detailed steps to download the code bundle are mentioned in the Preface of this book. Please have a look.

The code bundle for the book is also hosted on GitHub at https://github.com/PacktPublishing/Unity-5.x-Game-Development-Blueprints. We also have other code bundles from our rich catalog of books and videos available at https://github.com/PacktPublishing/. Check them out!!

The engine knows that if we refer to a class that isn't located inside this file, then it has to reference the contents within these namespaces for the referenced class before giving an error. We are currently using two namespaces.

The `UnityEngine` namespace contains interfaces and class definitions that let MonoDevelop know about all the addressable objects inside Unity.

The `System.Collections` namespace contains interfaces and classes that define various collections of objects, such as lists, queues, bit arrays, hash tables, and dictionaries. But we will not be using it in this file so you can remove that line.

The next line you'll see is:

```
public class PlayerBehaviour : MonoBehaviour {
```

You can think of a class as a kind of blueprint for creating a new component type that can be attached to GameObjects, the objects inside our scenes that start out with just Transform and then have components added to them. When Unity created our C# stub code, it took care of that; we can see the result, as our file is called PlayerBehaviour and the class is also called PlayerBehaviour. Make sure that your .cs file and the name of the class match, as they must be the same to enable the script component to be attached to a game object. Next up is the: MonoBehaviour section of the code. The : symbol signifies that we inherit from a particular class; in this case, it is set to MonoBehaviour. All behavior scripts must inherit from MonoBehaviour directly or indirectly by being derived from it. This idea of having classes inherit behavior is known as **inheritance**.

Inheritance is the idea of having an object to be based on another object or class using the same implementation. With this in mind, all of the functions and variables that exist inside the MonoBehaviour class will also exist in the PlayerBehaviour class, because PlayerBehaviour is a MonoBehaviour with the ability to add more to it.

> Checking Unity's Script Reference can be quite useful when determining what has already been done for you in Unity. For more information on the MonoBehaviour class and all of the functions and properties it has, check out http://docs.unity3d.com/ScriptReference/MonoBehaviour.html.

Directly after this line, we will want to add some variables to help us with the project. Variables are pieces of data that we wish to hold on to for one reason or another, typically because they will change over the course of a program, and we will do different things based on their values.

Add the following code under the class definition:

```
// Movement modifier applied to directional movement.
public float playerSpeed = 4.0f;

// What the current speed of our player is
private float currentSpeed = 0.0f;

// The last movement that we've made
private Vector3 lastMovement = new Vector3();
```

Between the variable definitions, you will notice comments to explain what each variable is and how we'll use it. To write a comment, you can simply add a // to the beginning of a line and everything after that is commented upon so that the compiler/interpreter won't see it. If you want to write something that is longer than one line, you can use /* to start a comment, and everything inside will be commented until you write */ to close it. It's always a good idea to do this in your own coding endeavors for anything that doesn't make sense at first glance.

> For those of you working on your own projects in teams, there is an additional form of commenting that Unity supports, which may make your life much easier: XML comments. They take up more space than the comments we are using, but also document your code for you. For a nice tutorial about that, check out http://bit.ly/xmlComments.

One of the things you'll notice is the public and private keywords before the variable type. These are access modifiers that dictate who can and cannot use these variables. The public keyword means that any other class can access that property, whereas private means that only this class will be able to access this variable. Here, currentSpeed is private because we want our current speed not to be modified or set anywhere else. But, you'll notice something interesting with the public variable that we've created. Go back into the Unity project and drag and drop the PlayerBehaviour script onto the playerShip object. Before going back to the Unity project though, make sure that you save your PlayerBehaviour script. Not saving is a very common mistake made by people when starting to code. Have a look at the following screenshot:

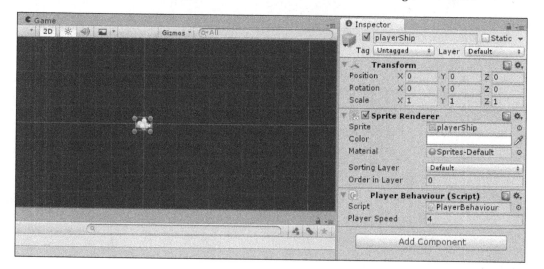

You'll notice now that the `public` variable that we created are located inside **Inspector** for the component. This means that we can actually set those variables inside **Inspector** without having to modify the code, allowing us to tweak values in our code very easily, which is a godsend for many game designers. You may also notice that the name for **Player Speed** has been changed to be more readable. This is because of the naming convention that we are using where each word starts with a capital letter. This convention is called `CamelCase` (more specifically `headlessCamelCase`).

Now that we have our variables set, go back to `MonoDevelop` for us to work on the script some more.

The line after that is a function definition for a method called `Start`; it isn't a user method but one that belongs to `MonoBehaviour`. Where variables are data, functions are the things that modify and/or use that data. Functions are self-contained modules of code (enclosed within braces { and }) that accomplish a certain task. The nice thing about using a function is that once a function is written, it can be used over and over again. Functions can be called from inside of other functions:

```
void Start () {

}
```

`Start` is only called once in the lifetime of the behavior when the game starts and is typically used to initialize data.

If you're used to other programming languages, you may be surprised that initialization of an object is not done using a constructor function. This is because the construction of objects is handled by the editor and does not take place at the start of gameplay as you might expect. If you attempt to define a constructor for a script component, it will interfere with the normal operation of Unity and can cause major problems with the project.

However, for this behavior, we will not need to use the `Start` function. Perform the following steps:

1. Delete the `Start` function and its contents.

   The next function that we see included is the `Update` function. Also inherited from `MonoBehaviour`, this function is called for every frame that the component exists in and for each object that it's attached to. We want to update our player ship's rotation and movement every turn.

2. Inside the Update function (between { and }), put the following lines of code:

```
// Rotate player to face mouse
Rotation();
// Move the player's body
Movement();
```

Here, I called two functions, but these functions do not exist because we haven't created them yet (and will possibly show up as red in your IDE because of that). Let's do that now!

3. Below the Update function and before the } that closes the class, put the following function to close the class:

```
// Will rotate the ship to face the mouse.
void Rotation()
{
  // We need to tell where the mouse is relative to the
  // player
  Vector3 worldPos = Input.mousePosition;
  worldPos = Camera.main.ScreenToWorldPoint(worldPos);

  /*
    * Get the differences from each axis (stands for
    * deltaX and deltaY)
  */
  float dx = this.transform.position.x - worldPos.x;
  float dy = this.transform.position.y - worldPos.y;

  // Get the angle between the two objects
  float angle = Mathf.Atan2(dy, dx) * Mathf.Rad2Deg;

  /*
    * The transform's rotation property uses a Quaternion,
    * so we need to convert the angle in a Vector
    * (The Z axis is for rotation for 2D).
  */
  Quaternion rot = Quaternion.Euler(new Vector3(0, 0, angle +
90));

  // Assign the ship's rotation
  this.transform.rotation = rot;
}
```

In this code, we are changing the rotation of the object we attached this script to (our player) based on where the player has put the mouse. Now, if you comment out the Movement line (by putting // in front of it) and run the game, you'll notice that the ship will rotate in the direction in which the mouse is. Have a look at the following screenshot:

If you did comment out the line, be sure to remove the // before continuing.

4. Below the Rotation function, we now need to add the following code in our Movement function:

```
// Will move the player based off of keys pressed
void Movement()
{
    // The movement that needs to occur this frame
    Vector3 movement = new Vector3();

    // Check for input
    movement.x += Input.GetAxis ("Horizontal");
    movement.y += Input.GetAxis ("Vertical");

    /*
      * If we pressed multiple buttons, make sure we're only
      * moving the same length.
    */
    movement.Normalize ();

    // Check if we pressed anything
    if(movement.magnitude > 0)
    {
        // If we did, move in that direction
        currentSpeed = playerSpeed;
        this.transform.Translate(movement * Time.deltaTime *
        playerSpeed, Space.World);
        lastMovement = movement;
    }
    else
    {
```

```
    // Otherwise, move in the direction we were going
    this.transform.Translate(lastMovement * Time.deltaTime *
currentSpeed, Space.World);
    // Slow down over time
    currentSpeed *= .9f;
  }
}
```

Now, inside this function, we use Unity's built in Input properties in order to set the x and y aspect of our movement vector and then move (or Translate) the ship in that direction. **Edit | Project Settings | Input** will open up Unity's **Input Manager**, which will have a list of different Axes that can be used for input.

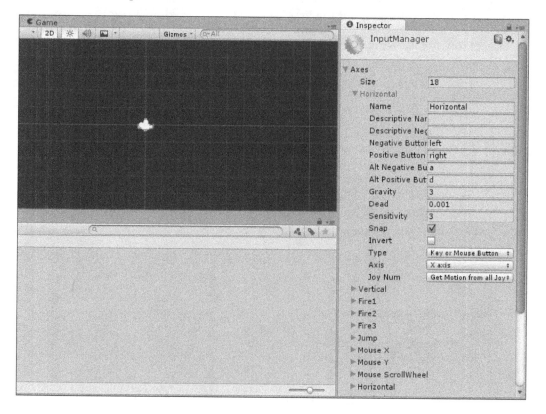

As you can see here, `left` and `a` are used in the **Negative Button** and **Alt Negative Button** properties respectively, so if we press either of those two it will give you a number between -1 and 1, with positive giving you a value between 0 and 1.

For more information on the Input Manager, check out:
`http://docs.unity3d.com/Manual/class-InputManager.html`.

5. Now, save your file and move back into Unity. Save your current scene as `Chapter_1.unity` by going to **File | Save Scene**. Make sure to save the scene to our `Scenes` folder we created earlier.

6. Run the game by pressing the play button on the top toolbar. And you should see something like the following screenshot:

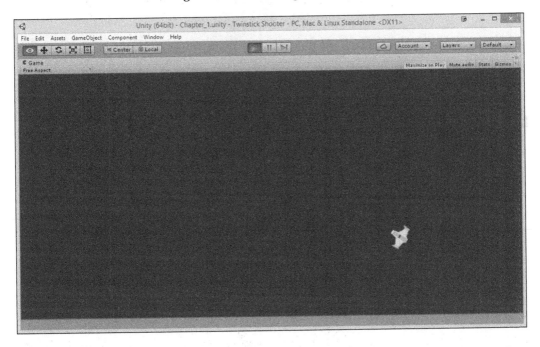

Now, you'll see that we can move using the arrow keys or the *W A S D* keys, and our ship will rotate to face the mouse. Great!

If you'd like to make your ship move faster and/or slower, increase or decrease the PlayerBehavior component's **Player Speed** variable inside the **Inspector** tab.

Shooting behavior

The next thing we will do is give our player the ability to shoot:

1. Open up the `PlayerBehaviour` script. In the top section where the other variables are present, we need to add some additional ones that we'll use:

```
// The laser we will be shooting
public Transform laser;

// How far from the center of the ship should the laser be
public float laserDistance = .2f;

// How much time (in seconds) we should wait before
// we can fire again
public  float   timeBetweenFires = .3f;

// If value is less than or equal 0, we can fire
private float timeTilNextFire = 0.0f;
```

One thing you may have noticed is that we have a `laser` variable that is of the type `Transform`. This is the laser we'll fire, which we will create shortly.

In our game, the player may want to shoot using either my clicking or the *Space* key. You may even want to use something else. Rather than restricting the player to just having one button or using an Axis like we did previously, we will store all of the possible ways to shoot in their own container. To do this, we are going to use a **list**, which is a holder for multiple objects that we can add or remove while the game is being played. However, to use a list, we will need to add the following to the top of our code:

```
using System.Collections.Generic; // List
```

 For more information on lists, check out `http://msdn.microsoft.com/en-us/library/6sh2ey19(v=vs.110).aspx`.

Afterwards, add the following variable below the others:

```
// The buttons that we can use to shoot lasers
public List<KeyCode> shootButton;
```

2. Inside our `Update` function, we will need to add some additional code, which is as follows:

```
// a foreach loop will go through each item inside of
// shootButton and do whatever we placed in {}s using the
// element variable to hold the item
foreach (KeyCode element in shootButton)
{
  if(Input.GetKey(element) && timeTilNextFire < 0)
  {
    timeTilNextFire = timeBetweenFires;
    ShootLaser();
    break;
  }
}

timeTilNextFire -= Time.deltaTime;
```

In this code we check each of the keys we allow the player to shoot with (such as the spacebar and *Enter* keys). If they press any of these keys and can fire again, then we will reset our timer and shoot a laser. However, we haven't made the `ShootLaser` function. Let's do that now.

3. Underneath the functions, add the following function:

```
// Creates a laser and gives it an initial position in
// front of the ship.
void ShootLaser()
{
  // We want to position the laser in relation to
  // our player's location
  Vector3 laserPos = this.transform.position;
  // The angle the laser will move away from the center
  float rotationAngle = transform.localEulerAngles.z - 90;
  // Calculate the position right in front of the ship's
  // position laserDistance units away
  laserPos.x += (Mathf.Cos((rotationAngle) *
              Mathf.Deg2Rad) * -laserDistance);
  laserPos.y += (Mathf.Sin((rotationAngle) *
              Mathf.Deg2Rad) * -laserDistance);

  Instantiate(laser, laserPos, this.transform.rotation);
}
```

4. Save your file, and go back into Unity. You'll now see a number of additional variables that we can now set.

 If, for some reason, your **Inspector** window doesn't update, save your project and restart Unity. Upon reset, it should be updated.

5. Now, change the **Size** of each of the **Shoot Button** variables to 2, and fill in the **Element 0** value with Mouse0 and **Element 1** with Space. When you've finished, it should look something like the following screenshot:

Inspector

	playerShip		Static ▾
Tag	Untagged ⬍	Layer	Default ⬍

Transcript

Transform

Position	X 0	Y 0	Z 0
Rotation	X 0	Y 0	Z 0
Scale	X 1	Y 1	Z 1

Sprite Renderer

Sprite	playerShip
Color	
Material	Sprites-Default
Sorting Layer	Default
Order in Layer	0

Player Behaviour (Script)

Script	PlayerBehaviour
Player Speed	4
Laser	None (Transform)
Laser Distance	0.2
Time Between Fires	0.3
▾ Shoot Button	
Size	2
Element 0	Mouse 0
Element 1	Space

Add Component

6. Next, we will need to create our laser to fill in the **Laser** variable. Go back into our Assets folder from the example code, and move the laser.png file into our **Project** tab's Sprites folder.

7. Following that, drag and drop it into your scene from the **Scene** tab to place it in the level.

8. Right-click the `Scripts` folder you created earlier, click on **Create**, and select the **C# Script** label. Call this new script `LaserBehaviour`. Go into your IDE, and use the following code:

```
using UnityEngine;
using System.Collections;

public class LaserBehaviour : MonoBehaviour
{
    // How long the laser will live
    public float lifetime = 2.0f;

    // How fast will the laser move
    public float speed = 5.0f;


    // How much damage will this laser do if we hit an enemy
    public int damage = 1;

    // Use this for initialization
    void Start ()
    {
        // The game object that contains this component will be
        // destroyed after lifetime seconds have passed
        Destroy(gameObject, lifetime);
    }

    // Update is called once per frame
    void Update ()
    {
        transform.Translate(Vector3.up * Time.deltaTime * speed);
    }
}
```

9. Attach `LaserBehaviour` to the laser object. Finally, add a **Box Collider 2D** component by first selecting the laser object and then going to **Component | Physics 2D | Box Collider 2D**. The collision box, by default, will be the size of the image, but I want to shrink it to fit what is inside of it. To do that, we will change the **Size** attribute's **X** property to `.09` and **Y** to `.5`. To see exactly what we're modifying, you can zoom in the camera by using the mouse wheel in the **Scene** tab:

Now, the laser will move in the direction that it's facing and die after a period of two seconds! Next, let's make it so that the player can shoot them.

10. To differentiate this object from the `laser` sprite that we used to create it, select your laser object in the **Hierarchy** tab and then under the **Inspector** change its name to `Laser`.

11. In the **Project** tab, go to the **Assets | Prefabs** folder, and drag and drop the Laser object from our **Hierarchy** tab into it. You'll notice that the object **Hierarchy** will turn blue to show that it is a prefab.

Prefabs or prefabricated objects are the objects that we set aside to make copies during runtime, such as our bullets and eventually enemies that we'll spawn into the world, and we can create as many as we want. When you add a prefab to a scene, you create an instance of it. All of these instances are clones of the object located in our `Assets`. Whenever you change something in the prefab located in our `Prefab` folder, those changes are applied to all of the objects that are already inside of your scene. For example, if you add a new component to `Prefab`, all of the other objects we have in the scene will instantly contain the component as well. We can also apply any of the ones in our scene to be the blueprint for the others as well, which we will do later on. However, it is also possible to change the properties of a single instance while keeping the link intact. Simply change any property of a prefab instance inside your scene, and that particular value will become bolded to show that the value is overridden, and they will not be affected by changes in the source prefab. This allows you to modify prefab instances to make them different (unique) from their source prefabs without breaking the prefab link.

Have a look at the following screenshot:

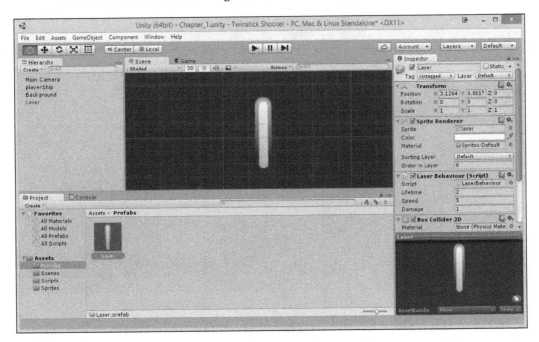

12. Now, because we have the prefab created, we don't need the original in the scene because we'll be spawning them instead. With that in mind, delete the Laser object from our scene, and then go to the playerShip object. For clarity, rename it to Player Ship and then drag and drop the Laser prefab from the **Project** tab into the **Laser** property of the PlayerBehavior component.

13. Finally, we want our player to have collision as well, so let's add a circle collider to our ship by going to **Component | Physics 2D | Circle Collider 2D.** Change the **Radius** property to 0.3.

Generally, in games, we want to be as efficient as possible toward calculations. Polygon collision is the most accurate collision, but it is much slower than using a box or a circle. In this case, I wanted to use a circle, because not only is it more efficient but also allows the player some leeway in how close they can get to enemies without being hurt. Players will always think it's their skill if they get away, but if the collider is too big they will think the game is broken, which we want to avoid.

Have a look at the following screenshot:

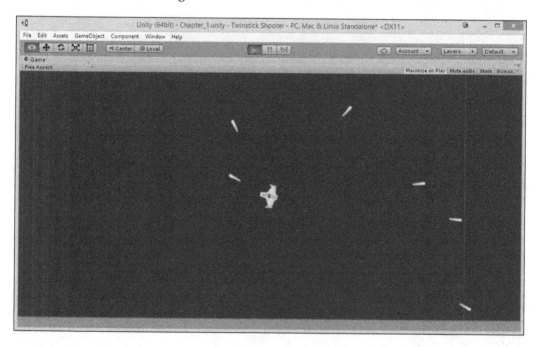

Now, our ship can shoot in the direction that the mouse is currently facing.

Creating enemies

Now, it's really cool that we have a player, but it'll get really boring if all we can do is move around and shoot some lasers in the dark. Next, we'll introduce some simple enemies that will move toward the player that we'll be able to shoot later. Perform the following steps:

1. Leave the game by pressing the Play button again and then access our example code's `Assets` folder; move the `enemy.png` file into our `Sprites` folder.

2. Following that, drag and drop it into your scene from the **Scene** tab to place it in the level.

3. Right-click on the **Scripts** folder you created earlier, click on **Create**, and select the **C# Script** label. Call this new script `MoveTowardsPlayer`. Go to `MonoDevelop` and use the following code:

```csharp
using UnityEngine;
using System.Collections;

public class MoveTowardsPlayer : MonoBehaviour
{
  private Transform player;
  public float speed = 2.0f;

  // Use this for initialization
  void Start ()
  {
    player = GameObject.Find("playerShip").transform;
  }

  // Update is called once per frame
  void Update ()
  {
    Vector3 delta = player.position - transform.position;
    delta.Normalize();
    float moveSpeed = speed * Time.deltaTime;
    transform.position = transform.position + (delta *
    moveSpeed);
  }
}
```

In the beginning of the game, I find the player ship and get his `Transform` component. Then, in every frame of the project, we move the enemy from where it currently is to the direction where the player is at.

The GameObject.Find function is very useful as it allows us to access objects at any time, but is computationally expensive, so don't put it in a function that gets called often (such as Update) when you can just save a reference to it. It's also important to note that the spelling of the parameter has to be exactly the same as the object's name in the hierarchy; so be sure to double check when you use it.

 If you ever want to have objects run away from the player, use a negative speed.

4. Drag and drop this newly added behavior onto our enemy object and rename it to Enemy.

5. Next, add a circle collider to our enemy by going to **Component | Physics 2D | Circle Collider 2D**. Change the **Radius** property to .455, and run the game. Have a look at the following screenshot:

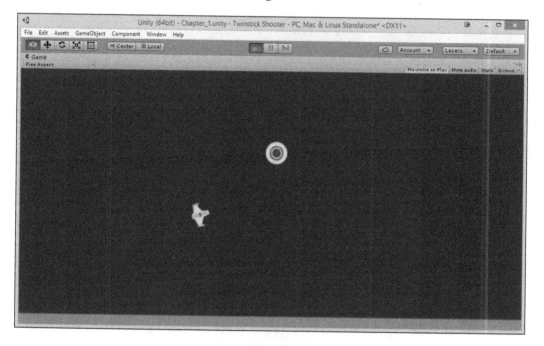

Now, you'll see that the enemy will always move toward you! But if we shoot it, nothing happens. Let's fix that as follows:

1. Right-click on the **Scripts** folder you created earlier, click on **Create**, and select the **C# Script** label. Call this new script `EnemyBehaviour`. Go to `MonoDevelop` (your IDE of choice,), and use the following code:

```csharp
using UnityEngine; // MonoBehaviour

public class EnemyBehaviour : MonoBehaviour
{

    // How many times should I be hit before I die
    public int health = 2;

    void OnCollisionEnter2D(Collision2D theCollision)
    {
        // Uncomment this line to check for collision
        //Debug.Log("Hit"+ theCollision.gameObject.name);

        // this line looks for "laser" in the names of
        // anything collided.
        if(theCollision.gameObject.name.Contains("laser"))
        {
            LaserBehaviour laser =
            theCollision.gameObject.GetComponent
            ("LaserBehaviour") as        LaserBehaviour;
            health -= laser.damage;
            Destroy (theCollision.gameObject);
        }

        if (health <= 0)
        {
            Destroy (this.gameObject);
        }
    }
}
```

Now, you will notice that we have commented a line of code calling the function `Debug.Log`. This function when called will print something onto your console (in this case, name the object that we collided with), which may help you when debugging your own code in the future.

It's also important to note the reason we ask if the name contains Laser instead of is equal to is because when you create an object using Instantiate, by default it will add " (Clone)" to the end of the name of the object.

2. We also want to tell the objects to actually react to collision events so we will need to add **Rigidbody 2D** physics to the object, which is required one of the two objects involved in a collision in order for OnCollisionEnter2D to be called.

3. Select the Enemy object and then select **Component | 2D Physics | Rigidbody 2D**. From there, change the **GravityScale** value to 0 so that the object will not fall down by default due to gravity.

4. Save your script, and then go back into Unity. Attach the EnemyBehaviour behavior to your enemy object, save your project, and run the game. If all went well, we should have something like the following screenshot:

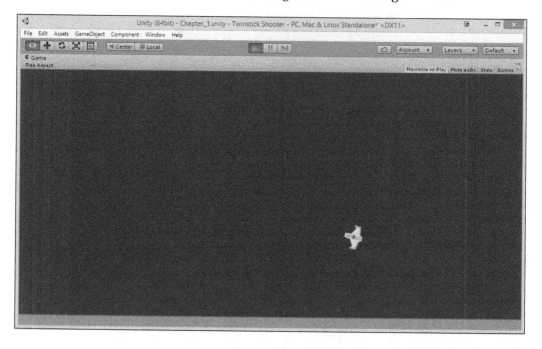

Now, whenever we hit the enemy with our bullets twice, it will die. Nice!

Adding GameController to spawn enemy waves

We have all of the mechanics of our game completed at this point. Now, we need to actually create the game or manage what happens in the game. This game controller would be required to run our game, keep track of and display the game's score, and finally end the game whenever the player dies. Later on, we'll discuss a game state manager, which we can use for larger projects with multiple states, but for the sake of this simple project, we will create a simple game controller, and that's what we'll do now:

1. First, create an empty game object by going to **Game Object | Create Empty**. From there, with the object selected, go to **Inspector** and set its name to **Game Controller**, and optionally, for neatness sake, set its **Position** to (0, 0, 0). As this is our main game object, I'm also going to drag it up on the **Hierarchy** tab so that it is the top object on the list.

2. Underneath the name, you'll see the **Tag** property. Change it from **Untagged** to **GameController**.

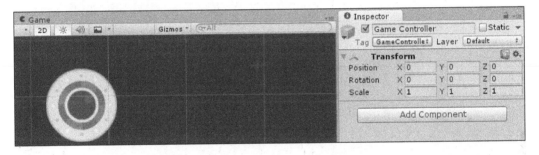

> A **Tag** is a way to link to one or more game objects in a collected group. For instance, you might use **Player** and **Enemy** tags for players and enemies respectively; a **Collectable** tag could be defined for power-ups or coins that are placed in the scene, and so on. This could also have been used with **EnemyBehaviour** to check whether something was a bullet or not. One thing to note is the fact that **GameObject** can only have one tag assigned to it. Tags do nothing to the scene but are a way to identify game objects for scripting purposes.

3. Next, let's see another way that we can create scripts quickly. From the **Inspector** tab, select **Add Component | New Script**, and once you are brought to the next menu, change the language to C#, and set the name of the script to GameController.

4. Select the newly created script, and move it to the `Assets\Scripts` folder. Go to your IDE of choice by double-clicking on the script file.

   While our game does many things, the most important thing is the spawning of enemies, which is what we'll be adding in first. Let's create a variable to store our enemy.

5. Inside of the class definition, add the following variable:

```
// Our enemy to spawn
public Transform enemy;
```

6. Now, we can set the enemy that we currently have in the scene, but we should instead make the enemy a prefab and use it. To do so, drag the enemy from **Hierarchy** into your `Assets\Prefabs` folder. Once we've created the prefab, we can remove the enemy object from our scene by deleting it.

7. Next, drag and drop the enemy prefab into the **Enemy** variable in the **GameController** component.

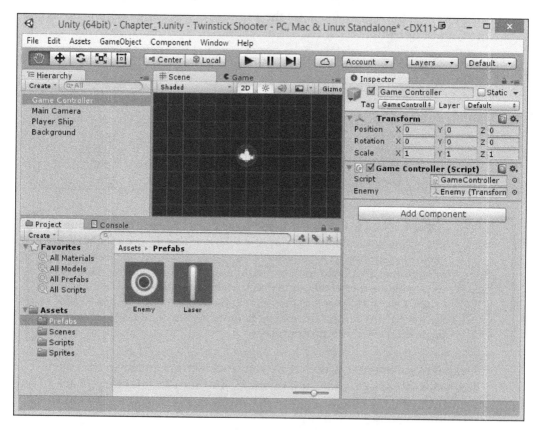

8. Next, go back into our `GameController` script by double-clicking it to go into **MonoDevelop**. Add the following additional variables to the component:

```
[Header("Wave Properties")]
// We want to delay our code at certain times
public float timeBeforeSpawning = 1.5f;
public float timeBetweenEnemies = .25f;
public float timeBeforeWaves = 2.0f;

public  int enemiesPerWave = 10;
private int currentNumberOfEnemies = 0;
```

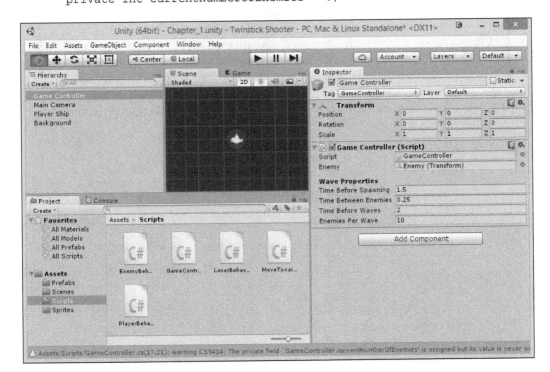

Now, if we save the script and go back into the editor, you'll notice a couple of interesting things. First of all, you'll see that due to the Header that we added to our script, the script has been separated into sections to make it easier to compartmentalize our code. In addition, we also see a warning on the bottom-left of the screen saying that we haven't used our variables yet. You can click on it to open up the Console window to look at it, but with that in mind, let's make it so that we are actually using the variables.

We now need a function to spawn enemies; let's call it SpawnEnemies. We don't want to spawn all of the enemies at once. What we want is a steady stream of enemies to come to the player over the course of the game. However, in C#, to have a function pause the gameplay without having to stop the entire game, we need to use a coroutine that looks different from all of the code that we've used so far.

9. Inside the Start method, add the following line:

```
StartCoroutine(SpawnEnemies());
```

 A **coroutine** is like a function that has the ability to pause execution and continue where it left off after a period of time. By default, a coroutine is resumed on the frame after we start to yield, but it is also possible to introduce a time delay using the WaitForSeconds function for how long you want to wait before it's called again.

10. Now that we are already using the function, let's add in the SpawnEnemies function as follows:

```
// Coroutine used to spawn enemies
IEnumerator SpawnEnemies()
{
    // Give the player time before we start the game
    yield return new WaitForSeconds(timeBeforeSpawning);

    // After timeBeforeSpawning has elapsed, we will enter
    // this loop
    while(true)
    {
        // Don't spawn anything new until all of the previous
        // wave's enemies are dead
        if(currentNumberOfEnemies <= 0)
        {

            //Spawn 10 enemies in a random position
            for (int i = 0; i < enemiesPerWave; i++)
            {
                // We want the enemies to be off screen
                // (Random.Range gives us a number between the
                // first and second parameter)
                float randDistance = Random.Range(10, 25);

                // Enemies can come from any direction
```

```
    Vector2 randDirection =
      Random.insideUnitCircle;
    Vector3 enemyPos =
      this.transform.position;

    // Using the distance and direction we set the
    // position
    enemyPos.x += randDirection.x * randDistance;
    enemyPos.y += randDirection.y * randDistance;

    // Spawn the enemy and increment the number of
    // enemies spawned
    // (Instantiate Makes a clone of the first
    // parameter
    // and places it at the second with a rotation of
    // the third.)
    Instantiate(enemy, enemyPos, this.transform.rotation);
    currentNumberOfEnemies++;
    yield return new
    WaitForSeconds(timeBetweenEnemies);
    }
  }
  // How much time to wait before checking if we need to
  // spawn another wave
  yield return new WaitForSeconds(timeBeforeWaves);
  }
}
```

The ++ operator will take the current value of a number and increment it by 1.

11. Now, when we destroy an enemy, we want to decrement the number of currentNumberOfEnemies, but it's a private variable, which means that it can only be changed inside the GameController class or one of the methods inside of the class. Simple enough? Now, let's add a new function in our GameController class:

```
// Allows classes outside of GameController to say when we
// killed an enemy.
public void KilledEnemy()
{
  currentNumberOfEnemies--;
}
```

12. Finally, let's go back into our EnemyBehaviour class. Inside the
    OnCollisionEnter2D function under the Destroy function call,
    add the following lines:

    ```
    GameController controller = GameObject.FindGameObjectWithTag("Game
    Controller").GetComponent<GameController>();
    controller.KilledEnemy();
    ```

    The preceding line gets the script GameController from the game object that
    has the GameController tag.

    This will call the KilledEnemy function from GameController, onto which
    we set the GameController tag in step 2.

13. With all those changes, save both script files and run the game! Have a look
    at the following screenshot:

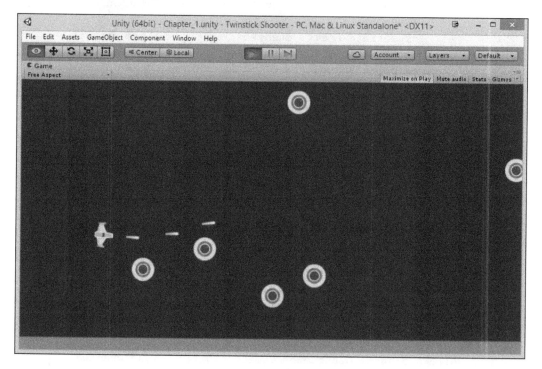

We now have waves of enemies that will now move toward the player! When we kill
all of the enemies inside a wave, we will spawn the next wave. In such a short period
of time, we already have so much going on!

Particle systems for enemy explosion

Now that we have the basis for our game, let's spend some time to make the project look nicer. Particle systems are one of my go-to things to add juiciness to a game project and helps to set your project apart from others. Particle systems are composed of two separate parts: a particle and the thing that emits it (called an emitter). A particle is a small object that stores properties; generally, we try to make these objects as simple as possible, as we want to spawn a large number of them. The emitter's job is to spawn a number of these and initialize their properties. Thankfully, Unity has a fully featured particle editor that's included with the engine, and we're going to use it in this section. Perform the following steps:

1. Create a new particle system by going to **GameObject | Particle System**. Have a look at the following screenshot:

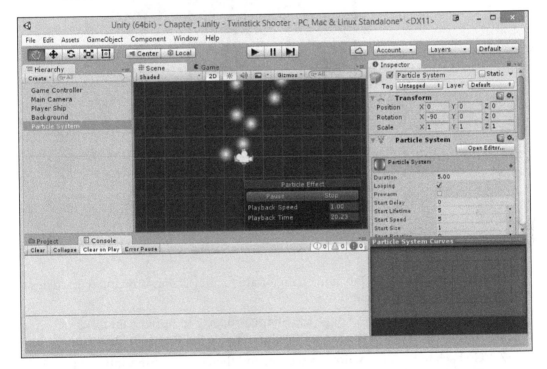

Once you do this, you should see a default particle system show up. Do note that the system will only animate if it is the object selected and Unity is the active window.

2. Change the object's name to `Explosion`. First, under the **Particle System** tab, change **Duration** to `1.00`.

3. Click on the arrow on the right-hand side of **Start Lifetime**, and change the values to be **Random Between Two Constants**. Change those values to 0 and 1. Do the same with **Start Speed**. Make **Start Size** use random values between 0 and .5.

4. Next, we will set the object's **Start Color** value to the same color as the UFO ship (you can use the eyedropper tool or set it to 210, 224, 230) and an **Alpha** value of 125. Have a look at the following screenshot:

5. Open the **Emission** tab, and change **Rate** to 200. This is how many particles are spawned at a time.

6. Open the **Shape** tab, change the **Shape** property to **Sphere**, and then set **Radius** to .35 to fit the rim of the ship. Enable the **Random Direction** option.

7. Go back to the top **Explosion** section and then change **Simulation Space** to **World**; that way, if this object moves, the already-spawned particles will not move. After this, still in the **Explosion** section, uncheck **Looping**.

8. At this point, you'll need to click on the **Stop** and **Simulate** buttons to see how the properties change while we make adjustments.

9. Now, make this object a prefab by dragging and dropping it into the Prefabs folder. After that, delete the Explosion object in your **Hierarchy** object.

10. Go back to your `EnemyBehaviour` script file. We will first want to add in a new variable for us to use to spawn this explosion when it dies:

```
// When the enemy dies, we play an explosion
public Transform explosion;
```

11. Back in the **Project** tab, drag and drop your new Explosion prefab to fill in the explosion variable slot in our Enemy prefab.

12. Coming back to the `EnemyBehaviour` script, let's spawn an explosion whenever we die. Inside your `if(health <= 0)` section of `OnCollisionEnter2D`, add in the following lines:

```
// Check if explosion was set
if(explosion)
{
    GameObject exploder = ((Transform)Instantiate(explosion, this.
transform.position, this.transform.rotation)).gameObject;
    Destroy(exploder, 2.0f);
}
```

As you can see here, we use the Instantiate function in order to create an explosion and we call the Destroy function to have it automatically delete itself (the first parameter) after 2 seconds as passed (the second parameter).

13. Save your script and scene files, and run your project! Have a look at the following screenshot:

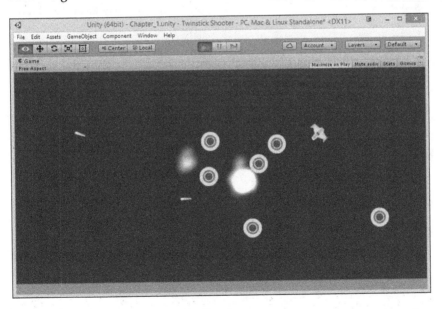

And now, whenever an enemy dies, it will spawn an explosion for us to see!

Adding in sound effects/music

Another thing that we can do to give the project a little more polish is add in sound effects and background music. Let's do that now. Perform the following steps:

1. Select your **enemy** prefab, and add an **Audio Source** component to it by selecting **Component | Audio | Audio Source**.

2. From there, go into the **Inspector** and uncheck the **Play On Awake** property. Otherwise, if there is something attached to **AudioClip** it will play that sound automatically.An **audio source** lets the audio listener attached to the **Main Camera** object know that this is an object that can play sounds.

3. After this, let's go into our `EnemyBehaviour` script! As usual, we'll need to add in a new variable for us to use to play whenever we're hit:

    ```
    // What sound to play when hit
    public AudioClip hitSound;
    ```

4. Next, go into the `CollisionEnter2D` function. After the `Destroy(theCollision.gameObject)` line, add the following code:

    ```
    // Plays a sound from this object's AudioSource
    GetComponent<AudioSource>().PlayOneShot(hitSound);
    ```

    In this instance, I used the `GetComponent` function to access the `AudioSource` component that is attached to the game object this is attached to. It is important to note that `GetComponent` is a fairly expensive function to call. Since this will only be used once, it's OK to use like this; but if you were to use this more than once, I would suggest creating an `AudioSource` variable and setting it in the `Start` function instead like we will be doing in the next section.

    > For more information about the `PlayOneShot` function, check out `http://docs.unity3d.com/ScriptReference/AudioSource.PlayOneShot.html`.
    >
    > For more information on the **Audio Source** component (audio), check out `http://docs.unity3d.com/ScriptReference/AudioSource.html`.

5. Now, we need some actual sounds to play. I've set aside a folder of assets for you in the `Example Code` folder, so open your project folder via your **Explorer** and move the folder into your project's `Assets` and then return to Unity.

6. Back in the inspector for our enemy, let's set the `Hit Sound` variable in the `EnemyBehaviour` script to the hit sound that we've imported by using drag and drop. Now, if we play the game, when we hit an enemy, the sound will be played! Now, let's have a sound if we destroy the enemy!

7. Go to the **Explosion** prefab, and add an **Audio Source** component in the same way we did in step 1; however, make sure that the **Play On Awake** property is still checked. After this, set the **Audio Clip** property in the component to the `explode` sound.

   Now, if you play the game, hitting the object will play one sound, and when the object is destroyed, the explosion will play a sound. Because the sound is in the **Audio Clip** property, we can just check **Play On Awake** or call the `Play` function. However, if you want an object to play multiple sounds, it's better to have separate `AudioClip` variables just as we did with `EnemyBehaviour`.

8. Finally, I want to play a sound whenever we fire a shot. To do that, let's go to `playerShip` and add an audio source.

9. Next, go into `PlayerBehaviour`, and add in two new variables, as follows:

   ```
   // What sound to play when we're shooting
   public AudioClip shootSound;

   // Reference to our AudioSource component
   private AudioSource audioSource;
   ```

10. Then, we need to initialize the audio property, so add a `Start` function with the following:

    ```
    void Start()
    {
      audioSource = GetComponent<AudioSource>();
    }
    ```

11. After this, whenever we shoot a bullet, let's play the new sound at the beginning of the `ShootLasers` function:

    ```
    audioSource.PlayOneShot(shootSound);
    ```

12. Coming back to **Inspector**, set the **Shoot Sound** property in the `PlayerBehaviour` component to the `shoot` sound effect.

13. Finally, let's add in our background music. Go to your **Main Camera** object in **Hierarchy**. Add an **Audio Source** component. Change **Audio Clip** to **bgm**, check the **Loop** option, and set **Volume** to `.25`.

[The background music is provided for this project by Stratkat (Kyle Smith). If you are interested in more of his work, check out his website at http://daydreamanatomy.bandcamp.com/.]

14. Save everything, and run the game!

Although we won't see any changes at this point for those of you actually running the game, you'll notice quite a change when the game is started. It's already feeling much more like a game.

Adding in points, score, and wave numbers

One of the most important things to do in a game is reward the player and give them a sense of progression. For now, let's reward the player with a score we will display for them and also let the player know exactly which wave he is on. Perform the following steps:

1. Create a new **Text** object by going to the **Hierarchy** tab and selecting **Create | UI | Text**.

   You'll notice that three objects get created at this point: **Canvas, Text**, and **Event System**. Right now, we only need to worry about **Text**; however, the three objects are all needed in order for Unity's new UI system to function properly. We will be discussing this in much more detail in a later chapter.

2. Next, select the **Text** object again and notice that the top of it has a **Rect Transform** component instead of a **Transform**. This is a special transform that is used to position UI elements on the screen relative to other objects that are also part of the UI.

3. In this case, we want the text to be located in the top-left, but currently you may not be able to see the text at all. You can double-click on the object to zoom out and see it more clearly.

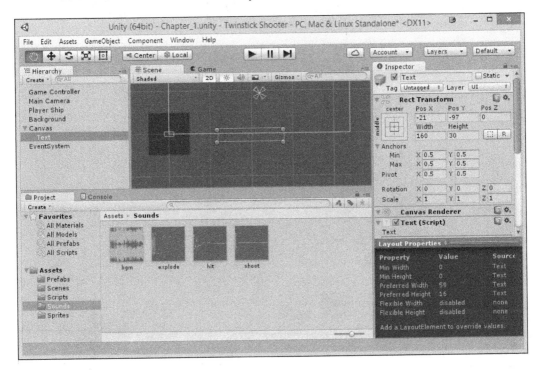

As you can see, the text is much larger than the player, and there seems to be a white box surrounding the object. This is a representation of what the UI will look like, with the white box being the screen. Rect Transform is currently set up to represent a position of (0,0) to be the center of the world and currently the text is -21 pixels away from the center in the x axis and -97 in the y. If we were to change it to (0,0), you'd notice that the text would now be centered.

4. Rename the Text object to Score Counter and then change the **Anchors Min Max** and **Pivot** properties to (0, 1); then reset **Pos X** to 10 and **Pos Y** to -10 to move them slightly away from the edge of the screen. Lastly, change the **Color** to white to make it easier to see.

5. Now that we have the text set up, let's set the font. Bring the **Font** folder into your project. Then, set **Font** to OSP-DIN and **Font Size** to 25.

> The font used in this project was created by the OSP Foundry. For more information about their stuff, check out http://ospublish. constantvzw.org/foundry/.

6. Next, duplicate the **Score Counter** object by right-clicking and selecting **Duplicate**. Set this duplicate's name to `Waves Counter`, and change its text to `Wave: 0`.

7. Set the **Waves Counter** object's **Anchors Min Max** and **Pivot** properties to (1, 1) and then reset **Pos X** to -10 and **Pos Y** to -10 to move them slightly away from the edge of the screen. Afterward, in the text component, change the **Alignment** to be right aligned horizontally.

8. Now that we have our text files created, let's now have them function correctly! First, let's go into the `GameController` class. Inside, we will first need to let the script know to use Unity's new UI system:

    ```
    using UnityEngine.UI;
    ```

9. Afterward, we need to create some new variables as follows:

    ```
    [Header("User Interface")]
    // The values we'll be printing
    private int score = 0;
    private int waveNumber = 0;

    // The actual GUI text objects
    public Text scoreText;
    public Text waveText;
    ```

10. Next, we will need to add a function to call whenever our score increases, as follows:

```
public void IncreaseScore(int increase)
{
  score += increase;
  scoreText.text = "Score: " + score;
}
```

The += operator will take the current value of the variable and add something additional to it.

11. Then, we'll need to call this function inside our EnemyBehaviour component. After the controller.KilledEnemy() line, add the following line:

```
controller.IncreaseScore(10);
```

12. Finally, whenever we increase the wave number, we need to change its text as well. Back in the GameController class after the opening { of the if(currentNumberOfEnemies <= 0) block, add the following lines:

```
waveNumber++;
waveText.text = "Wave: " + waveNumber;
```

13. Save all of the script files, go back to **Inspector**, and set the **Score Text** and **Wave Text** objects to the proper variables in the Game Controller object. After that, save your project and run the game. Have a look at the following screenshot:

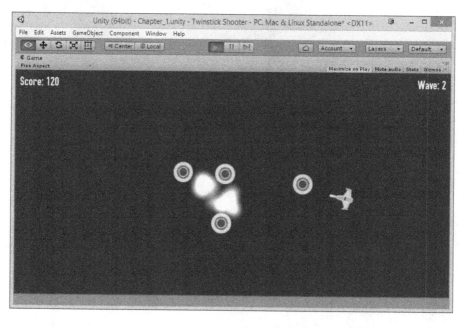

And with that, you can see that everything is working together, killing enemies will reward the player points, and killing all of the enemies in a wave triggers the next wave to start!

Publishing the game

The final thing that we are going to touch on for the project is actually publishing it:

1. Go to **File | Build Settings**. From here, you can decide which platforms and/or scenes to include with your project.

2. Click on the **Add Current...** button to add our current scene to the game, as follows:

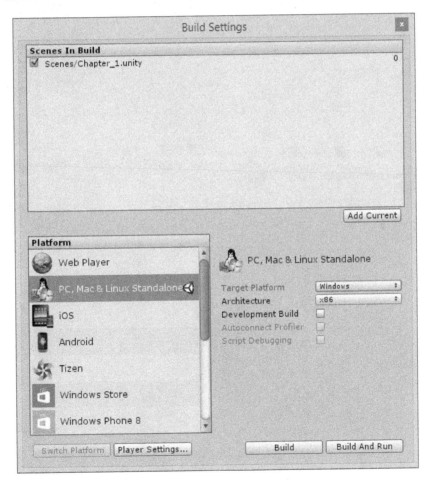

3. After that, since we are just publishing to our current platform, confirm that the settings are correct, and click on the **Build and Run** button.

4. Once you press the button, you'll be brought to a menu to name your application that you are going to save. Give it a name, save it, and wait. If all goes well, you should be brought to a menu allowing you to set some options before the game starts:

5. After that, click on the **Play!** button to see your completed project. Have a look at the following screenshot:

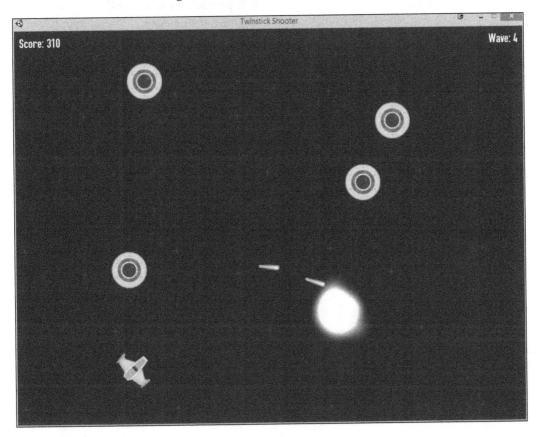

Summary

And there we have it! Within this first chapter, you've already completed an entire game project and learned how to publish it. Moving on, in the next chapter, we will tackle more advanced game types, learn additional things about Unity, and do more to push Unity to do as much as possible.

Challenges

For those of you who want to do more with this project, there are still plenty of things you can do, especially after finishing the rest of this book. Here are some ideas to get your mind thinking:

- Add in feedback whenever the player hits an enemy – perhaps an animation or change the sprite used.
- **Give the player lives**, and each time he is hit by an enemy, have him lose one life. Add Text to display lives as well.

Once you learn how to use use Unity's GUI system even more, create a main menu, pause screen, and restart button using UI as well!

- Add in Xbox controller and mobile touch support!

2
Creating GUIs

A **Graphical User Interface (GUI)** is the way players interact with your games. You've actually been using a GUI in the previous chapter and also to interact with the operating system of your choice. You wouldn't be able to make your electronics do anything without the use of a GUI such as a command prompt similar to DOS and UNIX.

When working on GUIs, we want them to be as intuitive as possible and only contain the information that is pertinent to the player at any given time. There are people whose main job is programming and/or designing user interfaces and they have college degrees on the subject. So, although we won't talk about everything that we have to work with on GUIs, I do want to touch on the aspects that should be quite helpful when working on your own projects in the future.

Project overview

Over the course of this chapter, we will be expanding on our twin-stick shooter by adding additional UI elements that will include a main menu, a pause menu, and an options menu and will give us the ability to restart our project. It is important to note that unlike the previous edition of this book, in this second edition of the book we will be creating these menus using the new UI system that was introduced in Unity 4.6.

Your objectives

This project will be split into a number of tasks. It will be a simple step-by-step process from beginning to end. Here is the outline of our tasks:

- Creating a main menu
- Customizing the GUI

- Implementing a pause menu
- Restarting the game
- Adding an Options screen

Prerequisites

This chapter assumes that you have completed the previous chapter and are working with that project. If you have not completed the project yet, please use the `Twinstick Shooter` folder from Chapter 1's example code and open it up in Unity.

We will also need some graphical assets for use in our project. These can be downloaded from the example code provided for this book on the Packt Publishing website.

Browse through the code files; inside the `Chapter 2` folder, there are a number of things, including an `Art Assets` folder that will have the art, sound, and font files that you'll need for the project as well as the `Twinstick Shooter with GUI` folder which contains the final project.

Creating the main menu level

At this point, I have assumed that you have the twin-stick shooter project created from the last chapter open. With that in mind, we will create an introduction level, or rather a main menu to let the player know the game's name and be able to start or quit the game.

1. Open the previous project. Now, let's first create a new scene by navigating to **File | New Scene**. With the new scene created, save it by navigating to **File | Save Scene**. Name it `Main_Menu.unity` and place it inside your `Scenes` folder.

2. Let's first grab the background from our previous level so that we do not need to create it once again. To do that, double-click on the scene you created in the first chapter. Left-click on the **Background** object in the **Hierarchy** view and navigate to **Edit | Copy**. Go back to your Main_Menu scene and paste it into the world by navigating to **Edit | Paste**:

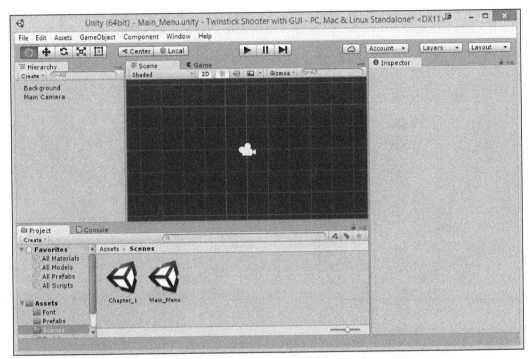

At this point, you should see the background object added to the Hierarchy and our Scene view

Now we have our level with a background! Perfect for us to start creating our main menu.

Adding a header text object

Of course, one of the best things to begin a game with is a title screen and that title screen will need to display the game's name. Let's learn how to do that while also learning more about how Unity's UI system works:

1. Just like we did in the previous chapter, we will first create a text object with the name of our game, so with that in mind go to **GameObject | UI | Text**.

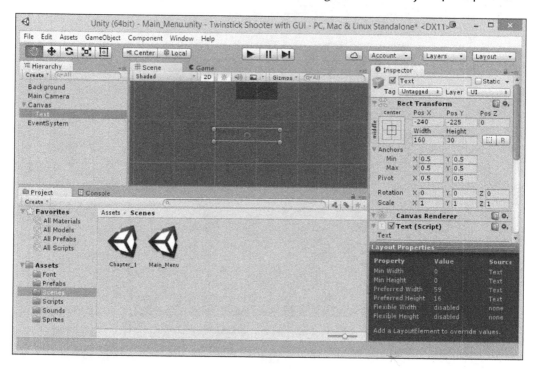

Just like before, this will create three objects, which we'll talk about in more detail now:

   °   **Canvas** – This is the area where all of the UI elements will reside and if you try to create a UI element without one, Unity will create one for you like it did here. From the **Scenes** view, it will draw a white rectangle around itself to show you how large it is. The game object contains a **Canvas** component which allows you to dictate how the image will be rendered, as well as **Canvas Scaler** to make your art scale depending on the resolution of the device the game is running on and **Graphic Raycaster** which determines whether any objects on the Canvas have been hit.

> [For more information on the Canvas object, check out
> http://docs.unity3d.com/Manual/UICanvas.html.]

- ° **Text** – This object is our actual text object and has all of the properties to allow us to position the object anywhere on the **Canvas** and change what text, color, size, and more will be displayed.

- ° **EventSystem** – This object allows users to send events to objects in our game based on various input types, from keyboard to touch events to gamepads. There are properties here that allow you to specify how you'd like users to interface with your UI and if you try to create a UI element without one, Unity will create one for you like it did here.

> [For more information on EventSystem, check out:
> http://docs.unity3d.com/Manual/EventSystem.html.]

2. To make it easier to see our text object, go to the **Hierarchy** tab and double-click on the Text object. It may be a little difficult to see, so from the **Inspector** tab scroll down to the **Text** component and change the **Color** property to white.

> If you cannot see the text after this, confirm that the **A** value for the color is 255 (with colors, A is the alpha channel in which 0 means fully transparent and 1 is fairly opaque).

3. The next thing we are going to do is make it easier to tell what this object is, so with that in mind scroll all the way up on the **Inspector** tab with the Text object selected and change its name to Game Title.

   After this, we are going to want to move this object to its proper place in the world; however, just like in the last chapter, you'll note that instead of the default **Transform** component we've been seeing our text object has a **Rect Transform** component in the same place. The **Rect Transform** component is probably the most different thing about working in the UI system, so it's a good idea to learn as much as we can about it.

   Rect Transform is different from regular **Transform** in the sense that whereas **Transform** represents a single point or the center of an object, **Rect Transform** represents a rectangle that the UI element will reside in. If an object with **Rect Transform** has a parent that also has **Rect Transform**, the child will specify how the object should be positioned relative to the parent.

> For more information on positioning objects and **Rect Transform**, check out http://docs.unity3d.com/Manual/UIBasicLayout.html.

4. Now, to get a better idea of what the properties of the **Rect Transform** component mean, change the **Pos X** and **Pos Y** values to 0, which will center our object around the object's anchors.

Our object's anchors are visible from the **Scene** tab via the four small rectangles creating the X shape in the center of our **Scene** tab if you have the **Game Title** object selected. (Double-click on it to center the object on the screen.)

> Note that the white box that is displayed above for the **Canvas** may look different on your screen based on the **Aspect Ratio** you've set from the **Game** tab (mine is set to **Free Aspect** so it scales based off of that).

Anchors give you the ability to "hold on" to a corner or part of the canvas so that if the canvas were to move and/or change, the pieces of UI will stay in an appropriate place. This can be quite useful when it comes to things like supporting multiple resolutions without scaling the art assets created. In our case, we will want to have our title position itself relative to the top of the level.

5. Click on the **Anchor Presets** menu in the upper-left corner of the **Rect Transform** component. From there, it shows some of the most common anchor positions that are used in games for easy selection. In our case, we will want to pick the top-center option.

Notice that now the **Pos Y** value has become -93. This is saying that our object is positioned 93 units below the anchor's y position. If we change the **Pos Y** value to 0, the object would be centered along the y axis' anchor, which would put the object half off the screen, which is not good.

However, if we changed our Game Title object's **Pos Y** to -15 (subtracting half its **Height** value), it would be positioned correctly; however, if we decided we wanted to change the **Height** later on, we would have to remember to adjust this as well. It would be a lot nicer if we had something to make **Pos Y** at 0 be the edge of the map relative to our height and thankfully we have the **Pivot** property to fix that.

6. Next, change the **Pivot Y** property to 1 and then change **Pos Y** to 0.

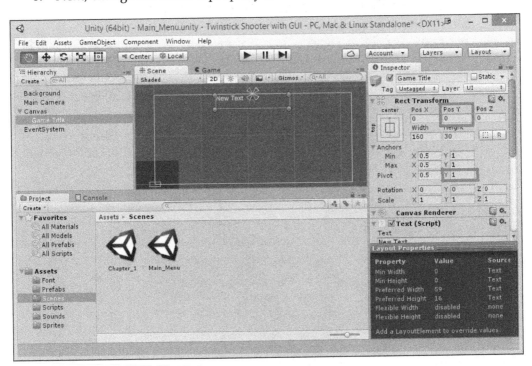

Pivots are markers that inform the other values in the **Rect Transform** component saying where we want to affect things, relative to this position on our object. This means that objects will be moved, rotated, and/or scaled via this position. To note how things react and what changing the values does, try changing the **Rotation Z** property with **Pivot Y** of 0, 0.5, and 1 and see the differences in how things are rotated.

Note that it is possible to set the **Pivot, Position**, and **Anchors** of an object via the **Anchors Preset** menu I mentioned previously if you hold down the *Alt* and *Shift* keys while clicking on the desired spot. This way, all of the steps we discussed will happen all at once, but it's a good idea to get an understanding of what everything means before jumping straight into using the shortcuts.

7. Now that we have our object positioned correctly, let's give it some visual flair. Select the Game Title object from the **Hierarchy** tab and then move over to the **Inspector** tab and scroll down to the **Text** component. From there, change the **Text** property to Twinstick Shooter and change **Alignment** of the object to the center vertically and horizontally. Afterward, change **Font** to the OSP-DIN we used in the last chapter and then change **Font Size** to 35 and **Color** to white. Notice that now the text doesn't show up, because we've made the text too big for the **Rect Transform** that we defined.

8. With that in mind, scroll up to **Rect Transform** and change **Height** to 200 and **Width** to 50. We will also want it to be offset from the top of the world, so let's change **Pos Y** to -30 to give it a little offset.

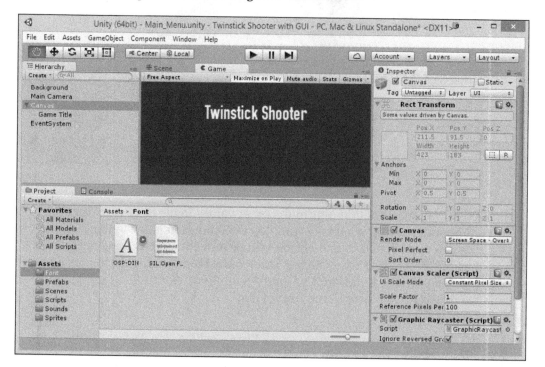

Now, this looks great for this resolution, but if we were to play the game at a higher resolution, it may look like this:

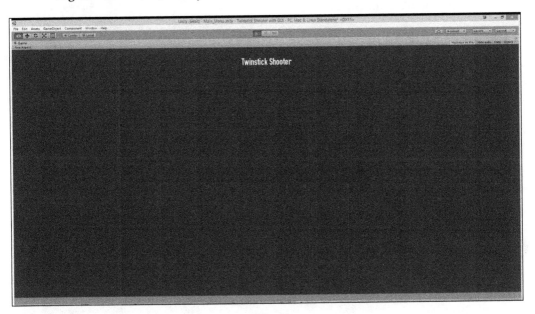

This can be good if you're trying to do a HUD in your game, but for the title screen it's usually a good idea to make things large, so with that in mind we will use the **Canvas Scaler** component to adjust the size of the objects automatically.

9. Select the `Canvas` object from **Hierarchy** and then in **Inspector** from **Canvas Scaler** change **Ui Scale Mode** to **Scale with Screen Size**. From there, change **Reference Resolution** to 800 x 600 if it isn't there already.

10. Next, let's make the text a bit larger. With that in mind, from **Rect Transform** change **Width** to 400 and **Height** to 100 and then change the **Text** component's **Font Size** to 70.

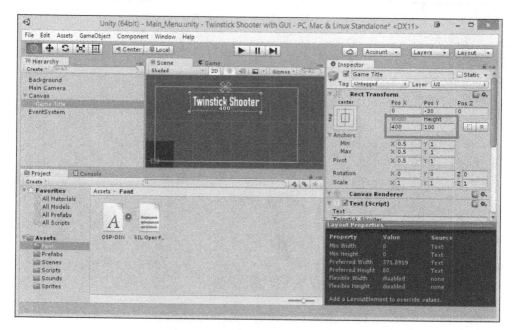

Now, if we play the game from a higher resolution, it will display our title nicely:

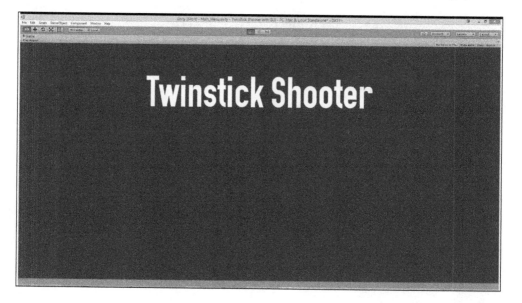

As we can see, it's working great!

> For more information on **Canvas Scaler**, check out: `http://docs.unity3d.com/Manual/script-CanvasScaler.html`.

Adding main menu buttons

Now that we have the text displaying correctly, let's add in the ability to move from the main menu into the game and quit the game.

1. Start off by going to the top menu bar and then selecting **GameObject | UI | Button**.

   At this point, you will see a new child object to the **Canvas** called **Button** and if you were to extend that object, you'd see that it has a Text child as well.

2. Next, let's learn a new way that we can position objects. From the **Hierarchy** tab, select the `Button` object and open up the **Anchors Preset** menu and from there select the **bottom-stretch** option.

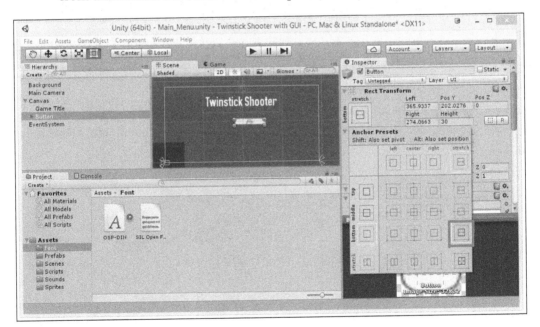

Notice now that **Pos X** and **Width** have been replaced with a **Left** and **Right** value. When we use the stretch option, it will scale the object either horizontally or vertically depending on your choice. The **Left** and **Right** values are how far to the left or right in pixels that the center of the object will be based.

3. Change the **Left** and **Right** values to 300 to center the object with 300 pixels on each side. Then, change **Pivot Y** to 0 to base our positions to offset via the top and then change the **Pos Y** value to 100 to move the object 100 pixels above the bottom of the screen.

4. From the **Hierarchy** tab, expand the Button object and change the button's text child's text value to Start Game.

5. Now that our button exists and is positioned correctly, let's customize how it looks. Change **Font** to OSP-DIN and change **Font Size** to 25.

6. Now that we have the text customized, let's customize the button's visibility. From **Hierarchy**, select the Button object and from **Inspector** scroll down to the **Button** component. From there, you'll see a number of colors and a target graphic that will be tinted when you mouseover or click on the button (try playing the game and interacting with the button to see the default behaviour).

7. We'll be replacing this default behavior so that instead of using colors, we will be changing the image used. To do that, go into the Example Code folder and bring the contents of the Art Assets folder for *Chapter 2* into the Sprites folder from our **Project** tab.

8. After that, change **Transition** to Sprite Swap and then for **Highlighted Sprite** put in buttonYellow, **Pressed Sprite** to buttonGreen, and **Disabled Sprite** to buttonDisabled.

9. Finally, in the **Image** component under **Source Image**, put in buttonBlue. Afterward, change **Image Type** to **Sliced**. You'll notice that there is an error saying it doesn't have a border, and that's true.

10. From the **Project** tab, open up the **Sprites** folder and then select the buttonBlue sprite. From **Inspector**, you'll see the properties for **Sprite** and a button called **Sprite Editor**. Click on it and you'll be able to see properties for how the sprite will be drawn. It's also used for animations, but in this case we are going to establish a border. For L (left), R (right), T (top), and B (bottom) put in 10 and then click on the **Apply** button.

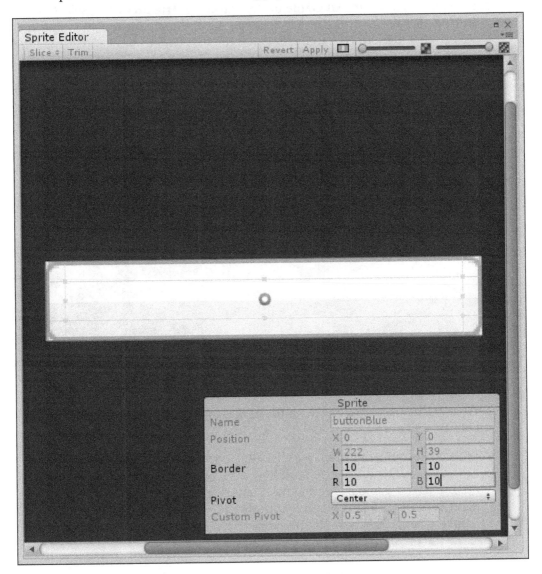

What this will do is anytime we create a sprite using the Sliced type and change the width and height, the four non-cardinal corners will not scale but the others will, allowing us to create boxes of whatever size we want. Pretty nifty, huh?

11. Create the same borders for the other button sprites.

12. Now, let's create our **Exit Game** button. From the **Hierarchy** tab, select the **Button** object and press *Ctrl + D*. Change the object's name to **Exit Game** and **Pos Y** to 50. Back in **Hierarchy**, open up the **Exit Game** object and change the Text's text to **Exit Game**.

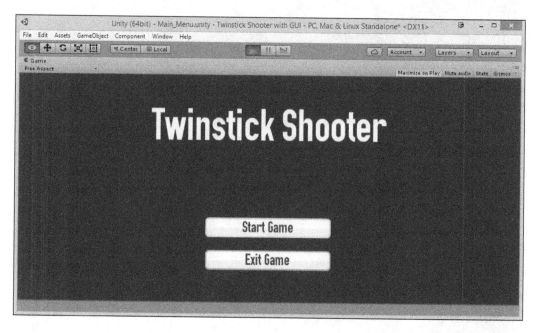

We now have two customized buttons that look great, but aren't functional. Let's fix that now.

13. To have functionality when we click the button, we will need to have a method to call, and for us to be able to set it up via **Inspector** that means we need to have a game object that has that function as part of it. So with that in mind, let's create a new empty game object by going to **GameObject | Create Empty**. Change this new object's name to MainMenuBehaviour and drag it up to the top of your **Hierarchy** for easy access.

14. Now that we have an object, let's give it a script to contain the functionality that we want. Select the **Main Menu Behaviour** object and click on the **Add Component** button from **Inspector**. From there, give it a name of `MainMenuBehaviour`, make sure the language is set to C#, and then select **Create** and **Add**. This will create a new script and attach it for us automatically. This is created in the `Assets` folder, so go ahead into the **Project** tab and move the script into the `Scripts` folder and then double-click on it to enter your IDE of course.

15. Once your IDE has opened, use the following code:

```
using UnityEngine;
using UnityEngine.SceneManagement;

public class MainMenuBehaviour : MonoBehaviour
{

    public void LoadLevel(string levelName)
    {
SceneManager.LoadScene(levelName);
    }

    public void QuitGame()
    {
        #if UNITY_EDITOR
            UnityEditor.EditorApplication.isPlaying=false;
        #else
            Application.Quit();
        #endif
    }
}
```

The `LoadScene` function will load a level based on a name that we provide to it and the `QuitGame` function will either set the editor to no longer play if we are in the Unity Editor, and will quit the game if we are playing an exported version.

16. Save the script and go back to the Unity editor. Currently, our gameplay level is named `Chapter_1`, but that's not terribly descriptive. From the **Project** tab, open the **Scenes** folder and rename the level to `Gameplay` by selecting it and then clicking on its name.

17. Select your **Start Game** button and from there go to the **Inspector** tab and scroll down to the `Button` component. From there, in the `On Click ()` section, click on **+** to add something for our button to do.

18. From there, drag and drop the `Main Menu Behaviour` object from the **Hierarchy** tab to the area that currently says None (Object) that's just been added to the list.

19. Click on the dropdown that currently says **No Function** and then select **MainMenuBehaviour | LoadLevel**. Then in the textbox that appeared below, type in `Gameplay`.

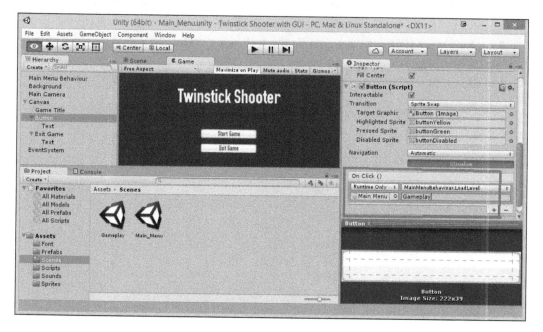

20. Next, select the **Exit Game** object and then add an `OnClick` action just like we did before, except this time call **MainMenuBehaviour | Quit Game**.

21. Lastly, open up our **Build Settings** like before by going to **File | Build Settings** and add our `Main_Menu` to your list at index 0 by selecting **Add Open Scenes** and then dragging the `Main_Menu` level to the top so it will be the level that starts off when we start the game.

22. Save your project and scene and hit the **Play** button.

23. At this point, our main menu is working perfectly!

Pausing the game

Now that we have started on our main menu, let's add some additional GUI functionality to our game, adding in the ability to pause our game and restart it. However, before we do that, let's take a look at some stuff we can do to make our lives easier when it comes to customization:

1. We also want to make these buttons have the same appearance as the stuff we've done previously. So I'm going to create a **Prefab** of one of our buttons so we can create them easily in the future. So with that in mind, select our **Start Game** button and duplicate it by pressing *Ctrl + D* and renaming our previous one **Start Game**.

2. We don't want every single button we create to load the gameplay level, so click on the outside part of the On Click () property, then click on the – button to remove it.

3. Next, rename the button **Base Button** and then from the **Project** tab, open up the Prefabs folder and drag and drop our **Base Button** object into the folder.

4. After the prefab has been created, we can now remove **Base Button** from **Hierarchy**.

5. Now, go to the **Project** tab and select the **Base Button** object and change the **Anchor** preset to middle-center and then change **Width** to 150.

6. Next, go to the **Scenes** folder and open up our **Gameplay** scene, saving Main_Menu as we go.

7. Go to **GameObject | UI | Panel**. Panels fill the entire screen, and we don't want that, so let's go ahead and change Anchor Presets to middle-center and change **Width** to 450 and **Height** to 150.

8. Like before, we will want to use **Canvas Scaler**, so select the Canvas object from **Hierarchy** and then in **Inspector** from **Canvas Scaler**, change **Ui Scale Mode** to **Scale with Screen Size**. From there, change **Reference Resolution** to 800 x 600 if it isn't there already.

9. Next, select the **Panel** object and then add a **Vertical Layout Group** component to it. (By clicking on **Add Component**, you can type in the name of components and hit *Enter* to select them.) From there, change **Padding** to 10 in all directions and under **Spacing** put in 10.

10. Then, drag and drop our **Base Button** object on top of the **Panel** name in **Hierarchy** to make it a child of the object. Then, duplicate it twice.

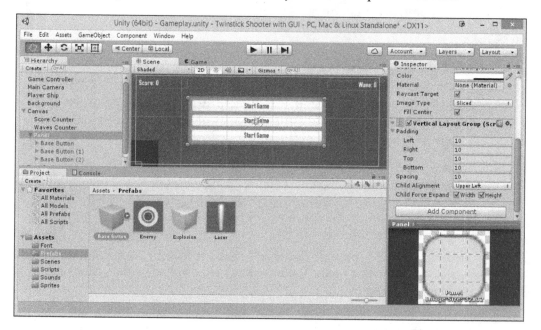

11. You'll notice that the buttons have resized themselves to fit the area that the panel had, with the spacing and padding we created taken into consideration.

12. Change the text and name of the three buttons to **Resume, Main Menu,** and **Quit Game**.

13. Now, just like before, we will need to create the functionality for these items, as well as the way to have the menu appear and disappear properly, so with that in mind, let's go ahead and create an empty game object with a name of **Pause Menu Behaviour** with a PauseMenuBehaviour script attached to it.

Use the following code:

```
using UnityEngine;

public class PauseMenuBehaviour : MainMenuBehaviour
{
    public static bool isPaused;
    public GameObject pauseMenu;
    public void Start()
    {
        isPaused = false;
        pauseMenu.SetActive(false);
    }
    public void Update()
    {
        if (Input.GetKeyUp("escape"))
        {
            // If false becomes true and vice-versa
            isPaused = !isPaused;
            // If isPaused is true, 0 otherwise 1
            Time.timeScale = (isPaused) ? 0 : 1;
            pauseMenu.SetActive(isPaused);
        }
    }
    public void ResumeGame()
    {
        isPaused = false;
        pauseMenu.SetActive(false);
        Time.timeScale = 1;
    }
}
```

Note that this time PauseMenuBehaviour inherits MainMenuBehaviour, which means all of the main menu stuff will be included here as well.

14. Next, save your script and move back into the Unity editor. Once there, set the **Panel** object of our **Pause Menu** to the pause menu variable. Then, set the **Resume** button's OnClick to call the **Pause Menu Behaviour's** Resume function. Then, the **Main Menu** button call LoadLevel with a parameter of Main_Menu, and **Quit Game** with QuitGame.

15. Finally, to make it a little easier for you to see, go ahead and select the **Panel** object, rename it **Pause Menu**, and then click on the checkmark to the left of the name in Inspector to disable it, making it disappear. However, due to **Pause Menu Behaviour**, we still have a way to access it.

16. At this point, the game will work correctly, but when you pause the game the player still seems to rotate and can shoot. So, let's fix that real quick. Open up the **PlayerBehaviour** script and modify the Update function to check if the game is paused before doing anything with the following bolded lines:

```
// Update is called once per frame
void Update ()
{
    if (!PauseMenuBehaviour.isPaused)
    {

        // Rotate player to face mouse
        Rotation();
        // Move the player's body
        Movement();


// a foreach loop will go through each item inside of
// shootButton and do whatever we placed in {}s using the
//element variable to hold the item
        foreach (KeyCode element in shootButton)
        {
            if (Input.GetKey(element) && timeTilNextFire < 0)
            {
                timeTilNextFire = timeBetweenFires;
                ShootLaser();
                break;
            }
        }

        timeTilNextFire -= Time.deltaTime;
    }

}
```

17. Save your scene and level and go ahead to play the game!

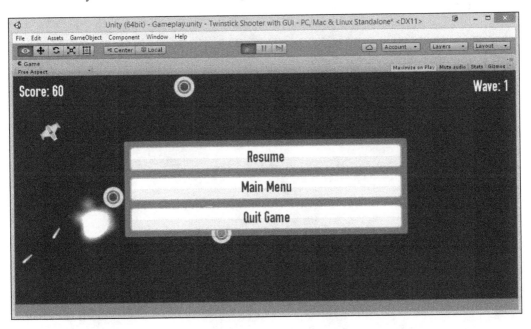

Now, we have a fully functional pause menu that will allow us to press the *Esc* key and leave what we're doing in the project. We've also made it incredibly easy for us to draw buttons in the style that we created for other sections.

Restarting the game

There may come a time in a game when a player makes a mistake and would like to restart the level in the game they're currently playing. If you prepared your project ahead of time like we have, it's actually quite easy to get this functionality placed into your game. With that being said, let's implement that functionality now! We will perform the following steps:

1. Select the **Panel** object and from there, create an empty child and drag it in the **hierarchy** to be the top child from the list. To that empty game object, rename it to Top Row and add a **Horizontal Layout Group** component to it.

2. Next, drag and drop **Resume** object to it to make it a child and then duplicate it (*Ctrl + D*) to create a copy.

3. As you can see, we now have two buttons on the same row.

4. Rename the second **Resume** button to **Restart** and change the text to reflect that.

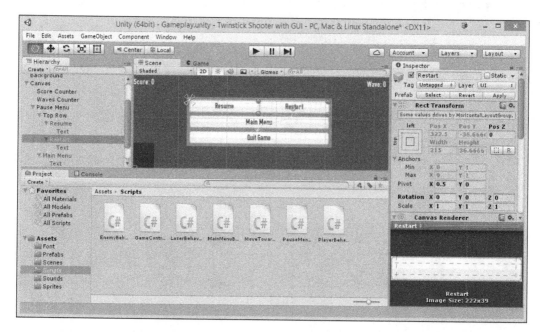

5. Next, open up the **PauseMenuBehaviour** script and add the following line at the top of the file:

```
using UnityEngine.SceneManagement; // LoadScene
using UnityEngine;
```

6. Then, add the following code as a new function:

```
public void RestartGame()
{
    SceneManager.LoadScene(SceneManager.GetActiveScene().name);
}
```

7. Next, have the **Restart** button now call this newly created `RestartGame` function.

8. Once finished, save your file and move back into Unity and play the game! The following screenshot depicts the game screen:

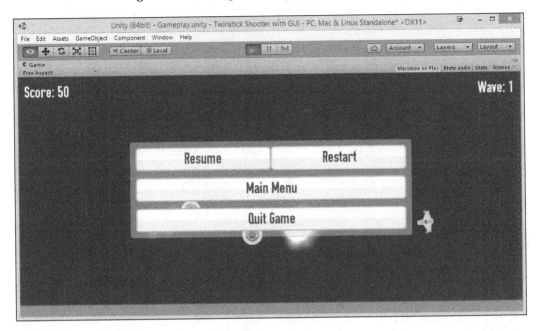

Simple enough! We've now added a new button to our menu and when we click on it, we load the currently loaded level.

If you use this implementation in your own projects, be sure to initialize all static variables inside your Start function unless you want them to be consistent between run-throughs.

Creating an Options menu

Something that many games also need is an **Options** menu, so let's create it by performing the following steps:

1. First, let's prepare **Pause Menu** to support an **Options** screen. Select the **Pause Menu** object and create an empty child called **Bottom Row** and then add a **Horizontal Group Layout** component to it.

2. Duplicate the **Main Menu** button and then drag and drop the original **Main Menu** and **Quit Game** to **Bottom Row**. Afterward, rename the **Main Menu** copy **Options** and change the text as well to reflect that.

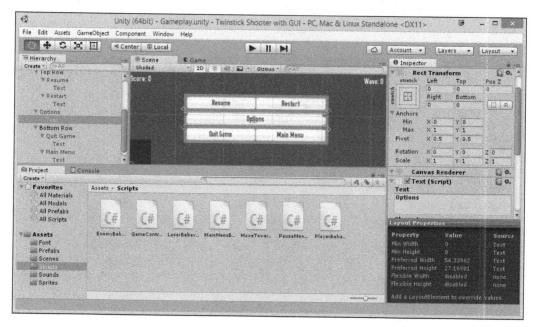

3. Now, we will need to create the **Options** menu. Duplicate the **Pause Menu** object and rename it **Options Menu**.

4. Then, move the **Options** button to the bottom and rename it **Back** and then changes the names of **Quit** and **Main Menu** to **Decrease** and **Increase Quality**.

5. Next, we want to add a slider to the menu to allow players to change the volume of the game. To do that, go to **GameObject | UI | Slider** and then drag it on top of **Options Menu** to add it to the menu.

6. Select the **Options Menu** object and set **Height** to 200 to account for us adding new things and then put a Text object above the **Slider** and **Quality** markers, saying **Master Volume** and **Quality Level**.

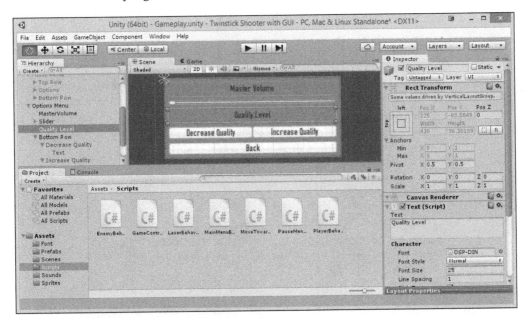

7. Next, we're going to need to write some functions and add a new property to our **PauseMenuBehaviour**, so with that in mind open it up and add the following variable:

```
public GameObject optionsMenu;
```

8. Then, update the script to have the following new functions:

```
public void IncreaseQuality()
{
    QualitySettings.IncreaseLevel();
    UpdateQualityLabel();
}

public void DecreaseQuality()
{
    QualitySettings.DecreaseLevel();
    UpdateQualityLabel();
}

public void SetVolume(float value)
{
```

```
        AudioListener.volume = value;
        UpdateVolumeLabel();
    }


    private void UpdateQualityLabel()
    {
        int currentQuality = QualitySettings.GetQualityLevel();
        string qualityName =
        QualitySettings.names[currentQuality];

        optionsMenu.transform.FindChild("Quality
        Level").GetComponent<UnityEngine.UI.Text>().text =
        "Quality Level - " + qualityName;
    }


    private void UpdateVolumeLabel()
    {
        optionsMenu.transform.FindChild("Master
        Volume").GetComponent<UnityEngine.UI.Text>().text =
        "Master Volume - " + (AudioListener.volume *
        100).ToString("f2") + "%";
    }
```

In the following code we use the ToString function to convert the AudioListener's volume property (a float) into a string which we can print. We provide "f2" to the function to say we want to format the text as a float with 2 decimal points.

> For more info on the ToString function, check out: https://msdn.microsoft.com/en-us/library/f71z6k0c(v=vs.110).aspx.

9. Then, we need to have to update the **Start** function of have the following bolded lines:

```
public void Start()
{
    isPaused = false;
    pauseMenu.SetActive(false);
 optionsMenu.SetActive(false);

    UpdateQualityLabel();
    UpdateVolumeLabel();
}
```

10. Save the script and move back into the Unity editor. From there, go to **Pause Menu Behaviour** and set the **Options Menu** property to our **Options Menu** object.

11. Next, select the **Slider** object and scroll down to the **Slider** component and add an On Value Changed event with **Pause Menu Behaviour** attached and call the **Dynamic float** version of SetVolume.

12. Afterward, change the **Value** of the **Slider** component to 1 to reflect full volume.

13. Then, have **Decrease** and **Increase Quality** call their respective functions.

14. Next, we need to be able to go from **Options** to the **Pause** menu and vice versa, so add in two more functions for us to work with in **Pause Menu Behaviour**:

```
public void OpenOptions()
    {
        optionsMenu.SetActive(true);
        pauseMenu.SetActive(false);
    }


public void OpenPauseMenu()
    {
        optionsMenu.SetActive(false);
        pauseMenu.SetActive(true);
    }
```

15. Then, assign `OpenPauseMenu` to the **Back** button and `OpenOptions` to the **Options** button on the **Pause** menu.

16. Then, we need to adjust our **Escape** button behavior in `Update`:

```
public void Update()
    {
    if (Input.GetKeyUp("escape"))
        {
            if (!optionsMenu.activeInHierarchy)
            {
                // If false becomes true and vice-versa
                isPaused = !isPaused;

                // If isPaused is true, 0 otherwise 1
                Time.timeScale = (isPaused) ? 0 : 1;

                pauseMenu.SetActive(isPaused);
            }
            else
            {
                OpenPauseMenu();
            }

        }
    }
```

17. It looks fine now, but we also want our text to look easy to read, so go to the **Options Menu** object and change the **Image** component's **Color** to have an Alpha to 200. Then, do the same to the **Pause Menu** panel.

18. Lastly, hide the **Options Menu** object from the **Hierarchy** tab.

19. After this, we save all of our files and then go back into Unity and run the game, as shown in the following screenshot:

Over the course of this section, we've done two things. First of all, we changed the pause menu to now have an additional **Options** menu.

And when we click on the **Options** button, we will see a separate menu that will allow users to modify the **Master Volume** value as well as the **Graphics Quality** value of their project. This is shown in the following screenshot:

Summary

With that, we now have most of the commonly needed features for most games to be completed. With the basics created here, you can easily add additional menus and features to make your game great! In the next chapter, we will start up a new project with more exciting things for us to work with and explore even more of what Unity has to offer!

Challenges

For those of you who want to do more with this project, there are plenty of things you can do, especially after finishing the rest of this book. Here are some ideas to get you thinking:

- Add a **Credits** screen to your main menu
- Add in three color sliders to customize your ship's color (`renderer.material.color`) with red, green, and blue values
- Add in **Music Volume** and **SFX Volume** sliders, and use those values to set the volume of sounds you play!
- Modify the style of the buttons to reflect your own game!

GUIs Part 2 – Clicker Game

3

In *Chapter 2, Creating GUIs*, we've seen how we can use Unity's powerful UI system to create something to complement a game title, but it's also possible for people to create entire games using only the UI interface.

Project overview

Over the course of this chapter, we will be creating a clicker game named **Code Clicker**. Code Clicker will be similar in some respects to the popular clicker title **Cookie Clicker** created by Orteil (playable at `http://orteil.dashnet.org/cookieclicker/`) except instead of clicking cookies, we will be clicking a button to write code. We'll also get exposure to how to create more complex menus, such as those with a scrollbar.

Your objectives

This project will be split into a number of tasks. It will be a simple step-by-step process from beginning to end. Here is the outline of our tasks:

- Starting our project
- Recording clicks
- Creating a shop
- Purchasing upgrades

Prerequisites

We will need some graphical assets for use in our project. These can be downloaded from the example code provided for this book on the Packt website.

Starting our project

To get started, let's create a new project for us to work with:

1. With Unity started from the launcher, select **File | New Project**. From there, give it a name (I used `ClickerGame`) and a **Project Location** of your choice and make sure that **2D** is selected. Afterwards, click on **Create project**:

2. Now that we are inside the editor, let's start off by creating our button, which we will use to click. From the **Project** tab, create a folder named `Sprites` and open it up. Then, right-click from the folder and select **Import New Asset...** and select the `button.png` file from inside of the **Art Assets** folder. Alternatively, you can use your own asset as it's just a way to make the button different from the default one.

3. To create the basic button, we will customize start off by going to **GameObject | UI | Button**. From the **Hierarchy** tab, open up the `Button` object by clicking on the triangle next to the name and then delete the `Text` object by selecting it and then pressing the *Del* key. Then, select the `Button` object and drag and drop the button **Sprite** from the **Project** tab into the **Inspector** tab's **Source Image** property from the **Image** component.

4. From there, click on the newly created **Set Native Size** button, and the image will resize to be the same as the image provided:

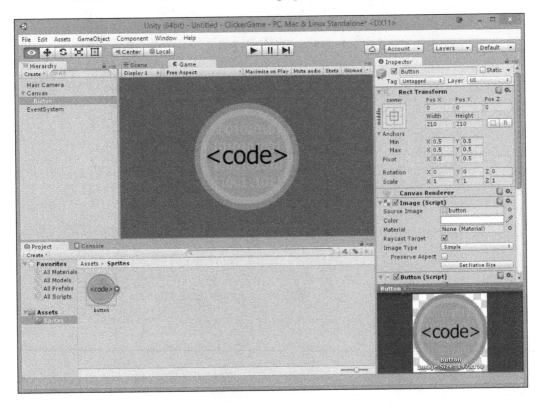

5. This will be the button that we will be using to click on in order to write a line of code. Currently, if we were to play the game, we would note that the button uses changing colors to indicate it's been pressed, due to the **Button** component's **Transition** property being set to **Color Tint**. However, I feel that instead of just being confined to the color or the sprite to use, it would be more impressive for it to modify other properties as well. So with that in mind, we are going to learn about Unity's **Animation** window and how to create basic animations.

6. With the Button object selected, move to the **Inspector** tab and scroll down to the **Button** component. From there, change the **Transition** to **Animation**. Afterwards, click on the **Auto Generate Animation** button. It will ask you where you'd like to save the controller; create a new folder named Animations and save it there.

7. This creates an **Animator Controller**, which allows us to dictate how animations should be played and when while allowing them to blend together by using something called a state machine. Now, this one is automatically created for us due to the selection that we just made, but later on, we can learn how to create our very own from scratch.

 For more information on the **Animator Controller** asset, check out `http://docs.unity3d.com/Manual/Animator.html`.

8. Now select the `Button` object from the **Hierarchy** and then go to **Window | Animation** or hit *Ctrl+6*. This will bring up a new window or show a tab where we can animate. Optionally, drag the tab on top of the bottom-left side where the **Project** tab is to place it inside that area to make it easier to see in the future:

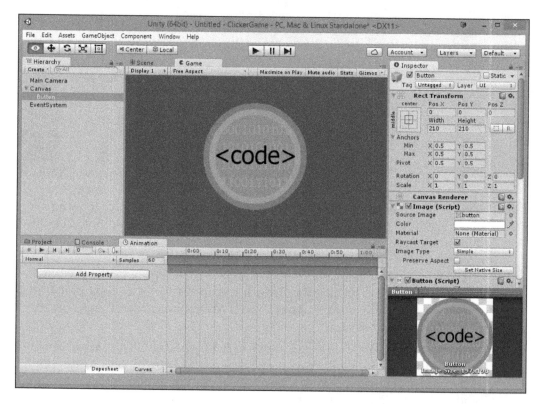

9. From the **Hierarchy** tab, select the **Button** object and you will notice that the **Animation** tab will no longer be grayed out. Under the record button, you will notice it'll display the name of the currently selected animation (**Normal** by default). Click on the **Normal** selection to then select **Highlighted** to switch animations to look at:

10. Next, click on the red circle **Record** button to save any changes we make to the object. Afterwards from the **Inspector**, set **Scale** to **1.25**, **1.25**, **1** by typing it in and then from the **Image** component's **Color** property, change it to green:

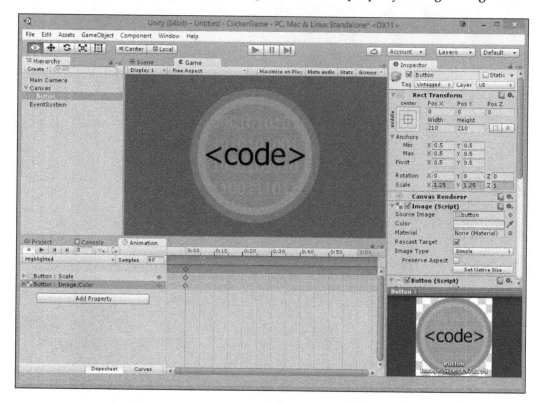

> Note that even though I just modified these properties, any public property from any of the components on the object or its children can be modified from here.
>
> For more information on the **Animation** view and how to build more complex animations, check out http://docs.unity3d.com/Manual/AnimationEditorGuide.html.

11. We can just keep this as a single frame change, but I want to modify it a bit so click on the **0:20** section of the **Animation** tab to move the red line there, then click on the **Add Keyframe** button or right-click and select **Add Frame**. This will save all of the properties that we changed at the **0:00** time.

12. Now click on the **0:20** section and create another key for the **Image** component's **Color** property (**Image.Color**), and this time decrease the **Alpha** of the color to have the animation change over time:

13. To get an idea of what the animation looks like, go ahead and hit the **Play** button and you will notice the effect playing.

14. Now, we want to modify the animation when we click as well so go to where it says **Highlighted** and then click on it to bring up a drop-down menu to change the animation to **Pressed** and click on the **Record** button (the red circle) again if it isn't selected already while also moving the red bar back to 0:00. From there, change **Scale** to **.75**, **.75**, **1** and the color to a darker gray:

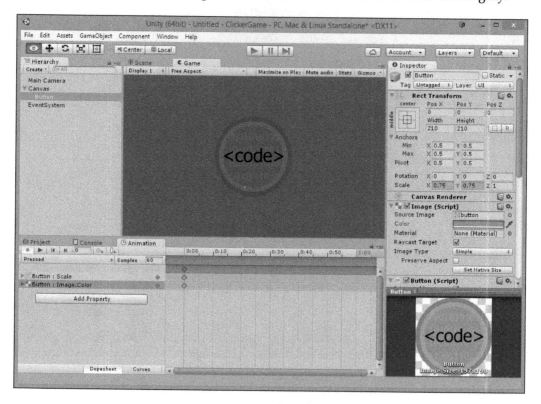

15. This works great, but once we click on the button, it no longer will go to the **Normal** state, so let's disable the navigation options of the **EventSystem** by going to the **Inspector** tab and changing the **Button** component's **Navigation** property to **None**.

16. Finally, the button always stays the same size, which is fine now, but for a larger screen may cause issues down the line so let's use the **Canvas Scaler** component that we used before. Select the Canvas object, and from the **Canvas Scaler** component, change **UI Scale Mode** to Scale With Screen Size and change the **Reference Resolution** to 1920 x 1080.

17. Save your scene as `CodeClicker` (creating a new folder named `Scenes` to hold it) and then hit the **Play** button to see your project!

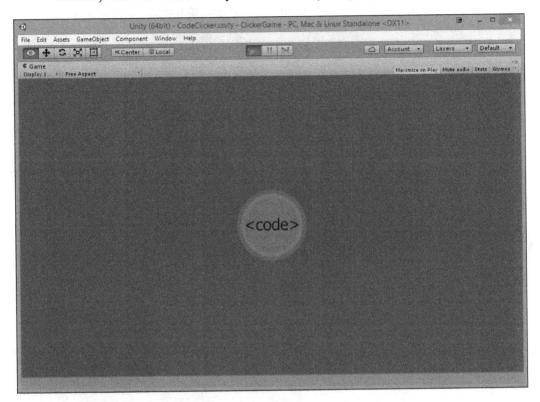

At this point, we have a button that can be interacted with!

Recording and displaying clicks

Now that we have this foundational button working, let's add some text to display information to the player.

1. Go to **GameObject | UI | Text**. From there, use the **Anchor Presets** tool, hold down *Alt + Shift*, and click on the top-center option. It may be hard to see, so let's fix that up next. Change the **Width** to 1920 and **Height** to 100. You will remember that 1920 is what we used in our **Reference Resolution**, so this will take up the entire size.

2. Then, change the **Font Size** to **75** and then change the **Paragraph Alignment** to be centered horizontally, change the **Text Color** to white, change the **Text** to You have: $0, and rename the Text object to CashText:

3. Now select the CashText object and duplicate it (*Ctrl+D*) and give it a name of RateText. Change the **Pos Y** to -75, the text to per second: 0.0 and change the **Font Size** to 50.

4. Next, let's write some code. Go to the **Project** tab, move to the Assets folder, and create a new folder named Scripts. From there, create a new script by selecting **Create | C# Script**, and once it's created, name it **GameController**. Once named, double-click on it to open up your IDE.

5. Use the following code:

```
using UnityEngine;
using UnityEngine.UI; // Text

public class GameController : MonoBehaviour {

    /// <summary>
    /// How much cash the player has
```

```
/// </summary>
private float _cash;
public float Cash
{
    get
    {
        return _cash;
    }
    set
    {
        _cash = value;
        cashText.text = "You have: $" + _
        cash.ToString("0.00");
    }
}

/// <summary>
/// How much cash is automatically earned per second
/// </summary>
private float _cashPerSecond;
public float CashPerSecond
{
    get
    {
        return _cashPerSecond;
    }
    set
    {
        _cashPerSecond = value;
        rateText.text = "per second: " +
        _cashPerSecond.ToString("0.0");
    }
}

[Tooltip("How much cash players will make when they hit
the button.")]
public float cashPerClick = 1;

[Header("Object References")]
public Text cashText;
public Text rateText;

// Use this for initialization
void Start ()
```

```
        {
            Cash = 0;
            CashPerSecond = 0;
        }

        // Update is called once per frame
        void Update ()
        {
            Cash += CashPerSecond * Time.deltaTime;
        }

    public void ClickedButton()
        {
            Cash += cashPerClick;
        }
```

There is a lot of stuff going on in the previous code, so we will start off talking about the new aspects of code we used and then explain the overall content and meaning.

Working with accessors (get/set functions)

One of the things you may have noted is the addition of the `get` and `set` functions for the two properties. This is referred to as **accessors** and is a way for us to protect data or do something whenever a certain value changes. In this case, anytime the value changes, we will change the text displayed from our text objects.

 For more information on that check out `https://msdn.microsoft.com/en-sg/library/aa287786(v=vs.71).aspx`.

Tooltip and Header attributes

You may have noticed the Header being used briefly in *Chapter 1*. These allow users to have additional behavior from the **Inspector** tab in the Unity editor. In this case, **Tooltip** will display a comment when you highlight the property in the **Inspector** tab, and **Header** will display a header before the next variable displayed.

Unity 5.3 has added a whole bunch of new attributes for people to use that still aren't put together easily within Unity's documentation yet, but Lior Tal put together a list of them with links to their documentation at `http://www.tallior.com/unity-attributes/`.

Explaining GameController's functionality

In the previously mentioned code, we have a number of new variables that we are going to be working with. cashText and rateText are references to the **Text** components of the two text objects we created earlier and will change their text whenever the value of Cash or CashPerSecond changes due to the set functions. To be as efficient as possible, we only want to change the text when the value changes so that this works perfectly.

In our Update function, we are changing the value of Cash by increasing it by the current value of CashPerSecond. Note that we also use Time.deltaTime as we did in *Chapter 1, 2D Twin-stick Shooter* to make it so that it will increase by the amount of time that elapsed in seconds since the previous frame.

Finally, we added a function that we will call whenever we click on the button to increase cash by whatever amount we set CashPerClick to.

1. Next, create an empty game object by going to **GameObject | Create Empty**. Rename it to GameController. Then, drag and drop the object to the top of the **Hierarchy**. Next, drag and drop the **GameController** script onto the object. Then, drag and drop the **CashText** and **RateText** objects to the respective properties in the newly added **GameController** component:

2. Now we need to call `ClickedButton` whenever the button is clicked, so from the **Hierarchy** tab, click on the `Button` object. From the `On Click ()` section, press the **+** button and then drag and drop the `GameController` game object into the slot (drag it from the **Hierarchy** tab). Then, from the function bar, call **GameController | ClickedButton**:

3. Save the scene and play the game!

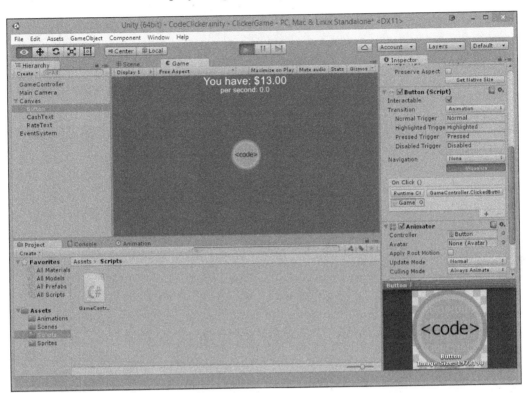

Now we have a way to increase the amount of cash we have by clicking on the button!

Creating a shop

Now that we have clicking working, let's add the ability to increase our cash per second or the amount we get per click!

1. Start off by going to **GameObject | UI | Panel** and then rename the object to `ShopPanel`. Change the values of **Left**, **Right**, **Top**, and **Bottom** to 150.

2. Now we need to create a holder for all of our buttons. Select the `ShopPanel` object from the **Hierarchy** and then create an **Image** object by going to **GameObject | UI | Image**.

Note that because we had the `ShopPanel` object selected, it automatically knew that we wanted the image object to be a child of the `ShopPanel` object.

3. Then, rename this new `Image` object to `ShopElements`. Open up the **Anchor Presets** menu and hold down *Alt + Shift* and then click on the **top-stretch** option on the bottom right:

4. Next, we will create a new component on this object to resize as needed, based on the size of our buttons. To do this, go to **Add Component** and search for `Content Size Fitter` by typing in the name to filter through all of the components until you see it. Under the newly created component, change the **Vertical Fit** to `Preferred Size` to make it change its size based on the eventual children we will be creating:

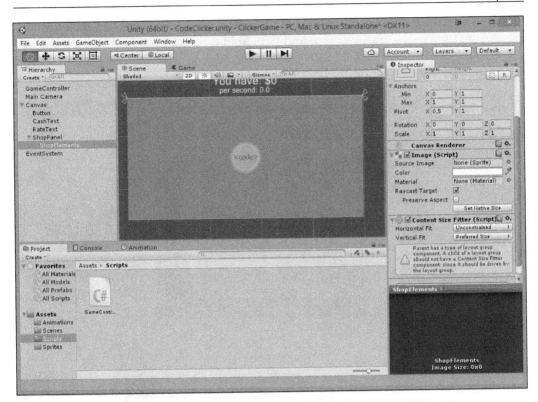

5. Now we will create our first button outside of the `ShopElements` object until we have it finished. The reason for this is that we don't want the fitter component to modify things until we are done with it. Right-click on the `ShopPanel` object and select **GameObject | UI | Button**.

6. From the **Scene** tab, change to the **Rect** tool (press *R* or press on the button on the top left of the screen) and then hold down *Alt* keys and drag from one of the edges of the button to have it resize to whatever height and width you'd like the buttons to be:

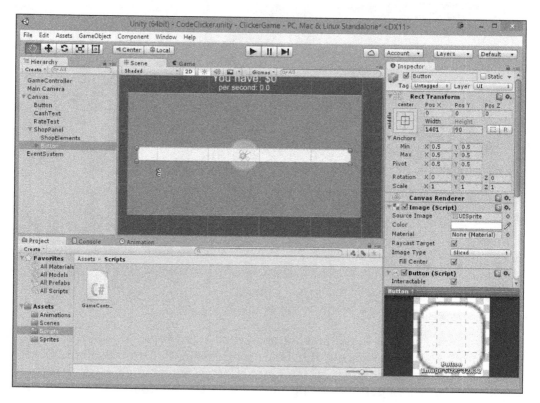

7. The text is a little difficult to read, so open up the Button text object and change the **Font Size** to 50.

8. Go back to the **Button** object and add a **LayoutElement** component, check the **Preferred Height** property, and check **Flexible Width** to let it know that we can modify how wide the button is but we prefer it to be where we have it currently:

9. We now have our base object created, so now it's time to make it possible to create many of them and work with our ShopElements object. To do that, drag and drop the Button object on top of the ShopElements object to make it a child.

10. Then, select the `ShopElements` object from the **Hierarchy** tab and add a **Vertical Layout Group** component to it (do a search like before):

11. Next go to the **Vertical Layout Group** component and extend the **Padding** property. From there, change **Left**, **Right**, **Top**, and **Bottom** to 20 as well as **Spacing** to 20 as well. This will give some much needed space between each of the objects we place as well as move them away from the center of their parent.

12. Let's get rid of the white image blocking the panel from being seen. To do this, select the `ShopElements` object and then under the **Image** component's **Color** property, change **Alpha** to 0.

We will be customizing the functionality of these buttons later on, but right now I want to point out as we keep adding new buttons to the list, it will be added to the bottom of the object, which is great but if we add too many:

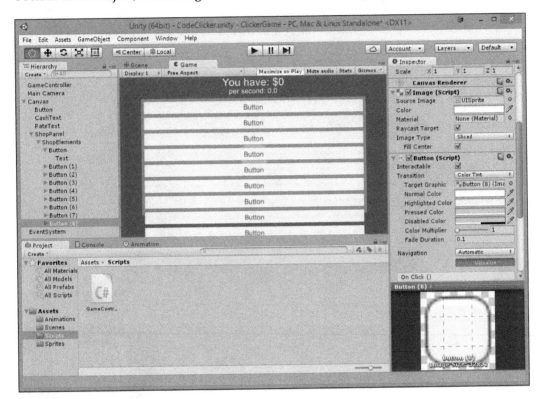

Making the list scrollable with ScrollView

As you can see, it goes off the screen. To avoid this, we will make use of the `ScrollView` component:

1. Go back to the `ShopPanel` object and then add a **Mask** component to it:

As you can see, this cuts off the contents of all of its children to fit within the Panel's image.

2. Select the `ShopPanel` object and add a **ScrollRect** component to it. Connect the **Content** component to the `ShopElements` object. We want it to just move vertically so uncheck the **Horizontal** option and change **Movement Type** to `Clamped`. To make it easier to scroll with the mouse's scrollwheel, change **Scroll Sensitivity** to `50`:

We can now scroll down the buttons by either clicking and dragging or using the mouse wheel, but we can make it easier to see by using a Scrollbar.

3. Right-click on the `Canvas` object and select **GameObject | UI | Scrollbar**. Under the **Scrollbar** component, change the **Direction** to `Bottom to Top`. Then to make it easier to work with, change the **Anchor Preset** to **stretch-right** and change the **Scale X** to 2. Then, move it over to the right of the window:

4. Select the ShopPanel object and then from **Vertical Scrollbar**, assign the newly created Scrollbar object:

5. Now, let's create an empty game object to hold the entire menu. To do this, right-click on the **Canvas** object and select **Create Empty**. From there, rename the object to ShopMenu and then drag and drop the ShopPanel and Scrollbar objects on top of it to become children. Finally, from the top of the **Inspector** tab, uncheck the ShopMenu object to easily hide the menu options:

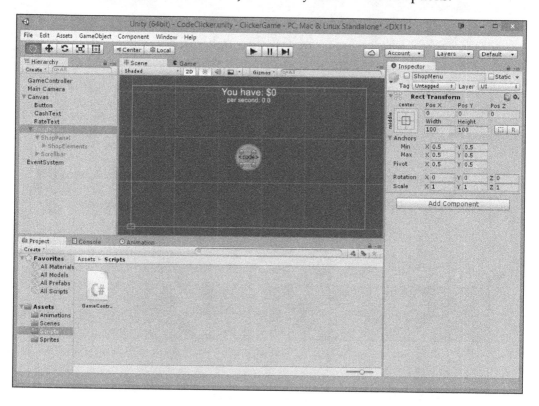

Opening/closing the shop

Now, let's make it so we can open up the shop. With this in mind, let's create a button to do just that:

1. Right-click on the Canvas object, select **GameObject | UI | Button** and then rename the object to ShopOpenButton. Change the **Width** to 300 and **Height** to 60. From there, extend the Text object by selecting it and then from the **Inspector** tab under the **Text** component, change the **Text** to Open Shop and change the **Font Size** to 40.

2. Now from the **Hierarchy** tab, select the ShopOpenButton object once again and then from the **Anchor Presets** window, hold down *Alt* and *Shift* and then click on **top-left**. Then, change **Pos X** to 20 and **Pos Y** to -20. Scroll down to the **Button** component, and from the **On Click ()** section, click on the + button. Connect the **ShopWindow** object and then from the dropdown, select **GameObject | Set Active**. Then, click on the checkmark to enable the shop. Click on + again and drag and drop the ShopOpenButton object to the list with an unchecked **SetActive** (so it'll turn itself off once pressed):

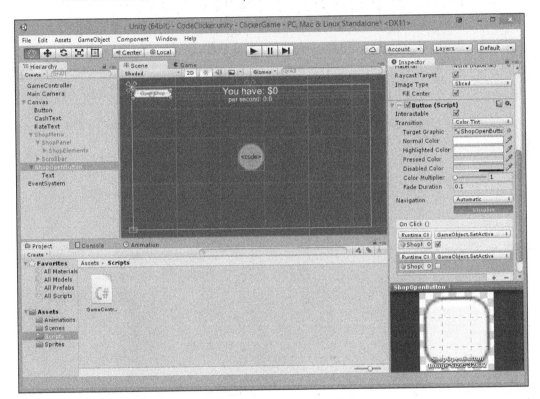

3. Now duplicate the `ShopOpenButton` (select from the **Hierarchy** tab and then press *Ctrl+D*) and rename the new one `ShopCloseButton`. Change the text of the close button to `Close Shop`, and from the object's **Button** component, add a **+** button to turn off the `OpenCloseButton` button (unchecked **SetActive**). Then, go to the `ShopOpenButton` and turn the `ShopCloseButton` object on (checked **SetActive**).

What we are doing here is so when one button is pressed, it will turn the shop on or off and then turn itself off and on:

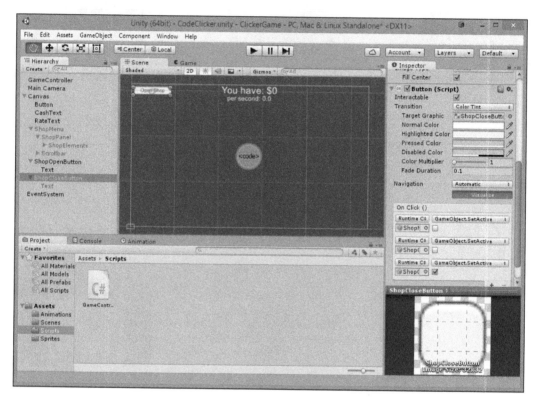

4. Save your scene and play the game:

Now when we open the shop, we will see the shop and be able to close it.

Purchasing upgrades

Now that we have the shop menu up and working, let's add in the functionality to purchase things:

1. Go to the **Hierarchy** tab and then toggle the ShopMenu back on and delete all of the other buttons except for one which will be our reference for others.

    We will want each button to have three texts – the name of the object, the number we have, and the cost to build another.

2. First, change this object's name to `Desc` and change the **Text** component's
Alignment to the left horizontally, then duplicate it (`Ctrl+D`) name the
duplicate `Cost` and center it. Finally, duplicate once more and change the
name to `Qty` and put it on the right. Fill in the values if you'd like, but we'll
be replacing the contents via code shortly:

3. Select the **Button** object and create a new C# Script named **StoreItem** and
open the script up in your IDE. Once opened, use the following code:

```csharp
using UnityEngine;
using System.Collections;
using UnityEngine.UI; // Text

public enum ItemType
{
    ClickPower, PerSecondIncrease
};


public class StoreItem : MonoBehaviour
{
```

```csharp
[Tooltip("How much will this upgrade cost.")]
public int cost;

public ItemType itemType;

[Tooltip("If purchased, how much will it increase this")]
public float increaseAmount;

private int qty;

public Text costText;
public Text qtyText;

private GameController controller;
private Button button;

// Use this for initialization
void Start ()
{
    qty = 0;
    qtyText.text = qty.ToString();
    costText.text = "$" + cost.ToString();

    button = transform.GetComponent<Button>();

    // Execute the ButtonClicked function when we click
    // the button
    button.onClick.AddListener(this.ButtonClicked);

    // Get a reference to our GameController via code
    controller =
    GameObject.FindObjectOfType<GameController>();
}

private void Update()
{
    button.interactable = (controller.Cash >= cost);
}

public void ButtonClicked()
{
    controller.Cash -= cost;
    switch (itemType)
    {
```

```
                case ItemType.ClickPower:
                    controller.cashPerClick += increaseAmount;
                    break;
                case ItemType.PerSecondIncrease:
                    controller.CashPerSecond += increaseAmount;
                    break;
            }

            qty++;
            qtyText.text = qty.ToString();
        }
    }
```

As before, let's dive into the new parts and then jump into an overall explanation as to what the code is doing.

Working with enumerations

At the top of this below the using statements, we make use of the enum keyword. Sometimes in code, we want to have a property that is used for a certain purpose, but it can be one and only one of a number of things.

For instance, if I'm having pizza for lunch, it can be in the oven cooking, on my plate, or in my mouth, but it can only be in one of those at a time.

We could use boolean values for each of these possibilities, switch one to `true` and the rest to `false`, but it's a hassle. We can also use an integer to store a number and then do different things based on a number, but then someone can put in any random number and you'd have to account for that. Instead, we create a new data type that can only have certain values for it. So in this case, `ItemType` can either be `ClickPower` or `PerSecondIncrease` but nothing else. Later on, you'll note that there will now be a variable of type `ItemType` in the class itself which we then use in the code to do something based on that value. This also makes it easier to create new types of item in the future as it'll require minimal changes to the code.

For more information on enums, check out `https://msdn.microsoft.com/en-us/library/sbbt4032.aspx`.

Switch statements

This may be the first time that has seen a switch statement before. A switch statement can be thought of as a nice way to compare a single variable against a number of different values. In this case, the switch statement mentioned previously could be rewritten as:

```
if (itemType == ItemType.ClickPower)
{
    controller.cashPerClick += increaseAmount;
}
else (itemType == ItemType.PerSecondIncrease)
{
    controller.CashPerSecond += increaseAmount;
}
```

This may not seem like a big deal with this simple example, but when we get to *Chapter 6*, we will be using a switch statement again and it'll be more apparent why switch statements are such a nice thing to use.

For those of you with a programming background, in C# you are required to put a break at the end of each case so fall-throughs are not possible by default.

Explaining the StoreItem class

As before, we've created a number of variables for us to work with, including references to text objects, which we then set whenever a value changes. Our items have a cost that the player has to pay to purchase them, and we can own more than one of them so we store how many have been purchased in the past.

The button's interactable property tells the UI system if the player can click on the button or not. In our case, we don't want the player to be able to buy anything unless they have enough money to purchase it, so in our `Update` function, we set the value to `true` if the player has enough money and `false` if not.

Finally, if the player clicks on the button and it is valid, then `ButtonClicked` will get called, which will alter a certain value based on the value of our item's type.

Note the use of the `AddListener` function, which allows us to add a function to be called whenever a `UnityEvent` is executed. For more information on that, check out `http://docs.unity3d.com/ScriptReference/Events.UnityEvent.AddListener.html`.

Filling in Item descriptions

Now that we have the functionality built in for the buttons, let's see how we can use them within the editor!

1. Save your script. Now back in the editor, attach the script to our **Button** object. In our newly added component, attach the **Cost** and **Qty** texts to the respective objects. Next, change the **Cost** to 5, set the **Item Type** to Per Second Increase, and change the **Increase Amount** to 0.1. Finally, select the **Desc** object and change the text to Hire Code Monkey.

2. Next, duplicate the button and then change the **Desc** text to Develop Game and then from the Button object, go to the **Store Item** component, change the **Cost** to 50, the **Item Type** to Click Power, and the **Increase Amount** to 1:

3. Finally, disable the `ShopMenu` object, save your scene, and start the game!

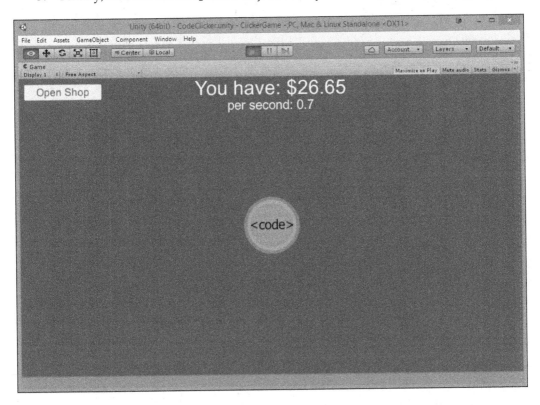

Now we have buttons that work for each of the types of thing that we can increase!

Summary

In this chapter, we have seen a simple foundation that can be expanded upon to create even more interesting projects down the road, learn how to create more complex menus and display text only when values changed.

In the next chapter, we will discover how to create an entirely different but popular title where we will see how to design a project so that it will work on multiple platforms such as mobile devices with minimal effort.

Challenges

For those of you who want to do more with this project, there are still plenty of things you can do, especially after finishing the rest of this book. Here are some ideas to get you thinking:

- Whenever you click on the button, spawn a particle system to float up with the amount of your click rate

- Use Unity's new IAP system in order to add in-app purchases to the game

- Add more graphical assets and flair to fit your own project

4
Mobile Endless Game – Procedural Content

In computing, a concept named procedural generation is a method of creating data algorithmically or rather through code as opposed to manually. This is successfully used in a lot of titles, such as in *Minecraft's* world generation and a lot of mobile games.

There are a number of advantages to this kind of development, such as the player being able to play the game forever, as well as being able to have additional replay value because every time you play it will be different.

Project overview

In this chapter, we will develop a game *Tappy Plane*, similar in gameplay to the popular mobile title *Flappy Bird*, which uses this concept to create an infinite amount of gameplay.

Your objectives

This project will be split into a number of tasks. It will be a simple step-by-step process from beginning to end. Here is the outline of our tasks:

- Adding the background
- Adding a simple animated character
- Making a repeating background
- Working with sorting layers
- Creating our player's behavior
- Creating obstacles

- Spawning obstacles at runtime
- Game starting and ending behaviors
- Keeping the score

Prerequisites

As in *Chapter 1, 2D Twin-stick Shooter*, you will need Unity installed on your computer, but we will be starting a new project from scratch.

The art assets required for this chapter, in addition to the completed project and source files, can be downloaded from the example code provided for this book on Packt's website.

Project setup

At this point, I have assumed that you have started Unity up:

1. With Unity started, go to **File | New Project**. Select a **Project Location** of your choice somewhere on your hard drive, ensure that you have 2D selected, and under **Project Name**, change it to Tappy Plane. Once completed, select **Create Project**. From there if you see the **Welcome to Unity** popup, feel free to close it as we won't be using it.

2. Create the following folders just as we described in the previous chapters:
    - Prefabs
    - Scenes
    - Scripts
    - Sprites

Adding the background

To get started, the first thing we'll need to do is add in our backgrounds:

1. From the Art Assets folder in the example code folder for this chapter, bring the background sprite into the **Project** tab under the Assets/Sprites folder by dragging and dropping it there.

 These assets are also created by Kenney and the art provided in addition to additional plane colors and assets can be found at http://kenney.nl/assets/tappy-plane.

2. If you select the `background` sprite from the **Project** tab, you'll notice that the **Inspector** tab should have **Texture Type** set to `Sprite (2D and UI)`. If not, change it and then press the **Apply** button.

   At this point, I want to point out the **Pixels Per Unit** property as it is important for our logic in the code we'll write later. By default, it is set to `100`, so the background image (which is **800 x 480**) will be 8 x 4.8 units in the Unity scene. This works out nicely for this case because we will mostly be using the width, but for traditional sprites that come in powers of 2 values (such as **64 x 64**), you may wish to change this value to the width or height value to make the image easier to work with.

3. Bring the background sprite into the world by dragging and dropping it into the **Scene** tab. Then, with the object selected, from the **Inspector** tab, right-click on the **Transform** component and then select **Reset Position**.

   We now have our background centered in the world, but you'll notice that if we play the game we see this blue background around our image, which is fairly unappealing:

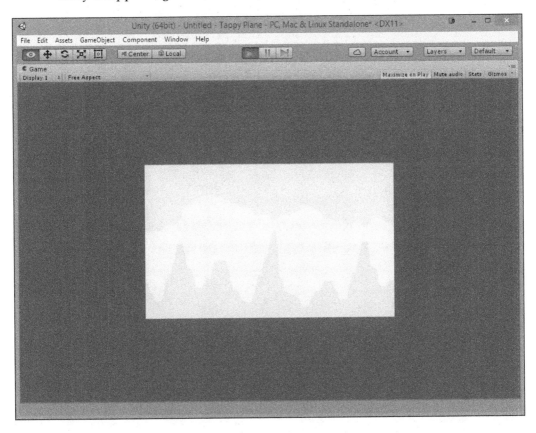

When dealing with mobile games, you want to have your project support many different resolutions and **aspect ratios**, so we will zoom our camera in so that if we're using many of the common aspect ratios seen for games it'll look correct for us.

4. From the **Hierarchy** tab, select the `Main Camera` object. From the **Inspector** tab, go to the **Camera** component and change the **Size** property to `2.2`.

    The **Size** property (known as the `orthographicSize` property in code) is half of the vertical size of the camera. Our background image is 480 pixels tall so setting the **Size** property to 2.4 would make the camera fit vertically exactly with the image. However, setting the **Size** property to 2.2 zooms us so that we have some leeway for working in different resolutions on the width side of things.

5. Now select the **Game** tab to see what the game looks like. Right under the tab, you'll see a dropdown beside **Display 1** that says what aspect ratio the game is currently testing for. Select it and go through each of them. Note that the background image will now cover the entire project. To make it easier to see, I'll be going to **16:9** for the rest of the project:

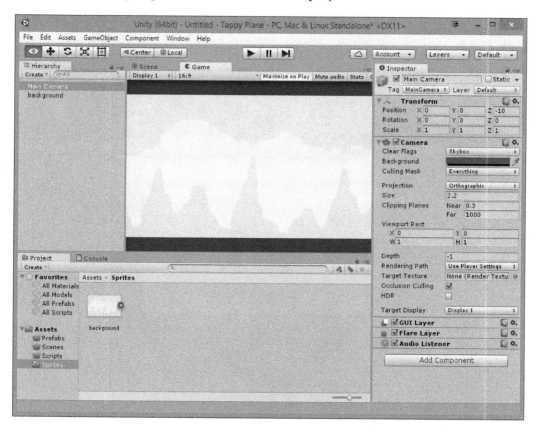

You can also press the **+** button and create your own custom resolutions to support such as the 1920x1080 of iPhone 6s Plus or qHD and wqHD of some more recent Android devices.

> For a very detailed solution towards the thinking of supporting multiple resolutions, though this is in a different game engine, it does a good job explaining the thought process for it. See `http://v-play.net/doc/vplay-different-screen-sizes/`.

Adding a simple animated character

Now that we have our background in the world, let's add in our player sprite:

1. From the `Art Assets` folder included in the example code for the chapter, bring the three sprites for the plane into the **Project** tab's `Assets/Sprites` folder.

2. Then, from the `Assets` folder, create a new folder named `Animations`.

3. From there, select all three images (hold *Ctrl* and then select each of them) and then drag and drop them into the **Scene** tab to bring them into the level. You'll see a new window pop up that says **Create New Animation**. From there, browse to the `Animations` folder we just created and then open it. Afterwards, change the **File name:** property to `PlaneFlying` and then press **Save**. This will create an animation and controller that will automatically play it. We will talk about animations in more detail in the next chapter, but currently, this will always just play an animation using these three frames over and over again unless we stop it via code.

4. The plane looks a bit large for me, so I'm going to change the **Scale** to `.5, .5, 1`. Next, we want the plane to be to the left side of the screen while also being seen from each resolution so then the **Position** to `-2.5, 0, 0`. In addition, let's rename the object `Plane`.

5. Save your `Gameplay` scene in the `Scenes` folder and project and then play the game!

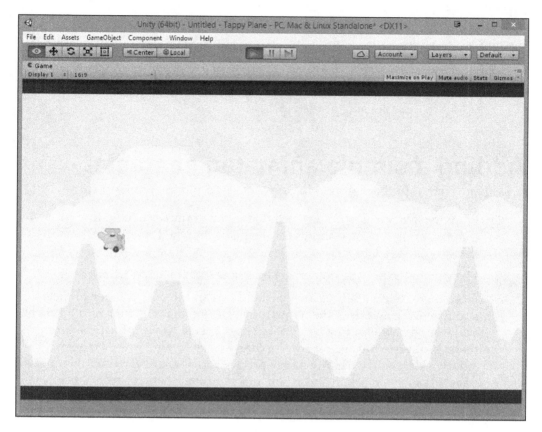

At this point, the plane animates for us automatically, and it fits in all of our aspect ratios nicely!

Making a repeating background

Of course, we could have the background remain static throughout the project, but that would get boring rather quickly and the plane will not appear to actually be moving. Instead, to make the game more visually interesting, let's have the background move to make the player's plane appear to be flying:

1. From the **Project** tab, open the `Scripts` folder and then select **Create | C# Script**. Name the newly created script `RepeatingBackground`.

2. Double-click on the script file to open it up in your IDE of choice and use the following code:

```csharp
using UnityEngine;

public class RepeatingBackground : MonoBehaviour
{

    [Tooltip("How fast should this object move")]
    public float scrollSpeed;

    /// <summary>
    /// How far to move until the image is offscreen.
    /// </summary>
    public const float ScrollWidth = 8;   // bg width /
                                          // pixels per unit


    /// <summary>
    /// Called at a fixed time frame, moves the objects and
    /// if they are off the screen do the appropriate thing
    /// </summary>
    private void FixedUpdate()
    {
        // Grab my current position
        Vector3 pos = transform.position;

        // Move the object a certain amount to the left
        // (negative in the x axis)
        pos.x -= scrollSpeed * Time.deltaTime;

        //Check if object is now fully offscreen
        if (transform.position.x < -ScrollWidth)
        {
            Offscreen(ref pos);
```

```
        }

        // If not destroyed, set our new position
        transform.position = pos;
    }

    /// <summary>
    /// Called whenever the object this is attached to goes
    /// completely off-screen
    /// </summary>
    /// <param name="pos">reference to position</param>
    protected virtual void Offscreen(ref Vector3 pos)
    {
        // Moves the object to be to off-screen on the
        // right side
        pos.x += 2 * ScrollWidth;
    }

}
```

Repeating background script

The repeating background script does a number of different things. First, we have two properties, scrollSpeed, which is the measure of how fast the background will move, and ScrollWidth, which is a const variable. The const keyword stands for constant, which means that this value cannot change from 8— the width of our background sprite.

We're also using a function named FixedUpdate, which unlike the regular update is called at a fixed time to keep the movement of our image steady. In this function, we set a helper variable pos to the object's current positon and then move it in the x axis negatively (to the left), and after we move it, we check whether it's completely off screen. If it is, then we call the Offscreen function. Afterwards, we set our position to the pos value.

The Offscreen function is something we would like to extend in the future. Instead of being public or private, we are using a new access modifier named **protected**, which means that it acts private, unless it is used by a child class, then it is still accessible. In addition, the function is also **virtual**, which means that we can override it in the future if we'd like to, which we will when we are creating our obstacles.

1. Save the script and move back to the Unity editor. Then, select the background object from the **Hierarchy** tab and add the **RepeatingBackground** component to it. From the **Inspector** tab, change the **Scroll Speed** property to 5 and then run the game:

You'll see that now the background image will move all the way over to the left and then repeat itself again! This is great, but half the time, there's some other background on our screen. Now we will see how we can easily fix this.

2. Create an empty game object, name it `Background`, and set its position to `0,0,0`. From there, drag and drop our background object on top of it to make it a child. Then, select the child again and duplicate it (*Ctrl + D*). Select the duplicate object from the **Hierarchy** tab and then change the **X** position to `8`:

This sprite on the right-hand side will move the same way as our original and will fill in the space that our left side leaves behind. It'll also be fully on the screen when we move the first image to the right via the `Offscreen` function.

With this, we now have an infinitely repeating background, but we can also reuse this same function in other interesting ways to create a more dynamic feel by adding some elements in front of the background.

3. From the **Art Assets** folder, bring in the `groundGrass` sprite and place it into the world at `0, -2, 0`.

4. Then, attach a **RepeatingBackground** component to the object with a **Scroll Speed** of 5 and change the two background object's **Scroll Speed** down to 2.

5. Make the `groundGrass` a child of the `Background` object as well and then duplicate (*Ctrl* + *D*) it with a position to 8, -2, 0.

6. Save the scene and play the game!

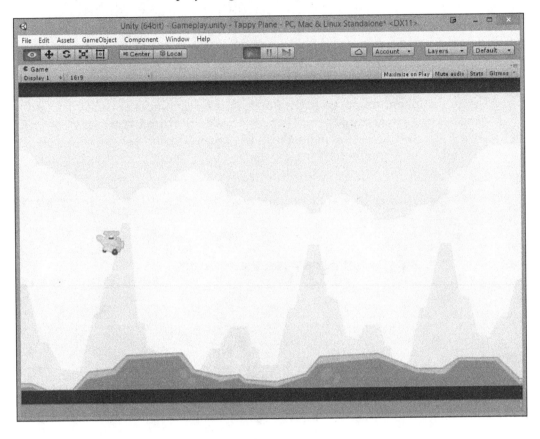

And with this, we have a much more realistic world, with objects closer to the camera moving faster than objects far away, in addition to repeating forever!

Working with sorting layers

Next, I want to ensure that the sprites that we added will actually be in the correct order from any of the other sprites that we add to the level. This is because when we place objects on the same Z position, we are telling the graphics card that we don't care what order the images are drawn to the screen (also known as z-fighting). In this case we do and even if it "looks right" in the editor right now, if you ever load or restart the scene it may not look correct so rather than wait for the problem I suggest we fix it now. I could change the Z position of the object, but rather that, we can make use of the sorting layers property instead:

1. Select one of the background objects from the **Hierarchy** tab and then from the **Inspector** tab, go to the **Sprite Renderer** component and click on the **Sorting Layer** dropdown. Then, select **Add Sorting Layer...** click on the + icon two times and name the newly created layers Background and Foreground. From there, bring the Background layer up (by dragging the = symbol on the left up) so that it's drawn first:

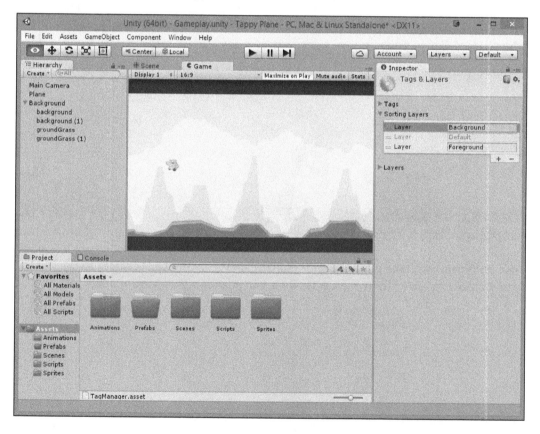

Now, the background will be drawn first, then the `Default` object (acting as our middleground), then the foreground.

2. Of course, this isn't doing anything just yet, so select the two background objects again and then under the **Sprite Renderer** component change the **Sorting Layer** to `Background`.

3. Afterwards, change the two `groundGrass` sprites to use the `Foreground` **Sorting Layer**. We'll keep the `Plane` object at the default so it'll stay as is.

At this point, the Sorting Layers are working correctly! If you want to see what happens when we change the order, go to the **Add Sorting Layer...** menu again (or click on **Layers | Edit Layers** from the top-right toolbar) and then drag and equals sign buttons in a different order. Note that if I bought `Background` all the way down, the following will happen:

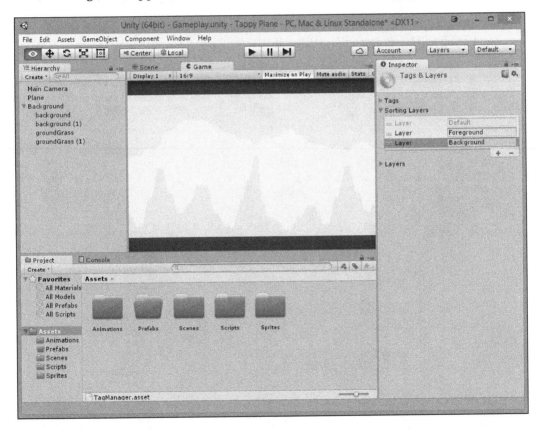

All of the other sprites would disappear because they'd be drawn first and then the background on top of them. Of course, change it back afterwards.

Creating our player behaviour

Now that we have the basic world created, let's add in the ability for our plane to actually move and interact with our world. To start off with, let's make it actually move:

1. From the **Hierarchy** tab, select the `Plane` object. Then, add a **Rigid Body 2D** component to it by selecting **Component | Physics 2D | Rigidbody 2D**.

2. We want the object to always check for collision, so from the **Inspector** tab, change the **Collision Detection** property to **Continuous**.

    Now the plane will fall but it falls directly off screen. We want it to react to being hit on the ground, so let's add collision data to it. Generally, we want to use whatever collider is simple enough to get the job done without adding complexity, but in this case, I really want to get realistic looking colliders, so we will add in the most detailed collider for 2D, the **Polygon Collider 2D**.

3. Next, add a **Polygon Collider 2D** component by selecting **Component | Physics 2D | Polygon Collider 2D**:

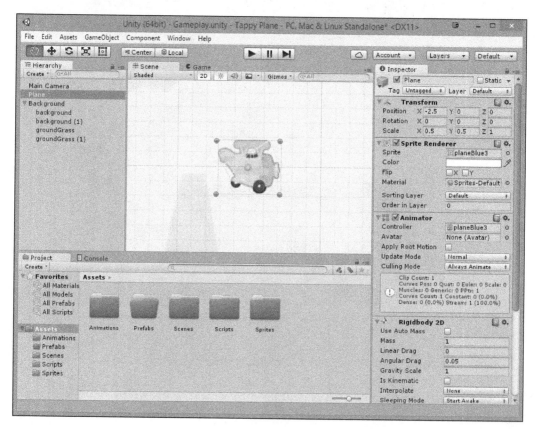

You may note the light green lines around the object. These are the parts of the object that will collide with other objects (if they have collision data as well).

4. With that in mind, select the two `groundGrass` objects and add a **Polygon Collider 2D** to it as well:

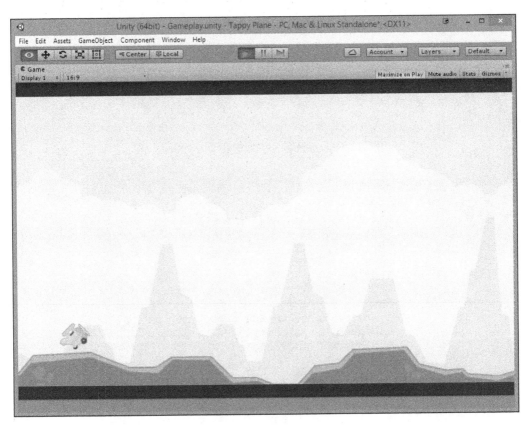

The plane will now react and stop falling once it hits the ground. Now of course the plane still moves at this point, which we'll fix later on, but for right now, we will add in the ability for the plane to "jump."

5. Now go to the **Project** tab and open up the `Assets/Scripts` folder and create a new C# Script to `PlayerBehaviour`.

6. Double-click on the newly created script and use the following code for it:

```
using UnityEngine;

[RequireComponent(typeof(Rigidbody2D))]
public class PlayerBehaviour : MonoBehaviour
{
```

```csharp
    [Tooltip("The force which is added when the player
jumps")]
    public Vector2 jumpForce = new Vector2(0, 300);

    /// <summary>
    /// If we've been hit, we can no longer jump
    /// </summary>
    private bool beenHit;

    private Rigidbody2D rigidbody2D;

    // Use this for initialization
    void Start ()
    {
        beenHit = false;
        rigidbody2D = GetComponent<Rigidbody2D>();
    }

    // Will be called after all of the Update functions
    void LateUpdate ()
    {
        // Check if we should jump as long as we haven't
        been hit yet
        if ((Input.GetKeyUp("space") ||
        Input.GetMouseButtonDown(0))
            && !beenHit)
        {
            // Reset velocity and then jump up
            rigidbody2D.velocity = Vector2.zero;
            rigidbody2D.AddForce(jumpForce);
        }
    }

    /// <summary>
    /// If we collide with any of the polygon colliders
    /// then we crash
    /// </summary>
    /// <param name="other">Who we collided with</param>
    void OnCollisionEnter2D(Collision2D other)
    {
        // We have now been hit
        beenHit = true;

        // The animation should no longer play, so we can
        // set the speed to 0 or destroy it
        GetComponent<Animator>().speed = 0.0f;
    }
}
```

7. Save the script and go back to the Editor. Then, attach the **PlayerBehaviour** component to the `Plane` object:

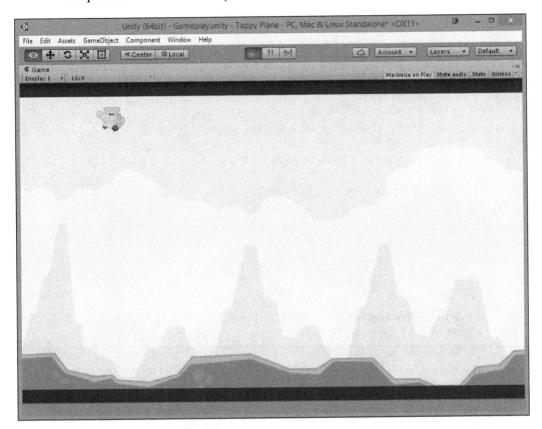

Stopping the game

Our plane will now jump up into the air, and upon hitting the ground, the plane will no longer animate. However, it would be better for the game to stop once we hit the ground, so let's add that in next. By using mouse input for jumping, this will also work by tapping on the phone:

1. Flappy Bird also has its objects falling at a faster rate than normal gravity. To change this, we can go to **Edit | Project Settings | Physics 2D** and then from there, change the **Gravity** property's **Y** value to -20. The higher the number the faster the plane will fall. However, note that this will also affect the player's jump force. Tweak these values until you get something that feels right for you.

2. Create a new C# Script named `GameController`. In it, use the
    following code:

```
using UnityEngine;

public class GameController : MonoBehaviour {

    [HideInInspector] // Hides var below
    /// <summary>
    /// Affects how fast objects with the
    /// RepeatingBackground script move.
    /// </summary>
    public static float speedModifier;

    // Use this for initialization
    void Start ()
    {
        speedModifier = 1.0f;
    }

}
```

3. Save the script and return to the Unity Editor. Create a new empty game
    object in the **Hierarchy** by selecting **GameObject | Create Empty**. Then,
    name it `GameController` and attach the **GameController** component to
    it. Finally, to make it easy to reference, drag the object to the top of the
    Hierarchy tab.

4. Next, open up the `PlayerBehaviour` script and add the following bolded
    line of code to the `OnCollisionEnter2D` function:

```
void OnCollisionEnter2D (Collision2D other)
{
    // We have now been hit
    beenHit = true;
    GameController.speedModifier = 0;

// The animation should no longer play, so we can set the speed
// to 0 or destroy it
    GetComponent<Animator>().speed = 0.0f;
}
```

5. Save that script and now open up the `RepeatingBackground` script, and from the `FixedUpdate` function, **add the following change in bold**:

```
// Move the object a certain amount to the left (negative in the
// x axis)
    pos.x -= scrollSpeed * Time.deltaTime *
            GameController.speedModifier;
```

6. Save that script and return to the Unity editor; save your project and play the game:

At this point, whenever we fall, the game will now stop the background objects! Perfect.

Creating obstacles

Of course, the game wouldn't be fun without any challenges so we're going to add in the pipe-like obstacles that the player will also need to avoid.

1. From the **Art Assets** folder, bring in the `rockGrass` and `rockGrassDown` sprite and place it into the `Assets/Sprites` folder from the **Project** tab.

2. Drag and drop the `rockGrass` object into the world. Change its position to `0`, `-2.5`, `0`. Then, add a **Polygon Collider 2D** component to it.

3. Afterwards, drag and drop the `rockGrassDown` object into the world. Change its position to `0`, `2.5`, `0`. Then, add a **Polygon Collider 2D** component to it.

4. Next, create an empty game object by selecting **GameObject | Create Empty**. Reset its position to `0,0,0` and then rename it to `Obstacle`. Afterwards, drag and drop the two `rockGrass` objects to it to become the `Obstacle` object's children:

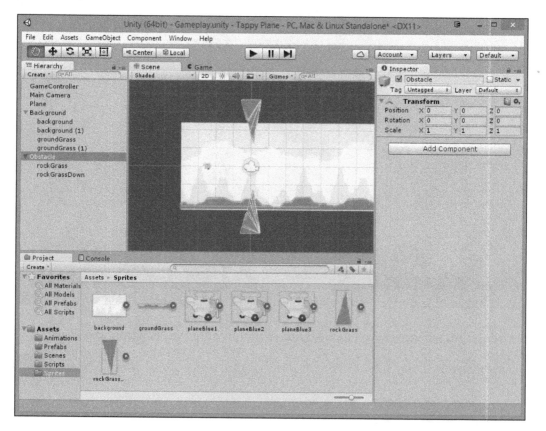

5. Now, we want the obstacle to move like the `RepeatingBehaviour` script does, except instead of repeating, we want to remove it so we can respawn. Create a new C# Script named `ObstacleBehaviour` and use the following code for it:

```
using UnityEngine;

public class ObstacleBehaviour : RepeatingBackground {

    protected override void Offscreen(ref Vector3 pos)
    {
        Destroy(this.gameObject);
    }
}
```

While it may not look like a lot, quite a lot is going on here. Note that instead of `MonoBehaviour` to the right of the `:`, we now have `RepeatingBehaviour`. What this does effectively is have `ObstacleBehaviour` inherit everything that the `RepeatingBehaviour` class has. This means that all of the properties and functionality are included from the previous script. This will allow us to only write code to extend or override the behavior from the original. In this case, we want to destroy the obstacle when it goes off screen, so all we do is override the `Offscreen` function (which we can only do if we made the function virtual earlier) to now destroy the game object this was attached to before.

 For more information on inheritance and derived classes, check out `https://msdn.microsoft.com/en-us/library/ms228387(v=vs.90).aspx`.

Save the script, then attach the newly created script to the `Obstacle` object, and set the **Scroll Speed** property to 5.

At this point, the obstacle will now go off screen, and afterwards, it'll destroy itself automatically!

Spawning obstacles at runtime

Now that we have a simple obstacle, we can now spawn a number of them through code using this object as a reference. To make this easier, let's make the obstacle a prefab:

1. Go to the **Project** tab and open up the `Prefabs` folder. Then, from the **Hierarchy** tab, drag and drop the `Obstacle` object into the **Project** tab's `Prefabs` folder. The obstacle object should turn the object.

2. Once this is done, select the `Obstacle` objects from the **Hierarchy** tab and delete it because we won't need it anymore.

3. Now that we have the obstacles, let's start spawning them. To do this, open up the `GameController` script and add the following variables:

```
[Header("Obstacle Information")]

[Tooltip("The obstacle that we will spawn")]
public GameObject obstacleReference;

[Tooltip("Minimum Y value used for obstacle")]
public float obstacleMinY = -1.3f;

[Tooltip("Maximum Y value used for obstacle")]
public float obstacleMaxY = 1.3f;
```

4. Next, add in the following function:

```
/// <summary>
/// Creates the obstacle an initializes its position.
/// </summary>
void CreateObstacle()
{
// Spawn offscreen with a random Y
Instantiate(obstacleReference,
            new Vector3(RepeatingBackground.
            ScrollWidth,
            Random.Range(obstacleMinY, obstacleMaxY),
            0.0f),
            Quaternion.identity);
}
```

5. Then, to have the function be called, add the following line to the end of the **Start** function:

```
InvokeRepeating("CreateObstacle", 1.5f, 1.0f);
```

6. Save the script and move back into the Unity editor. From the **Hierarchy** tab, select the `GameController` object and assign the `Obstacle` prefab to the **Obstacle Reference** property.

7. Save your scene and start the game!

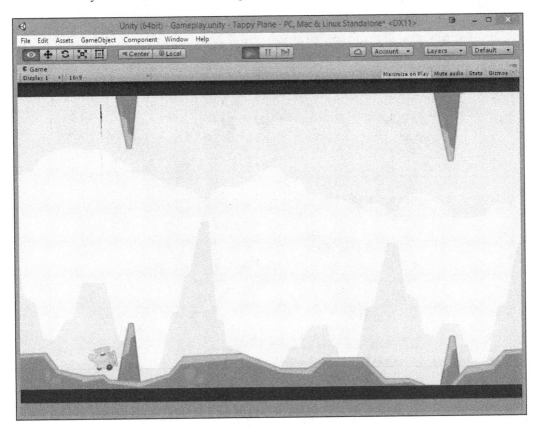

As you can see, we now have a number of different obstacles being created, each with their own different positions. Great!

Game start and end behaviours

Now, we don't want a game to automatically start as soon as we hit the play button. We want to give the player a chance to tap and then start spawning the obstacles. To do this, we'll create our own components that we will add and remove dynamically to contain this additional behavior.

1. Go to the **Project** tab, open up the Scripts folder, and create a new script named GameStartBehaviour. Open it up and use the following code:

```
using UnityEngine;

public class GameStartBehaviour : MonoBehaviour {
```

```csharp
/// <summary>
/// a reference to the player object.
/// </summary>
private GameObject player;

// Use this for initialization
void Start ()
{
    player = GameObject.Find("Plane");
    player.GetComponent<Rigidbody2D>().isKinematic =
    true;
}

// Update is called once per frame
void Update ()
{
    // Start the game
    if ((Input.GetKeyUp("space") ||
    Input.GetMouseButtonDown(0)))
    {
        // After 1 second, spawn obstacles every 1.5
        // seconds
        GameController controller =
        GetComponent<GameController>();
        controller.InvokeRepeating("CreateObstacle",
        1f, 1.5f);

        // We want the plane to start falling now
        player.GetComponent<Rigidbody2D>().isKinematic
        = false;

        // Just delete this component, not the object
        // it's attached to
        Destroy(this);
    }
}
}
```

2. Save the script and then open up the `GameController` script. Replace the `InvokeRepeating` line with the following:

```csharp
gameObject.AddComponent<GameStartBehaviour>();
```

3. Save the script and move back into the Unity Editor, save the project and play the game:

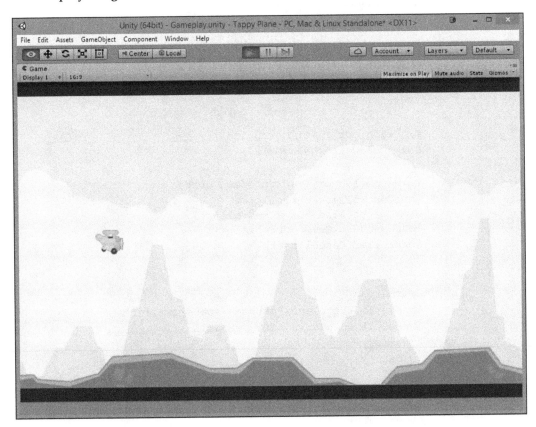

You'll note that now the game starts with the plane standing still. This is because we made the object kinematic, which means that it's not affected by other objects.

4. Now, let's make it so that when we crash, we can restart the game. To do this, let's add in a new C# script named `GameEndBehaviour`. Use the following code:

```
using UnityEngine;
using System.Collections;
using UnityEngine.SceneManagement;

public class GameEndBehaviour : MonoBehaviour {

    /// <summary>
```

```
/// Stops the player from quitting the game until a
/// certain amount of time has passed.
/// </summary>
private bool canQuit = false;

/// <summary>
/// We've lost the game so stop spawning obstacles
/// </summary>
void Start()
{
    // Start our timer coroutine
    StartCoroutine(DelayQuit());

    // We no longer need to spawn obstacles
    GameController controller =
    GameObject.Find("GameController").
    GetComponent<GameController>();
    controller.CancelInvoke();
}

/// <summary>
/// Checks if the player presses space or clicks the
/// mouse. If we can restart, we will
/// </summary>
void Update()
{
    if ((Input.GetKeyUp("space") ||
    Input.GetMouseButtonDown(0))
    && canQuit)
    {
        // Will restart up to the same level as we are
        // currently playing
        SceneManager.LoadScene(SceneManager.
        GetActiveScene().name);
    }
}

/// <summary>
/// Delays the player being able to restart instantly
/// </summary>
/// <returns>How long to wait before being called
again</returns>
```

```
IEnumerator DelayQuit()
{
    // Give the player time before we end the game
    yield return new WaitForSeconds(.5f);

    // After .5 seconds have passed it will come here.
    canQuit = true;
}
}
```

5. Now go back to `PlayerBehavior` and add the following bolded code to the end of the `OnCollisionEnter2D` function:

```
/// <summary>
/// If we collide with any of the polygon colliders
then we crash
/// </summary>
/// <param name="other">Who we collided with</param>
void OnCollisionEnter2D(Collision2D other)
{
    // We have now been hit
    beenHit = true;
    GameController.speedModifier = 0;

    // The animation should no longer play, so we can
    set the
    // speed to 0 or destroy it
    GetComponent<Animator>().speed = 0.0f;

    // Finally, create a GameEndBehaviour so we can
    restart
    if (!gameObject.GetComponent<GameEndBehaviour>())
    {
        gameObject.AddComponent<GameEndBehaviour>();
    }
}
```

6. Save all of the scripts and run the project.

At this point, whenever we lose, the game stops and after .5 seconds, we can then click once again in order to restart the project!

Keeping score

Now we have the basic gameplay in, but the player doesn't know how well they're doing to do that, we will.

1. Go to **GameObject | UI | Text**. Double-click on the Canvas object in order to see it and how the text looks compared to it.

2. Then, select the Text object and then from the **Anchors Presets** menu, hold down *Alt+Shift* and select the top-center option by clicking on it. Change the name of the object to Score Text.

3. Select the Score Text object and change the **Rect Transform** component's **Height** to 50. Under the **Text** component, change the **Text** property to 0 and change the **Alignment** to center horizontally. Then, change the **Font Size** to 40. I then changed the text color to a darker blue (If you want to use exactly what I did, you can click on the color and then for **Hex Color**, put in 7AA0ADFF).

4. We want this to be readable in most situations, so click on the **Add Component** menu and add an **Outline** component to this object as well with an **Effect Color** of white (**Hex Color** of FFFFFFFF) and an **Effect Distance** of 2, -2:

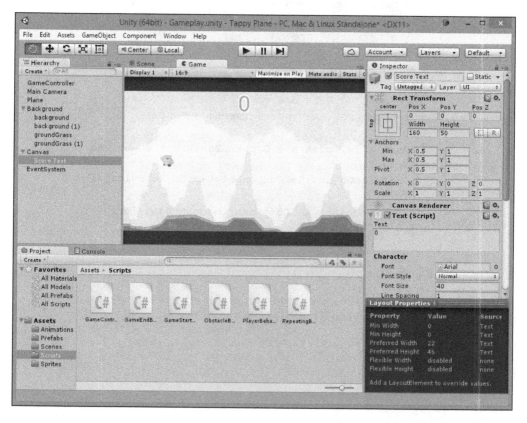

5. Now that we have the text created, let's add in the ability to gain a score. Go back to the **GameController** script add the following using:

```
using UnityEngine.UI;
```

6. Next, add the following variables to the file:

```
private static Text scoreText;
private static int score;

public static int Score
{
    get { return score; }
    set
    {
        score = value;
        scoreText.text = score.ToString();
    }
}
```

7. Afterwards, we need to initialize the variables, so add the following bolded lines to the **Start** function:

```
// Use this for initialization
void Start ()
{
    speedModifier = 1.0f;
    gameObject.AddComponent<GameStartBehaviour>();
    score = 0;
    scoreText =
    GameObject.Find("Score Text").GetComponent<Text>();
}
```

8. Save the script and now we need to increase the score when we go through the obstacles. To do this, we'll need to add in something to the obstacle prefab, so to make it easy to see the changes we'll be making, go to the **Project** tab and open up the `Prefabs` folder. From there, drag and drop an `Obstacle` object into the **Hierarchy** tab and double-click on to zoom the camera so that we can see it easily:

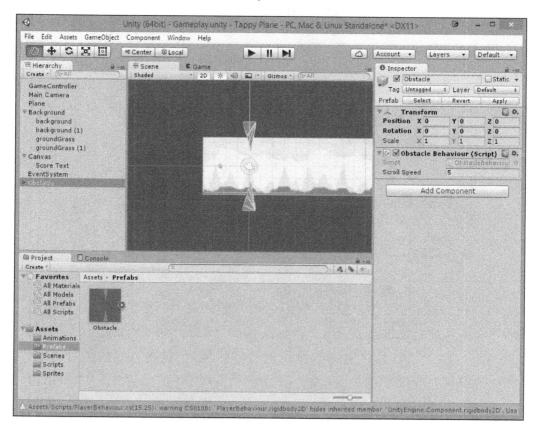

9. From here, let's add a box collider. To do this, go to **Component | Physics 2D | Box Collider 2D**. From there, click on the **Is Trigger** option and change the **Size** to `.5, 3`.

    The **Is Trigger** option allows us to tell when something collides with the collider, but instead of using physics to block the object from entering it, we can do something else using the `OnTrigger` functions instead of `OnCollision`. This is used oftentimes in games for things like spawning enemies when you enter a room. In this case, we will be increasing our score.

10. Open up the `ObstacleBehaviour` script and add the following function:

```
public void OnTriggerEnter2D(Collider2D collision)
{
    GameController.Score++;
}
```

11. Save your script and then go back to the Unity editor. From there, select the `Obstacle` objects and then from the **Inspector** tab under the **Prefab** section, click on the **Apply** button.

12. Delete the **Hierarchy** tab's `Obstacle` object and then save your project:

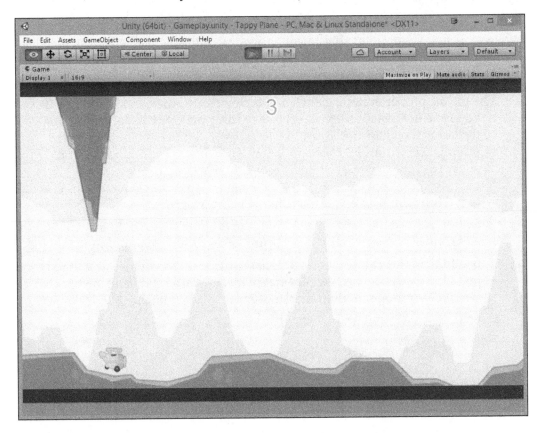

Now we can see our score increasing properly and with that our project is completed!

Summary

At this point, we have a project that will work fine on both PC as well as Mobile platforms. You also learned about sorting layers, as well as how to create gameplay that will go on forever as long as the player is skillful enough!

In the next chapter, we will be building yet another project that introduces us to create animations using tweening!

Challenges

For those of you who want to do more with this project, there are still plenty of things you can do, especially after finishing the rest of this book. Here are some ideas to get your mind thinking:

- Depending on what platform you'd like to place the title on, you'll need to have the proper module installed (which was introduced in Unity 5.3). If you have not installed it yet, feel free to run your Unity installation again including the platforms you'd like to support. For help on getting your projects onto Android, check out http://docs.unity3d.com/Manual/android-GettingStarted.html. For iOS, check out http://docs.unity3d.com/Manual/iphone-GettingStarted.html. Do note that in order to publish it on iOS, Apple may charge additional fees.

- Once you finish the next chapter and learn about iTween, add in a **Get Ready** and **Game Over** screen that will fly or fade in to add more polish to the title.

- In addition, you can add an additional text object that will tell you to tap or press the mouse depending on what platform you are on using defines. To see some examples on that, check out http://docs.unity3d.com/Manual/PlatformDependentCompilation.html.

5
Shooting Gallery – Working with Animations and Tweens

Now that we have some games under our belt, I thought it'd be a good idea for us to dive into how to make our games feel more "alive." One of the ways that we can do this is by adding animations to our worlds, so things aren't just static.

There are many different ways in which you can create animation, and in this chapter, we will be covering three different ways, using Unity's built-in animations, using a tweening library such as iTween, and moving objects ourselves via code.

Project overview

This project will teach us how to create a simple shooting gallery game in which players can shoot at targets before the time is up. In the meantime, we'll learn the various ways to animate things such as by Unity's built-in animations or a Tweening library such as `iTween`. Finally, we will use `PlayerPrefs` to set a new high score.

Your objectives

This project will be split into a number of tasks. It will be a simple step-by-step process from beginning to end. Here is the outline of our tasks:

- Creating the environment
- Adding our targets
- The animation via Unity's animation system
- The animation using iTween
- Creating moving targets

- Creating many targets
- Starting/ending the game
- Saving our high score

Prerequisites

The art assets required for this chapter, in addition to the completed project and source files can be downloaded from the example code provided for this book on Packt's website.

Project setup

To start this project, we will start off with creating a new project:

1. With Unity started, go to **File** | **New Project**. Select a **Project Location** of your choice somewhere on your hard drive and ensure that you have 2D selected, and under **Project Name**, change it to Shooting Gallery. Once completed, select **Create Project**. From there, if you see the **Welcome to Unity** popup, feel free to close it as we won't be using it.

2. Create the following folders, just as we described in the previous chapters:
   - Animations
   - Prefabs
   - Scenes
   - Scripts
   - Sprites

Creating the environment

To get started, the first thing we'll need to do is add in our backgrounds:

1. From the **Art Assets** folder in the example code folder for this chapter, bring the background sprite into the **Project** tab under the **Assets/Sprites** folder by dragging and dropping it there.

 These assets are also created by Kenney, and the art provided in addition to additional plane colors and assets can be found at http://kenney.nl/assets/shooting-gallery.

---

2. In this chapter, we will be creating a more detailed environment, which will consist of a sky layer, then a grass layer with three water layers on top of it. I have provided the completed level (`StartingMap`) for those who want to get started and you can skip to the next section, but for those who wish to know how to assemble the map, you'll need to do the following:

3. To start this off, bring the `bg_blue` sprite into the **Scene** tab and duplicate (*Ctrl+D*) four of them placing them horizontally away from each other while creating a `Background` sorting layer and assigning them to it. Then, create an empty game object named `Background` and place all of those objects inside of it.

4. Afterwards, create another layer using the two grass textures one after the other, then duplicate and drag it until the area created by the background is filled out. Create an empty game object to hold them all named **Grass Layer**. Feel free to place some trees up at the top to make it a bit more interesting.

5. Next, do the same thing as the grass with the water texture provided creating a parent object named **Water Row 1**. We want to make sure that this object is on top of the grass so change the z value to `-1`.

6. Duplicate the water layer twice by changing the z values to `-2` and `-3`, respectively, naming them **Water Row 2** and **Water Row 3**.

7. Finally, select the **Main Camera** object and zoom the camera in to have a **Size** of `3.9`. Once you're finished, you should have something like this:

Adding a target

In our shooting gallery, we will need to have something to shoot. In this case, we will need to create a target, which the player can shoot:

1. Create an empty game object by going to the **Hierarchy** tab and selecting **Create** | **Empty Game** object. Rename that object **Target** and change its **Position** to 0, 0,-4 so it'll be on top of other objects.

2. Add the wooden stick and the duck_outline_brown sprites to the **Target** object, giving the duck a **Position** of 0, 1.1,0 to place it on top of the stick.

3. We want the player to be able to touch the duck so next we will need to add a Polygon Collider 2D component to the duck_outline_brown object:

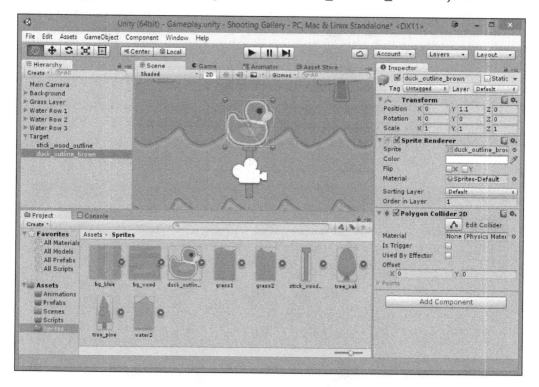

Animating the duck using Unity's animation system

1. Now, let's make it so that our duck will animate when we click on it, but before we do it, we first need to add a base animation for it to use. To do this, open up the **Animation** tab by going to **Window | Animation**. This will open the **Animation** tab by itself.

2. Next, from the **Hierarchy** tab, select the **Target** object and then from the **Animation** window, click on the **Create** button on the right-hand side:

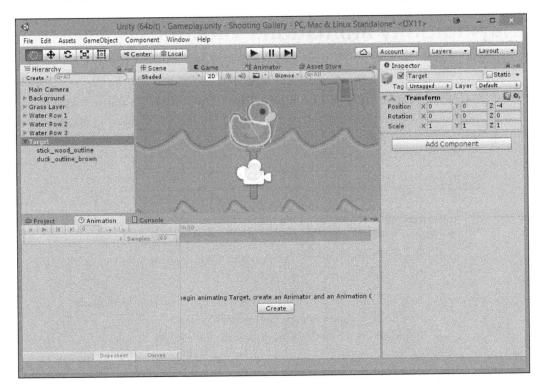

3. It will ask you where you want to save your animation. In this case, go to the Animations folder we created earlier and then give it a name of Idle before saying **OK**.

4. This animation we don't want to change due to the fact that we want it to not move, so let's click on the Idle drop-down and create a new clip, which will create a new animation and we will name Flip.

5. Once created, move the timeline to the 10th frame (0:10). From there, change the **Target** object's Y **Rotation** to `90`. Select the `duck_outline_brown` object and change its sprite to the `duck_outline_back` image. Then, create another `keyframe` at the 20th frame with a Y **Rotation** of `180`.

6. This animation currently will loop itself, which will look incorrect on our end, so let's fix that. Go to the **Project** tab, open the `Animations` folder, and select the `Flip` animation. From the **Inspector** tab, uncheck the **Loop Time** property. This will cause the animation to play once and then stop at the end, which is exactly what we want.

Playing Unity animations via code

Now that we have the animation working, let's make it so that we play the animation via code:

1. Go to the **Project** tab, open up the **Scripts** folder, and from there, create a new script named `TargetBehaviour`. Inside it, use the following script:

    ```
    using UnityEngine;
    using System.Collections;

    public class TargetBehaviour : MonoBehaviour {

        private bool beenHit = false;
        private Animator animator;
        private GameObject parent;

        void Start()
        {
            parent = transform.parent.gameObject;
            animator = parent.GetComponent<Animator>();
        }

        /// <summary>
        /// Called whenever the player clicks on the object.
        /// only works if you have a collider on the object
        /// </summary>
        void OnMouseDown()
        {
            // Is it valid to hit it
            if (!beenHit)
            {
                beenHit = true;
    ```

```
        animator.Play("Flip");
      }
    }
  }
```

This code will play the `Flip` animation on our target once we click on it. Note that the animator variable uses the object's parent. We need to do this because our collider is attached to the duck itself, not the **Target** object.

2. Save the script and then go to the `duck_outline_brown` image and then attach the `Target Behavior` to it.

3. Save the scene and play the game. Now you can click on the sprite:

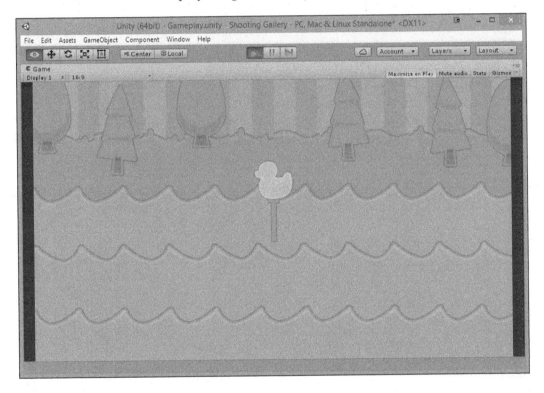

We have the animation playing correctly! This is a great start.

Animation using iTween

Being able to use Unity's built-in animation system is great and can be quite useful if you want to modify many different properties at once. However, if you're only modifying a single property or you want to animate something purely via code, you can also make use of a tweening library where given a start and an end the library will take care of all the work in the middle to get it there within a time and speed you specify.

One of my favorite tweening libraries is `PixelPlacement`'s `iTween`, which is open source and useable for free in commercial and noncommercial projects.

1. Open up the **Asset Store** tab by going to **Window | Asset Store**. Type in iTween from the search bar at the top and then press *Enter*:

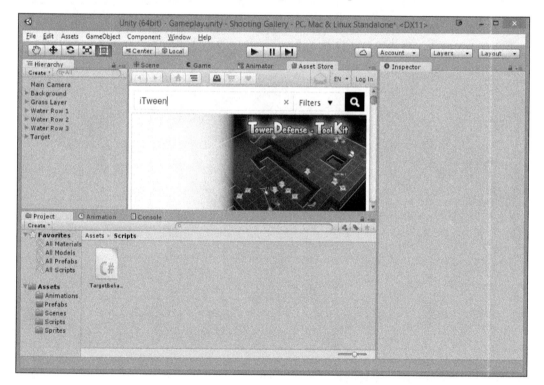

2. If the **Asset Store** tab is too small for you, as it is here, feel free to drag it out of the middle section and resize until it looks nice for you.

3. From there, you'll be brought to a list of items with the first one being **iTween**. Select it and you should be brought to iTween's product page. Click on the **Download** button:

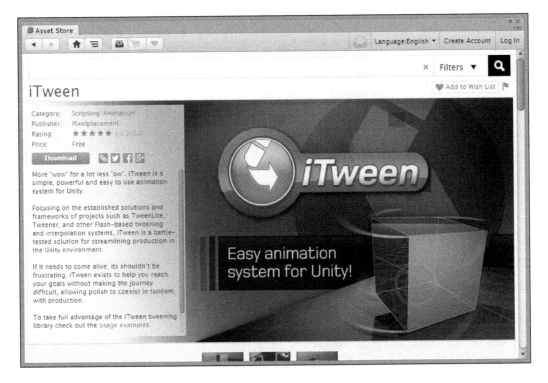

4. From there, you'll be asked to log in to your Unity account that you created when you installed Unity. If you don't have one, feel free to click on **Create Account** and do so. Once logged in, click on **Download** once again, and if it doesn't happen automatically, click on the **Import** button.

5. You should see an **Import Unity Package** window pop up. From there, you can check or uncheck whatever files you wish to keep. I will just be using **iTween.cs**, but the others may be useful to you and you should wish to use them on your own. Once you're finished selecting, click on the **Import** button:

6. We don't need the **Asset Store** anymore, so go ahead and close it out. You'll note that now we have the files we have selected inside our **Project** tab:

7. Now that we have **iTween** included in our project, we can now use it inside of our code. Open up our `Target Behavior` script in your IDE of choice and add the following variable:

```
private bool activated;
```

8. Next, add in the following function:

```
public void ShowTarget()
{
    if (!activated)
    {
        activated = true;
        beenHit = false;
        animator.Play("Idle");

        iTween.MoveBy(parent, iTween.Hash("y", 1.4,
                                        "easeType",
                                        "easeInOutExpo",
                                        "time", 0.5
                                        ));
    }

}
```

From here, we'll see our first function that we are calling from **iTween** the MoveBy function. This takes in two parameters—the first being the object we wish to move and the second being a Hash or hashtable. A **hashtable** is a data structure that creates an associative array such that certain keys will be mapped to certain values. In **iTween**, their implementation takes in sets of two with the first being a property and then second being the value we want it to be.

> For more information on hashtables, check out http://en.wikipedia.org/wiki/Hash_table.
>
> For more information on getting started with iTween, check out http://itween.pixelplacement.com/gettingstarted.php.

1. Now that we have this function, for testing purposes let's add to the end of the Start function the following line: ShowTarget();

2. Save your project and play the game!.

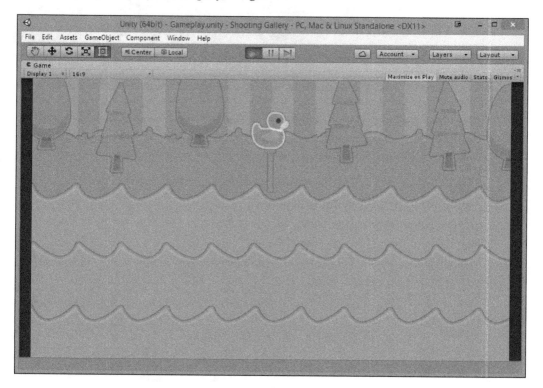

Once the game starts, you'll note that the duck flies up in the y axis by the amount we specified via the hash!

1. Now, let's make it so that the duck will move back down once we click on it. Add the following variable to the class:

```
private Vector3 originalPos;
```

2. Afterwards, add the following line inside the Start function so that we initialize it:

```
originalPos = parent.transform.position;
```

3. Then, add in this new function:

```
public IEnumerator HideTarget()
{
    yield return new WaitForSeconds(.5f);

    // Move down to the original spot
    iTween.MoveBy(parent.gameObject, iTween.Hash(
    "y", (originalPos.y -
    parent.transform.position.y),
    "easeType", "easeOutQuad", "loopType", "none", "time",
    0.5, "oncomplete", "OnHidden", "oncompletetarget",
    gameObject));
}
```

> Note that in this case, we added the oncomplete and oncompletetarget parameters to our hash map. oncomplete will call a function (in this case, OnHidden, which we will create after this) after the amount of time has elapsed and "oncompletetarget" will be what object iTween will look for the function with a name of whatever was provided in the oncomplete portion. This is only needed if the object you're animating is not the object that iTween is called on.

4. Add in the OnHidden function:

```
/// <summary>
/// After the tween finishes, we now make sure we can be shown
/// again.
/// </summary>
void OnHidden()
{
    //Just to make sure the object's position resets
    parent.transform.position = originalPos;
    activated = false;
}
```

5. And finally, we need to update the `OnMouseDown` button so that we will only flip when the animation is valid by adding in the following bolded code:

```
void OnMouseDown()
{
    // Is it valid to hit it
    if (!beenHit && activated)
    {
        beenHit = true;
        animator.Play("Flip");
        StartCoroutine(HideTarget());
    }
}
```

6. Save your level and project and start up the game!

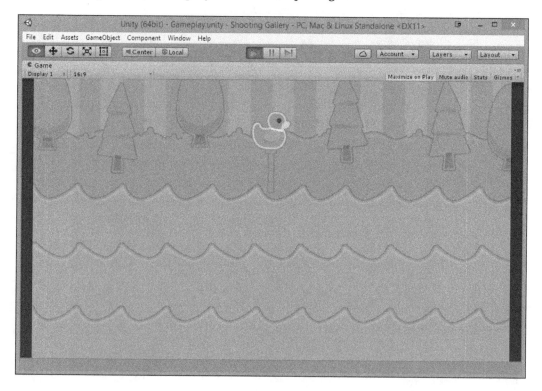

7. Our sprite pops up at the beginning and once we click on it:

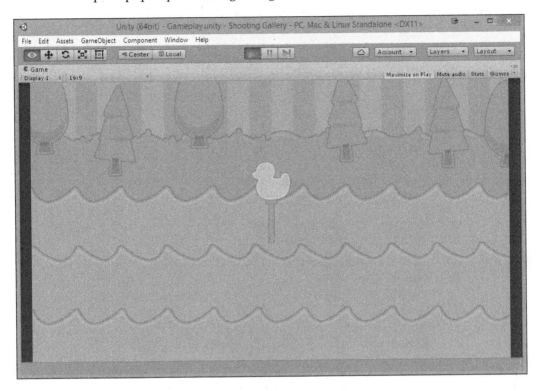

It flips and falls down, perfect!

Creating moving targets

Now we have our duck, and it can come up and down, it also needs to move rather than just stay in place:

1. First, let's make it so we can do something once the duck has risen all the way up. To do this, update the ShowTarget function to the following:

```
public void ShowTarget()
{
    if (!activated)
    {
        activated = true;
        beenHit = false;
        animator.Play("Idle");
```

```
        iTween.MoveBy(parent, iTween.Hash("y", 1.4,
        "easeType", "easeInOutExpo", "time", 0.5,
        "oncomplete", "OnShown", "oncompletetarget",
        gameObject));
    }

}
```

2. Now, let's add the `OnShown` function so that after the object has popped up, it can start moving:

```
void OnShown()
{
    StartCoroutine("MoveTarget");
}
```

3. Now, before we write the `MoveTarget` function, let's add in the variables needed to have our player move correctly:

```
public float moveSpeed = 1f;     // How fast to move in
// x axis
public float frequency = 5f;     // Speed of sine
// movement
public float magnitude = 0.1f;   // Size of sine
// movement
```

4. Now, let's create a coroutine to cause the target to move up and down over time while going towards the edge of the screen:

```
IEnumerator MoveTarget()
{
    var relativeEndPos = parent.transform.position;

    // Are we facing right or left?
    if (transform.eulerAngles == Vector3.zero)
    {
        // if we're going right positive
        relativeEndPos.x = 6;
    }
    else
    {
        // otherwise negative
        relativeEndPos.x = -6;
    }

    var movementTime =
    Vector3.Distance(parent.transform.position,
    relativeEndPos) * moveSpeed;
```

```
    var pos = parent.transform.position;
    var time = 0f;

    while (time < movementTime)
    {
        time += Time.deltaTime;

        pos += parent.transform.right * Time.deltaTime *
        moveSpeed;
        parent.transform.position = pos +
        (parent.transform.up *
        Mathf.Sin(Time.time * frequency) *
        magnitude);

        yield return new WaitForSeconds(0);
    }

    StartCoroutine(HideTarget());
}
```

Math is a game developer's best friend, and here we are using sin (pronounced sine) by using the `Mathf.Sin` function.

Taking the sin of an angle number gives you the ratio of the length of the opposite side of the angle to the length of the hypotenuse of a right-angled triangle.

If this didn't make any sense to you, don't worry. The neat feature of sin is that as the number gets larger, it will continuously give us a value between 0 and 1 that will go up and down forever, giving us a smooth repetitive oscillation.

 For more information on sine waves, visit http://en.wikipedia.org/wiki/Sine_wave.

This mathematical principle could be used in a lot of effects, such as having save points/portals bob up and down, or any kind of object you would want to have slight movement or some special FX:

1. Next, we need to update the `OnMouseDown` function so that the horizontal movement won't happen anymore if we click on the duck:

   ```
   /// <summary>
   /// Called whenever the player clicks on the object. Only works if
   ```

```
/// you have a collider
/// </summary>
void OnMouseDown()
{
    // Is it valid to hit it
    if (!beenHit && activated)
    {
        beenHit = true;
        animator.Play("Flip");

        StopAllCoroutines();

        StartCoroutine(HideTarget());
    }
}
```

2. Save your project and start the game!

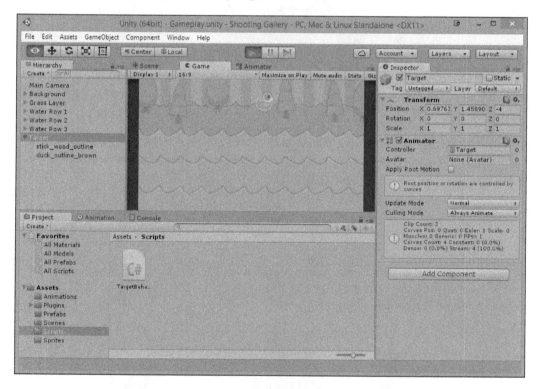

Now our target will move towards our edge with a slight bobbing motion and will automatically hide itself afterwards if it is not clicked! Perfect!

Creating many targets

Now that we have one target working correctly, let's make all of the others using the original as a template:

1. To start off with, let's make our **Target** a prefab, so let's do that by going to the **Hierarchy** tab and then dragging and dropping the object into the **Prefabs** folder from the **Project** tab. This will be useful if you later on decide to make changes to all of them. This way, you can just modify the one rather than having to do it over and over again.

2. We then will need to move our current target to a good spot. Let's go with **-5.75**, **-4.5**, and **2.5**.

 I'm doing **-2.5** because the front row is at -3 and the middle row is at -2.5, that is, we are going to be placed directly between them. A quick view in 3D will show us that as well:

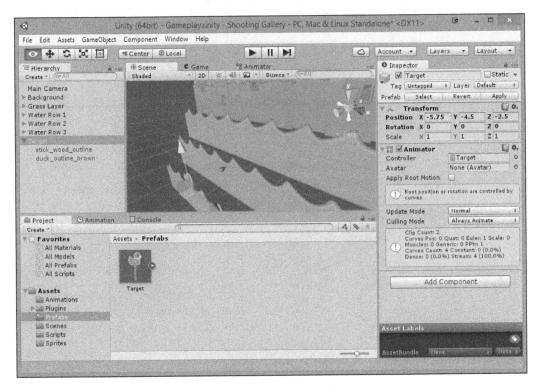

3. Duplicate that duck and then position the new one's **X position** to **-3.75** (2 units away) and do that four more times for a total of 6 ducks in the row:

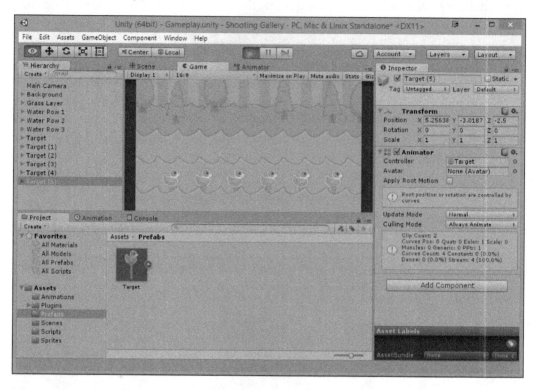

4. Create an empty game object with a **Position** of 0,0,0 and give it a name of **Duck Row 3** and then drag and drop our **Targets** into it.

5. Duplicate the **Duck Row 3** object, rename it to **Duck Row 2**, and change its **Position** to 0, 1.75, and 1.

6. Duplicate **Duck Row 2** and rename it to 1 with a position of 0, 3.4, and 2.

7. Finally, select the **Duck Row 2** object and then change the **Y Rotation** to **180** and **Z position** to **-4** (to make it fit between the two rows taking into consideration the rotation):

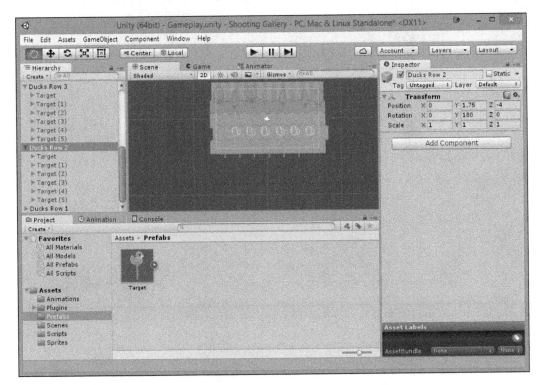

8. And with this, save your level and play the game!

As you can see, they're all moving and falling correctly!

Creating waves of targets

Now that we have all of the pieces together, let's make it so that we will only spawn a few ducks at a time and have a few of them appear at a time.

1. Open up the `TargetBehaviour` script, and in the `Start` function, remove the following line:

   ```
   ShowTarget();
   ```

   This will keep the targets in their original position until we are ready for them to be shown.

2. Next, we will create a new script named `GameController` by going to the **Project** tab and then selecting **Create | C# Script** and once it appears give it a name of `GameController`. Double-click on the file to open up your IDE of choice and add the following code:

```
using UnityEngine;
using System.Collections;              // IEnumerator
using System.Collections.Generic; // List

public class GameController : MonoBehaviour
{
    public static GameController _instance;

    [HideInInspector] // Hides var below from inspector
    public List<TargetBehaviour> targets = new
List<TargetBehaviour>();

    void Awake()
    {
        _instance = this;
    }

    // Use this for initialization
    void Start ()
    {
        StartCoroutine("SpawnTargets");
    }

    void SpawnTarget()
    {
        // Get a random target
        int index = Random.Range(0, targets.Count);
        TargetBehaviour target = targets[index];

        // Show it
        target.ShowTarget();
    }

    IEnumerator SpawnTargets()
    {
        yield return new WaitForSeconds(1.0f);

        // Continue forever
        while (true)
        {
            int numOfTargets = Random.Range(1, 4);

            for (int i = 0; i < numOfTargets; i++)
            {
                SpawnTarget();
```

```
                    }

           yield return new
           WaitForSeconds(Random.Range(0.5f *numOfTargets,
           2.5f));
        }
     }
}
```

3. Next, we need to fill the values of targets, so to do that, go back into the
   `TargetBehaviour` script and add the following function:

```
// Called before Start
void Awake()
{
    GameController._instance.targets.Add(this);
}
```

4. Then, add an empty game object to the scene (**GameObject | Create Empty**),
   center it at 0, 0, 0, and rename it **GameController**. Afterwards, add a
   GameController component to it.

5. Save your project and run the game:

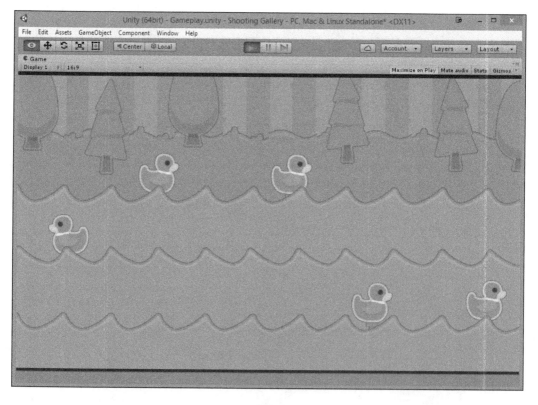

Now as you can see the ducks appear in waves with a random number of ducks appearing after a period of time. Excellent!

Adding in a time limit

Of course, if we kept playing the game, it would get boring over time due to their being no stakes, so let's add in a time limit to have the player hit as many ducks as possible within that time!

1. Let's add in a text to display to the player how much time they have left. To do this, go to **Game Object | UI | Text** and then switch over to the **Game** tab to see it.

2. Select the **Text** object from the **Hierarchy** and then from the **Inspector** tab, rename it to **Time Text**. Afterwards, open up the **Anchor Presets** menu on the left-hand side of the **Rect Transform** component, then hold *Alt+Shift* and then click on the top-center option to reposition the object.

3. Then, change **Height** to **100** and **Width** to **400,** so when we increase the size, it'll still show up.

4. After this, change the **Text** component's **Text** to **50** and then changes the **Font Size** to **60** and the **Horizontal Alignment** to **Centered**:

5. Next, let's add in an `Outline` component, change the color to white with 255 alpha and then change the **Effect Distance** to `2, -2`.

6. Now that we have this, open up the `GameController` and add the following line to the top include add:

```
using UnityEngine.UI; // Text
```

7. Next, add in the following variables:

```
private float timeLeft;
public Text timeText;
```

8. Afterwards, add the following to the `Awake` function:

```
timeLeft = 50;
timeText.text = timeLeft.ToString();
```

9. Update the `Start` function to the following:

```
// Use this for initialization
void Start ()
{
    iTween.ValueTo(gameObject, iTween.Hash(
            "from", timeLeft,
            "to", 0,
            "time", timeLeft,
            "onupdatetarget", gameObject,
            "onupdate", "tweenUpdate",
            "oncomplete", "GameComplete"
            ));
    StartCoroutine("SpawnTargets");
}
```

10. Then, add the following functions:

```
void GameComplete()
{
    StopCoroutine("SpawnTargets");
    timeText.color = Color.black;
    timeText.text = "GAME OVER";
}

void tweenUpdate(float newValue)
{
    timeLeft = newValue;
    if (timeLeft > 10)
    {
```

```
            timeText.text = timeLeft.ToString("#");
    }
    else
    {
        timeText.color = Color.red;
        timeText.text = timeLeft.ToString("#.0");
    }
}
```

11. Back in the editor, go back to the **Hierarchy** tab, select the `GameController` object, and assign the `Time Text` variable to our `Time Text` object.

12. Save your project and start the game!

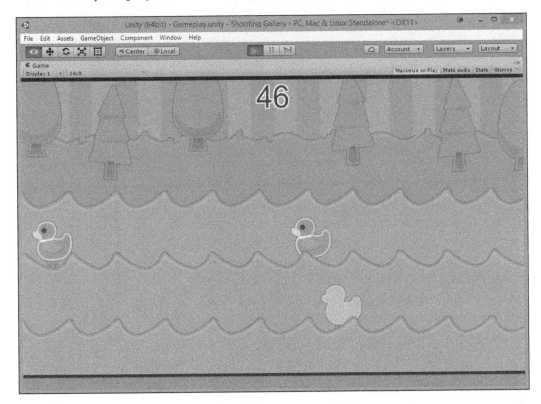

As expected, we now have a timer, and when we get to 10 seconds or less, it will turn red!

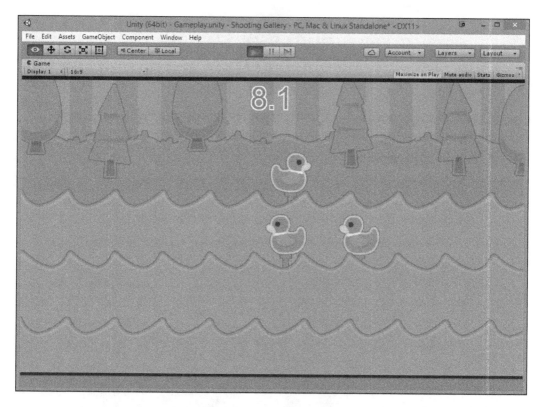

Adding in Score/High score

Now that the game has the start and ending, let's make it so that we can gain a score whenever we hit a duck:

1. From the **Hierarchy** tab, duplicate the Time Text object and rename it to Score Text. Go to the **Rect Transform's Anchor Presets** menu, hold down *Alt + Shift*, and click on the top-left option. Then, change **Pos X** to **10** and **Pos Y** to **-10** to push it a bit off from the edge of the screen.

2. Then, in the **Text** component, change the **Horizontal** alignment to the left and change the **Text** to **Score 0**.

3. Finally, change the `Outline` component's **Effect Distance** to 1.5, -1.5:

4. Next, we will want to duplicate the **Score Text object** and rename it **High Score Text**. From there, open up the **Anchor Presets** menu, hold down *Alt + Shift*, and click on the top-right option. Afterwards, change **Pos X** to **-10** and **Pos Y** to **-10**.

5. Afterwards, in the **Text** component, change the **Text** to **High Score 0**. Then, change the **Alignment** to the right side:

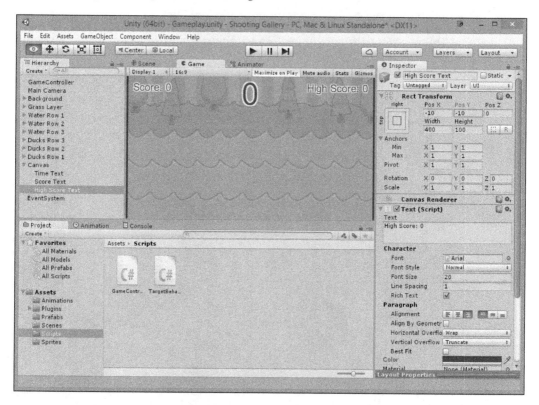

Now that we have the objects created, let's add in the functionality for scoring using what we already know and `PlayerPrefs` for the high score.

PlayerPrefs allow us to store small amounts of data on the end user's machine. Using `PlayerPrefs` is a great way to save data for user levels, the coordinates of where enemies are, or a high score so when the user comes back to the game, it will show the highest score achieved over the course of all games played.

6. Open up the `GameController` script and from there, add in the following variables:

```
private int score;
public Text scoreText;
public Text highScoreText;
```

7. Now in the `Start` function, add in the following bolded code:

```
// Use this for initialization
void Start ()
{
    iTween.ValueTo(gameObject, iTween.Hash(
                    "from", timeLeft,
                    "to", 0,
                    "time", timeLeft,
                    "onupdatetarget", gameObject,
                    "onupdate", "tweenUpdate",
                    "oncomplete", "GameComplete"
                    ));
    StartCoroutine("SpawnTargets");

    highScoreText.text = "High Score: " +
    PlayerPrefs.GetInt("highScore").ToString();
    score = 0;
}
```

PlayerPrefs

As I mentioned previously, the `PlayerPrefs` class allows us to save small parts of data on our player's computers for retrieval later. The `PlayerPrefs` can store the following types: `float`, `int`, and `string`. There are two key functions for each of the types `Get` and `Set` with the type added afterwards (`GetFloat`, `SetString`, and so on).

Set

The `Set` functions take in two parameters — the first being a string and the second being of the type you're trying to set. This will save the value in the second parameter to the registry on our computer with the string as a reference for us to get the data back with the `Get` function.

If there was a value previously saved with that variable name, it will be overwritten with the new value.

 To be sure that your variables do not get overwritten by other projects, it's important to make sure that you set the **Product Name** and **Company Name** in the **Project Settings**.

Get

The Get functions will retrieve the value that it currently has set, if there is one. If it cannot find a value (that variable doesn't exist yet), it will return 0, or whatever you put in as the second parameter. So as an example, I could do something like this:

```
void Start()
{
        print(PlayerPrefs.GetString("Player Name", "Bob"));
}
```

Then, if there already is a value assigned for **Player Name**, it will print out that, but otherwise, it will give you the value of Bob. This is great if you want to have a default value other than 0 or an empty string "".

Depending on what operating system you're currently using for this project or are porting to the location of where the values are saved to are different. For these locations, or for more information on the PlayerPrefs class, check out http://docs.unity3d.com/ScriptReference/PlayerPrefs.html.

Next, we need to create the functionality for hitting something, so add in the following function:

```
public void IncreaseScore()
{
    score++;
    scoreText.text = "Score: " + score.ToString();

    if (score > PlayerPrefs.GetInt("highScore"))
    {
        PlayerPrefs.SetInt("highScore", score);
        highScoreText.text = "High Score: " +
        score.ToString();
    }
}
```

Finally, we need to call the function, so go into the TargetBehaviour script and add in the following bolded line:

```
/// <summary>
/// Called whenever the player clicks on the object.
/// Only works if you have a collider
/// </summary>
void OnMouseDown()
{
    // Is it valid to hit it
```

```
if (!beenHit && activated)
{
    GameController._instance.IncreaseScore();
    beenHit = true;
    animator.Play("Flip");

    StopAllCoroutines();

    StartCoroutine(HideTarget());
}
}
```

Save both of your scripts and go back into the Unity editor. Select the **Game Controller object** and assign the **Score Text** and **High Score Text** variables to their respective game objects:

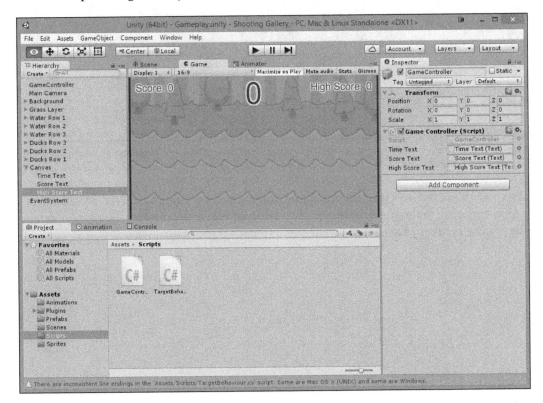

Save your project and run the game!

As you can see, when you play the game and exceed the high score, it will save that value and update the high score text. In addition, when you restart the game, your high score is saved! Excellent!

Summary

We created a project that will work fine on both PC as well as mobile platforms. You also learned about creating the environment, as well as how to add our targets and animate the iTween to start/end the game with saving our high score.

In the next chapter, we will be exploring how we can use the concepts that you've learned in 2D and use them with a 3D game with a 2D gameplay.

Project completed

And with this, we have all of the new parts needed to know to implement a shooting gallery game. With this in mind, you should be able to use what you learned in the previous chapters to make this a complete project!

Challenges

For those of you who want to do more with this project, there are still plenty of things you can do, especially after finishing the rest of this book. Here are some ideas to get your mind thinking:

- Add in the functionality from *Tappy Plane* for starting and restarting this game, so players don't need to restart the game every time the game ends.

- If you found yourself really enjoying using Unity's built-in animation system, you can find a more in-depth tutorial on creating a series of additional animations at `http://pixelnest.io/tutorials/2d-game-unity/animations-1/` and `http://www.raywenderlich.com/66345/unity-2d-tutorial-animations`.

- To learn more about iTween and what can be done with it, check out: `http://itween.pixelplacement.com/`.

6
Side-scrolling Platformer

At this point, we've gotten a chance to work on a number of games, but we've only been using 2D so far. In this chapter, we will be exploring how we can use the concepts that you've learned in 2D and use them with a 3D game with 2D gameplay.

As long as we have been playing games, there has been one particular genre that has stayed with us almost from the beginning, the platformer. Starting with *Donkey Kong* with the familiar content that we know, refined in *Super Mario Brothers*, given more action with *Mega Man*, taken faster with *Sonic the Hedgehog*, and used even today with games such as *Terraria*, *Super Meat Boy*, and *Child of Light* There is something that draws us to this specific type of game, especially within the indie game community.

A platform game (known commonly as a platformer) consists of a player controlling a character that can move around a game environment with extensive jumping between platforms, hence the name.

Project overview

Over the course of this chapter, we will be creating a complete side-scrolling platformer project. You will learn the similarities between working in 2D and 3D and the differences, in particular when it comes to physics.

Your objectives

This project will be split into a number of tasks. It will be a simple step-by-step process from beginning to end. Here is the outline of our tasks:

- Tile-based level creation
- Adding player functionality
- Adding collectibles/power-ups
- Designing the level layout and background

Prerequisites

As in previous chapters, you will need Unity installed on your computer, but we will be starting a new project from scratch.

This chapter uses no graphical assets; however, the completed project and source files can be downloaded from the example code provided for this book on Packt's website.

Project setup

At this point, I have assumed that you have a fresh installation of Unity and have started it up:

1. With Unity started, go to **File | New Project**. Select a **Project Location** of your choice somewhere on your hard drive and ensure that you have 3D selected (Note this is different than previous chapters). Once completed, select **Create project**:

2. At this point, we will not need to import any packages as we'll be making everything from scratch. From there, if you see the **Welcome to Unity** popup, feel free to close it out as we won't be using it.

3. Create the following folders just as we described in the previous chapters:

   ◦ Prefabs

   ◦ Scenes

   ◦ Scripts

Tile-based level creation

For most games with content, you'll typically have levels, each with their own environments. When building levels in games, there are some advantages to placing everything by hand, but if you're creating a game with many levels, that work will decrease your productivity. It's also important to note that the more assets you create for your game, the higher the cost will be in terms of development time and/or price to hire someone to do the art for you.

With that in mind, it's a much better idea to create parts that can be reused to create games. If you've played older 2D games in the past, such as an adventure, RPG, or platforming game, you may have realized that there were a lot of places in the world that looked similar to each other, such as the trees, a wall, chest, and door.

The reason they looked similar is due to the fact that they were using the same sprites. This is because they were tile-based games. A tile-based game is where the playing area consists of small rectangular, square, or hexagonal graphic images, referred to as tiles. Imagine a grid of blocks where every block is given a number or ID. Based on the ID, the game will determine how that grid is drawn and behaves when a player interacts with it.

An important thing to mention is that tile-based games are not a distinct genre; rather, the term refers to the technology a game engine uses for its visual representation. For example, most of the *Pokémon* series of games are top-down role-playing video games and the traditional *Mario* series of games are side-scrolling platformers, but both use a tile-based system for graphics. Tile-based techniques allow developers to create large levels quickly with relatively few art assets, which is great as a programmer.

To show how easy it is to build, we will be coding a tile-based system for this project:

1. The first thing that we're going to want to do is actually create the blocks we'll be placing for the world. Let's first create a **Cube** by selecting **GameObject | 3D Object | Cube**.

2. We want this cube to have collision so our player can collide against it, but this time, we will use a **Box Collider**. Check the **Inspector** to confirm that it is there. If not, add this component by selecting **Component | Physics | Box Collider**:

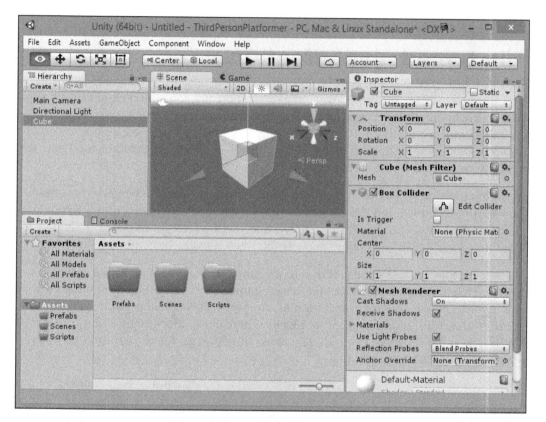

The **Box Collider** is the 3D equivalent of the **Box Collider 2D** component for 3D space.

1. Rename the cube to `Wall` by selecting the top bar on the **Inspector**, renaming it and pressing *Enter*:

2. In the **Project** tab, go to the **Prefabs** folder in the Project Browser and drag and drop the **Wall** object from our **Hierarchy** into it. Once that is finished, select the **Wall** object in the **Hierarchy** tab and then delete it by pressing the *Delete* key.

3. Now we will be spawning a large amount of objects into our world. It would be a good idea to have a parent object to store all of these objects. To do this, let's create an empty game object by going to **GameObject | Create Empty**. From there with the object selected go to the **Inspector** and set its name to `Dynamic Objects` and optionally for neatness sake, set its **Position** to (`0, 0, 0`).

4. The next thing we are going to do is create a **Game Controller** to hold the behavior to create our blocks. Create an empty game object with a name of Game Controller and reset its **Position** to (0, 0, 0). Once created, from the **Hierarchy** tab, drag and drop the object to the top of the **Hierarchy** to make it easier to access.

5. Underneath the name, you'll see the **Tag** property. Change it from Untagged to GameController:

6. Next, select **Add Component | New Script** once brought to the next menu, change the language to **C Sharp** (C#) and set the name of the script to **GameController** and then hit **Create and add**:

```
Q  out                                          ⊗

◄                  New Script

Name

GameController|

Language                              C Sharp  ⬍




                   Create and Add
```

7. Select the newly created script and move it to the Assets\Scripts folder. Go into your IDE of choice by double-clicking on the script file.

8. Inside the newly created code, we will first need to add two new variables for us to use—a level that will contain the data needed to create our level and Wall which will contain the block we want to spawn:

```
private int[][] level = new int[][]
{
    new int[]{1, 1, 1, 1, 1, 1, 1, 1, 1, 1, 1, 1, 1, 1, 1, 1, 1, 1, 1},
    new int[]{1, 0, 0, 0, 0, 0, 0, 0, 0, 0, 0, 0, 0, 0, 0, 0, 0, 1},
    new int[]{1, 0, 0, 0, 0, 0, C#, 0, 0, 0, 0, 0, 0, 0, 0, 0, 0, 1},
    new int[]{1, 0, 0, 0, 0, 0, 0, 0, 0, 0, 0, 0, 0, 0, 0, 0, 0, 1},
    new int[]{1, 0, 0, 0, 0, 0, 0, 0, 0, 0, 0, 0, 0, 0, 1, 1, 1, 1},
    new int[]{1, 0, 0, 0, 0, 0, 0, 0, 0, 0, 0, 0, 0, 0, 1, 1, 1, 1},
    new int[]{1, 0, 0, 0, 0, 0, 0, 0, 1, 1, 1, 1, 1, 1, 1, 1, 1, 1},
    new int[]{1, 1, 1, 1, 0, 0, 0, 0, 0, 0, 0, 0, 0, 0, 0, 0, 0, 1},
    new int[]{1, 0, 0, 0, 0, 0, 0, 0, 0, 0, 0, 0, 0, 0, 0, 0, 0, 1},
    new int[]{1, 0, 0, 0, 0, 0, 0, 0, 0, 0, 0, 0, 0, 0, 0, 0, 0, 1},
    new int[]{1, 0, 0, 0, 0, 0, 0, 0, 0, 0, 0, 0, 0, 0, 0, 0, 0, 1},
```

```
        new int[] {1, 1, 1, 1, 1, 1, 1, 0, 0, 0, 0, 0, 0, 0, 0, 0, 0, 0, 1},
        new int[] {1, 1, 1, 1, 1, 1, 1, 0, 0, 0, 1, 1, 1, 1, 0, 0, 0, 0, 1},
        new int[] {1, 0, 0, 0, 0, 0, 0, 0, 0, 0, 1, 1, 1, 1, 0, 0, 0, 0, 1},
        new int[] {1, 0, 0, 0, 0, 0, 0, 0, 0, 0, 0, 0, 0, 0, 0, 0, 0, 0, 1},
        new int[] {1, 0, 0, 0, 0, 0, 0, 0, 0, 0, 0, 0, 0, 0, 0, 0, 0, 1, 1},
        new int[] {1, 0, 0, 0, 0, 0, 0, 0, 0, 0, 0, 0, 0, 0, 0, 0, 1, 1, 1},
        new int[] {1, 0, 0, 0, 0, 0, 0, 0, 0, 0, 0, 0, 0, 0, 0, 1, 1, 1, 1},
        new int[] {1, 0, 0, 0, 0, 0, 0, 0, 0, 0, 0, 0, 0, 0, 1, 1, 1, 1, 1},
        new int[] {1, 0, 0, 0, 0, 0, 0, 1, 1, 1, 1, 0, 0, 1, 1, 1, 1, 1, 1},
        new int[] {1, 0, 0, 0, 0, 0, 0, 0, 0, 0, 0, 0, 0, 1, 1, 1, 1, 1, 1},
        new int[] {1, 0, 0, 0, 1, 1, 0, 0, 0, 0, 0, 0, 0, 1, 1, 1, 1, 1, 1},
        new int[] {1, 0, 0, 0, 1, 1, 0, 0, 0, 0, 0, 0, 0, 1, 1, 1, 1, 1, 1},
        new int[] {1, 0, 0, 0, 1, 1, 0, 0, 0, 0, 0, 0, 0, 1, 1, 1, 1, 1, 1},
        new int[] {1, 1, 1, 1, 1, 1, 1, 1, 1, 1, 1, 1, 1, 1, 1, 1, 1, 1, 1}
    };
        public Transform wall;
```

The wall variable looks similar to things we've created before, but the level variable looks a bit different.

Working with arrays

The level variable is an **array**. We could create an integer for each place inside of our level detailing what type is there; however, that is quite tedious and we'd have to remember each element's identifier. An array is a holder of multiple elements of the same type. To access an individual element of the array, we simply need to specify an index of where it is placed in between the square brackets (the [and] characters). Arrays are played sequentially in memory, which means that it's really easy to move between elements of them and it's a very fast operation to access an individual element.

The level variable is actually a multidirectional array, which can be thought of as an array of integers. We will use a multidirectional array because it allows us to "draw" with numbers like a grid to place each of the elements in our level.

This being said, now we actually need to build the level. To do this:

1. Let's create a function named BuildLevel:

```
    void BuildLevel()
    {
/*
Get the DynamicObjects object that we created already in the scene
so we can make it our newly created
objects' parent
*/
```

```
GameObject dynamicParent = GameObject.Find
    ("Dynamic Objects");
//Go through each element inside our level variable
for (int yPos = 0; yPos < level.Length; yPos++)
{
    for (int xPos = 0; xPos < (level[yPos]).Length;
    xPos++)
    {
        // Do nothing if the value is 0
        // If the value is 1, we want a wall
        if (level[yPos][xPos] == 1)
        {
        // Create the wall
        Transform newObject = Instantiate (wall,
        new Vector3(xPos, (level.Length - yPos),
        0), wall.rotation) as Transform;
/*
Set the object's parent to the
DynamicObjects variable so it doesn't clutter our Hierarchy
*/
            newObject.parent = dynamicParent.transform;
        }
    }
  }
}
```

The Quaternion class is what is used for rotations inside of Unity. In this instance, we are using the object's original rotation. For more information on quaternions, please check http://docs.unity3d. com/ScriptReference/Quaternion.html.

As you can see, we access each of the arrays stored in a level by using array[index] and for an index inside of that array we use array[index1] [index2].

2. Next, we need to actually call this function. Do so in your Start function:

```
void Start ()
{
    BuildLevel();
}
```

3. Save the script and exit out to the Unity Editor. When you get back, you
    should see under the **Game Controller** script that there is the Wall variable
    that still needs a value for its variable. In order to assign the prefab we
    created previously, we'll need to go to the folder and then drag and drop it
    there without releasing our mouse:

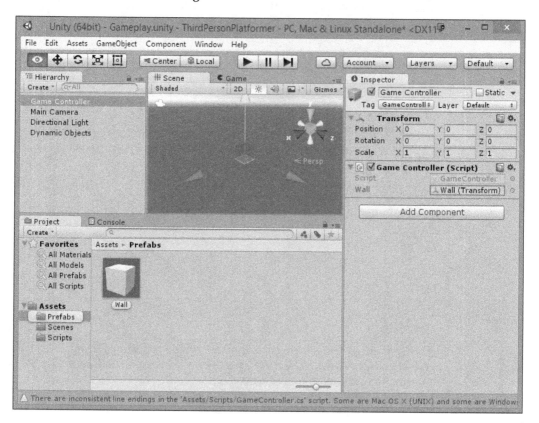

4. After this, press the **Start** button to see the code execute:

You may see a bit of the result in the **Game** screen that pops up, but if you click on the **Scene** tab, you'll see the level has been built for us!

You can drag and drop the **Scene** tab to share the space with the **Game** tab if you'd like, as you can see in the preceding picture.

There are a number of other ways you may modify your layout as well. There are also some provided ones as well, which may help your workflow.

To view them, you can go to the **Window** | **Layouts** menu or select the rightmost dropdown on the toolbar.

I personally use the **Default** layout for this book, but when I have two monitors, I like to spread things out with the **Game** tab on one monitor and everything else.

One of our technical editors prefers the 2 by 3 layout with a one-column project tab (right-click on the **Project** tab and then select one-column layout.

Creating our player

Having the basis of our world is great, but if we don't have a player, it doesn't matter how nice the level looks. In this section, we will create the actual player that will walk around and move in the world:

1. Let's first create a **Capsule** by selecting **GameObject | 3D Object | Capsule**.

2. Right now, the capsule is too big to fit our world due to being larger than our blocks. To easily fix this, we will set the **Scale** of our **Capsule** to be (**0.4, 0.4, and 0.4**). Also, set its **Position** to (**1, 2, 0**):

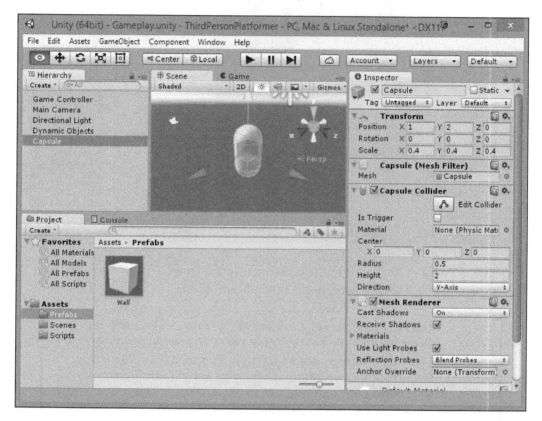

3. Now, we want our player to use gravity and forces, so we will need to add a **Rigidbody** component by going to **Component | Physics | Rigidbody**.

The 2D and 3D Physics systems are not interchangeable as in either can be used but they cannot interact with each other. You'll need to choose one or the other when working on a project. We're using 3D right now, so you can have a good idea of the differences between 2D and 3D and what to look out for.

4. Next, because we are doing a 2D game, we don't want our player to be moving in the Z axis, so under the **Rigidbody**, open up the **Constraints** box and check **Z** in the **Freeze Position** variable. After this, check each axis for the **Freeze Rotation** as we do not want our character to change its rotation via **Rigidbody** (we'll rotate it via code):

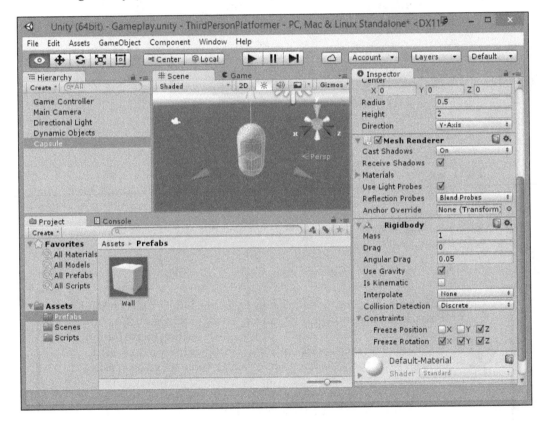

5. After this, all that's left is to create some custom functionality, which means that you guessed it, another script. Create a new C# Script file named `PlayerBehaviour` and open it up in your IDE of choice.

   With the `PlayerBehaviour` script opened, let's first write down each of the issues we need to solve and make them functions. As programmers, it's our job to solve problems, and separating problems into smaller pieces will make it easier to solve each part rather than try to solve the entire thing all at once.

6. Add in the following code:

```
void FixedUpdate()
{
    // Move the player left and right
    Movement();

    // Sets the camera to center on the player's position.
    // Keeping the camera's original depth
    Camera.main.transform.position = new
    Vector3(transform.position.x,
    transform.position.y,
    Camera.main.transform.position.z);
}
```

7. Next, we write the following in the `Update` function:

```
void Update()
{
// Have the player jump if they press the jump button
    Jumping();
}
```

> `Update()` is great and is called every frame, but it's called at random times, leading to more instant but less constant things, such as input. Instead of that, `FixedUpdate()` is a great function to use for things that need to happen consistently and for things like physics due to its fixed delta time (the `Time.deltaTime` value we've been using previously changes depending on the frame rate). However, in a platformer, the player needs to feel a jump instantly, so that's why I put the `Jumping` function inside of `Update`.

So at this point, we have broken the player's behavior into two sections—their movement and their jumping.

8. Next, we're going to need to declare some variables for us to use:

```
// A reference to our player's rigidbody component
private Rigidbody rigidBody;
// Force to apply when player jumps
public Vector2 jumpForce = new Vector2(0, 450);

// How fast we'll let the player move in the x axis
public float maxSpeed = 3.0f;

// A modifier to the force applied
public float speed = 50.0f;

// The force to apply that we will get for the player's
// movement
private float xMove;

// Set to true when the player can jump
private bool shouldJump;
```

9. I've initialized the public data here, but the user can modify the numbers in the **Inspector**. However, we still need to initialize the private variables in the Start function:

```
void Start ()
{
    rigidBody = GetComponent<Rigidbody>();
    shouldJump = false;
    xMove = 0.0f;
}
```

10. Now that we have the variables, we think that we need to fill in the implementation for the Movement function now:

```
void Movement()
{
    // Get the player's movement (-1 for left, 1 for right,
    // 0 for none)
    xMove = Input.GetAxis("Horizontal");

    if (xMove != 0)
    {
        // Setting player horizontal movement
        float xSpeed = Mathf.Abs(xMove *
        rigidBody.velocity.x);

        if (xSpeed < maxSpeed)
```

```
    {
        Vector3 movementForce = new Vector3(1, 0, 0);
        movementForce *= xMove * speed;
        rigidBody.AddForce(movementForce);
    }


    // Check speed limit
    if (Mathf.Abs(rigidBody.velocity.x) > maxSpeed)
    {
        Vector2 newVelocity;

        newVelocity.x =
        Mathf.Sign(rigidBody.velocity.x) *
                    maxSpeed;
        newVelocity.y = rigidBody.velocity.y;

        rigidBody.velocity = newVelocity;
    }
}
else
{
    // If we're not moving, get slightly slower
    Vector2 newVelocity = rigidBody.velocity;

    // Reduce the current speed by 10%
    newVelocity.x *= 0.9f;
    rigidBody.velocity = newVelocity;
}
}
```

In this section of code, we use a different way to get input from the player, the
GetAxis function. When called, GetAxis will return a value for the direction that
you are moving in a particular axis. In this instance, -1 for going all the way to
the left, 0 for stationary, and 1 for all the way to the right. GetAxis can return any
number between -1 and 1 as using a game controller you may only slightly move
the analog stick. This would allow you to sneak in an area rather than always be
running. In addition to the **Horizontal Axis**, there are a number of others included in
Unity by default, but we can also customize or create our own.

Adding Jump functionality

At this point, we can move left and right in the game, but we're unable to jump. Let's fix this now:

1. Access the **Input** properties by going to **Edit | Project Settings | Input**. Once there extend the **Jump** tab. In the **Alt Positive Button** put in up:

2. Next, let's implement the `Jumping` function:

```
void Jumping()
{
    if(Input.GetButtonDown("Jump"))
    {
        shouldJump = true;
    }

    // If the player should jump
    if(shouldJump)
    {
```

```
                    rigidBody.AddForce(jumpForce);
                    shouldJump = false;
            }
    }
```

Now, if we press *Spacebar* or *Up*, we will change the `shouldJump` Boolean value to true. If it's true, then we'll apply the `jumpForce` to our character.

3. With this completed, let's save our script and jump back into the Unity Editor. From there, go to the **Hierarchy** tab and select the **Capsule** object. Rename it to `Player` and then attach the newly created behavior to our player if you haven't done so already:

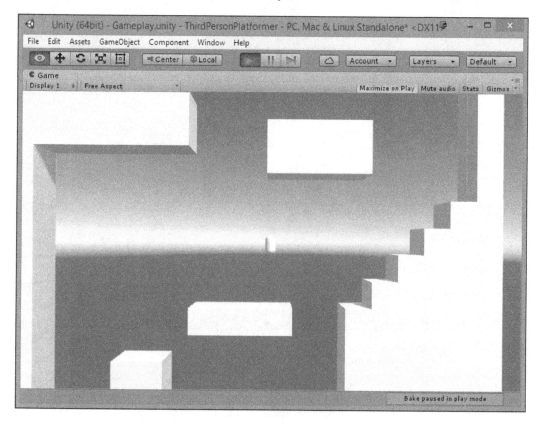

Great start! We now have a player in our world, and we're able to move around and jump. However, if you keep playing with it, you'll note some of the issues that this has, namely the fact that you can always jump up as many times as you want and if you hold a direction key hitting a wall, you'll stay stuck in the air. This could make for interesting game mechanics, but I'm going to assume that this is not what you're looking for.

Working with Gizmos

Next, before we solve our movement issues, I wanted to show you a tool that you can use as a developer to help you when working on your own projects. Add the following function to your script:

```
void OnDrawGizmos()
{
    Debug.DrawLine(transform.position, transform.position +
    rigidBody.velocity, Color.red);
}
```

OnDrawGizmos is a function inherited by the MonoBehaviour class that will allow us to draw things that will appear in the **Scene** view. Sure enough, if you play the game, you will not see anything in the **Game** view, but if you look at the **Scene** tab, you'll be able to see the velocity that our object is traveling by. To make it easier to see, feel free to hit the 2D button in the top toolbar on the **Scene** tab to get a side view:

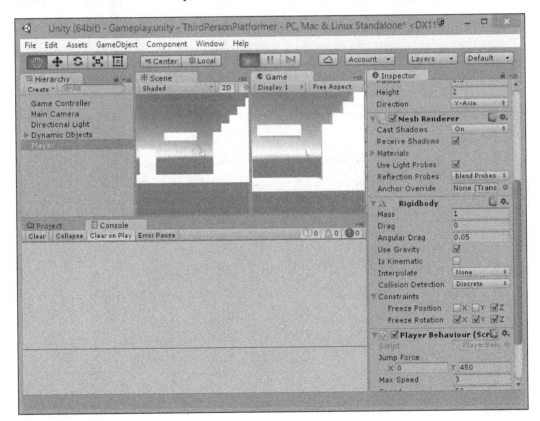

Note that the **Game** tab needs to be active before Input will register any pressed keys so I have both tabs open. Alternatively, you can add the gizmo to the Game view as well by going to the top right of the Game tab and toggling the Gizmos button.

Smoothing out player movement

In this example here, the red line is showing that I'm jumping up and moving to the left. If you'll look at the **Scene** view when the player is walking, you'll see little bumps occuring. This isn't something we'd like to see as we expect the collision to flow together. These bumps occur because the moment that we hit the edges of two separate boxes, the collision engine will try to push the player in different directions to prevent the collision from happening. After the collisions occur, the physics engine will try to combine both of those forces into one that causes these hickups. We can fix this by telling Unity to spend some extra time doing the calcuations.

Go into Unity's **Physics** properties by going to **Edit | Project Settings | Physics**. Change the **Default Contact Offset** property to **0.0001**:

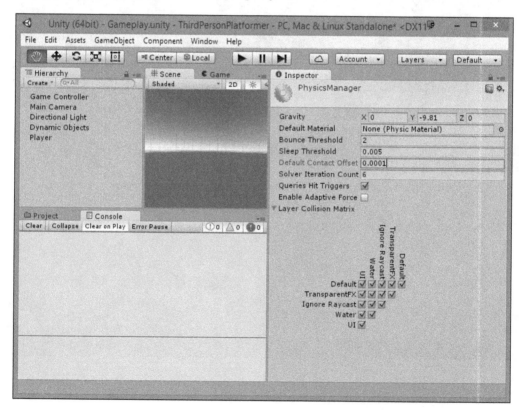

The **Contact Offset** property allows the collision detection system to predicatively enforce the contact constraint even when the objects are slightly separated, we decrease that number as we don't want the collisions to happen.

Restricting Jumping

Now there's the matter of being able to jump anytime we want. What we want to have happen is to have the player not be able to jump unless they're on the ground. This is to prevent the case of being able to jump while falling:

1. So to do this, we will need to introduce some new variables:

   ```
   private bool onGround;
   private float yPrevious;
   ```

2. Just like any private variables, we will need to initialize them in our Start function:

   ```
   onGround = false;
   yPrevious = Mathf.Floor(transform.position.y);
   ```

3. Now in our Jumping function, we just need to add the following code in bold:

   ```
   void Jumping()
   {
       if(Input.GetButtonDown("Jump"))
       {
           shouldJump = true;
       }

       // If the player should jump
       if(shouldJump && onGround)
       {
           rigidBody.AddForce(jumpForce);
           shouldJump = false;
       }
   }
   ```

4. And in our Update function, we will add in a new function for us to check whether we are grounded:

   ```
   // Update is called once per frame
   void Update ()
   {
       // Check if we are on the ground
       CheckGrounded();

       // Have the player jump if they press the jump button
       Jumping();
   }
   ```

5. Now we just need to add in the code for `CheckGrounded`. This isn't exactly a simple issue to solve without math, so we will actually need to use some linear algebra to solve the issue for us as follows:

```
void CheckGrounded()
{
    // Check if the player is hitting something from
    // the center of the object (origin) to slightly below
    // the bottom of it (distance)
    float distance =
    (GetComponent<CapsuleCollider>().height / 2 *
    this.transform.localScale.y) + .01f;
    Vector3 floorDirection = transform.TransformDirection(
    -Vector3.up);
    Vector3 origin = transform.position;

    if (!onGround)
    {
        // Check if there is something directly below us
        if (Physics.Raycast(origin, floorDirection,
        distance))
        {
            onGround = true;
        }
    }
    // If we are currently grounded, are we falling down or
    // jumping?
    else if ((Mathf.Floor(transform.position.y) !=
    yPrevious))
    {
        onGround = false;
    }

    // Our current position will be our previous next frame
    yPrevious = Mathf.Floor(transform.position.y);
}
```

This function uses a Raycast to cast an invisible line (ray) from origin in the direction of the floor for a certain distance, which is just slightly further than our player. If it finds an object colliding with this, it will return `true`, which will tell us that we are indeed on the ground.

Preventing the player getting stuck

In the game, we can leave the ground in two ways—by jumping or by falling down a platform. Either way, we will be changing our y position; if that's the case, we are no longer on the ground, so onGround will be set to false. The Floor function will remove the decimal from a number to allow for some leeway for a floating point error.

1. Now our only issue resides in the fact that the player sticks to walls if they press into it. To solve this, we will just simply not allow the player to move into a wall by not adding a force if we're right next to a wall. Add the following bolded code to this section of code in the Movement function:

```
// Movement()
// if xMove != 0...
if (xSpeed < maxSpeed)
{
Vector3 movementForce = new Vector3(1,0,0);
movementForce *= xMove * speed;

RaycastHit hit;
if(!rigidBody.SweepTest(movementForce, out hit, 0.05f))
{
rigidBody.AddForce(movementForce);
}
}
// Etc.
```

The SweepTest function will check in the direction the rigid body is traveling, and if it sees something within a certain direction, it will fill hit with the object that it touched and return true. We want to stop the player from being able to move into the wall, so we will not add force if that's the case.

2. Now, this works for the most part except for when we are already along the wall and jump up and other fringe cases. To fix these issues when we are touching a wall, we will add a variable that will keep track if we are touching a wall:

```
private bool collidingWall;
```

3. After this, we need to initialize it in Start:

```
collidingWall = false;
```

4. After this, we will use the 3D collision detection functions to determine if we're touching a wall:

```
// If we hit something and we're not grounded, it must be a wall
// or a ceiling.
    void OnCollisionStay(Collision collision)
    {
        if (!onGround)
        {
            collidingWall = true;
        }
    }

    void OnCollisionExit(Collision collision)
    {
        collidingWall = false;
    }
```

You'll note that the functions look quite similar to the 2D functions aside from not having the word 2D.

5. Next, inside of your Movement function, add the following bolded lines:

```
    void Movement()
    {
        //Get the player's movement (-1 for left, 1 for
        //right, 0 for none)
        xMove = Input.GetAxis("Horizontal");

        if(collidingWall && !onGround)
        {
            xMove = 0;
        }
        // Etc.
```

Now if we are colliding against a wall, we will stop the player from applying force.

6. Save the script and go back into Unity, refreshing the scripts if needed and hit the **Play** button:

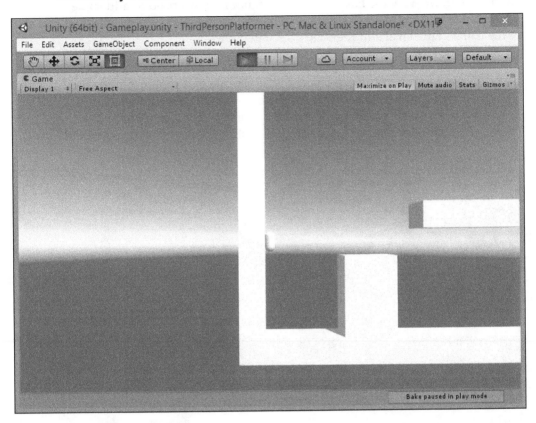

Now our player can jump along walls and fall like normal, and the player can jump only when he is on the ground! We now have the basis to make a platformer game completed!

Creating Collectibles

At this point, we have the basis of our game, but now we need to add some gameplay to our world. Perhaps we will have it so that we need to collect all of the coins in the level and then the goal will open:

1. Create a new **Particle System** by going into **GameObject | Particle System**. Change the name of the object to **Collectible** and center it in the world by changing its position to 0, 0, 0. Next, we need to assign the object's tag to **Orb**. To do so, select **Tag | Add Tag**. Once at the **Tag** menu, press the + button to the right of **Tags** and then from the assign Tag **0**, put in **Orb** and press *Enter*:

2. Then, select the **Collectible** game object in the **Hierarchy** again and then select the **Tag** as **Orb**. Under the **Shape** section, change the **Shape** variable to **Sphere** and the **Radius** to **0.01**:

3. Click on the Arrow on the right-hand side of **Start Lifetime** and change the values to be **Random Between Two Constants**. Change those values to 0 and .2. Do the same with **Start Speed** between 0 and 1. Make **Start Size** use random values between **0** and **1.5**:

4. Under **Start Color**, change the value to yellow by clicking on the color to bring up the **Color** select dialogue. Once there set the alpha (**A**) to **39**:

5. Next, click on the **Emission** section to open it up, and from there, **set** the **Rate** to **100**.

6. Now add a **Sphere Collider** by selecting **Component | Physics | Sphere Collider**. Inside of the **Inspector**, set the **Is Trigger** Boolean to `true`, set the **Center** to (0, 0, 0) and then set the **Radius** to **0.4**:

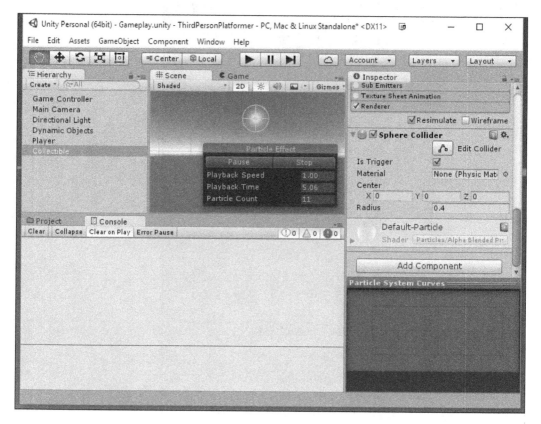

7. Finally, drag and drop the **Collectible** object into the **Prefabs** section of the **Project** folder and delete the object in the **Hierarchy**:

Adding new objects to our level builder

Now, we need to modify our original `Build Level` function to have support in order to add these collectibles as well to our level. While we're at it, let's make it so the level can spawn the `Player` as well. Rename our player object to `Player` if not done yet and drag and drop it to the `Prefabs` folder as well. After we've created the prefabs, go ahead and delete the `Player` object.

So because we're writing a new function, we have some new variables to introduce in the `GameController` class:

```
[Header("Object References")]
public Transform wall;
public Transform player;
public Transform orb;
```

 Note that in this case, I added in a Header as well, which will help you convey what these variables actually are.

Then change the `BuildLevel` function replacing what was inside our for loops to:

```
void BuildLevel ()
{
    // Get the DynamicObjects object so we can make it our
    // newly created objects' parent
    GameObject dynamicParent =
    GameObject.Find("Dynamic Objects");

    // Go through each element inside our level variable
    for (int yPos = 0; yPos < level.Length; yPos++)
    {
        for (int xPos = 0; xPos < (level[yPos]).Length;
        xPos++)
        {
            Transform toCreate = null;
            switch(level[yPos][xPos])
            {
                case 0:
                // Do nothing because we don't want anything
                // in this place
                break;

                case 1:
                toCreate = wall;
                break;

                case 2:
                toCreate = player;
```

```
                            break;

                            case 3:
                            toCreate = orb;
                            break;

                            default:
                            print("Invalid number: " +
                            (level[yPos][xPos]).ToString());
                            break;
            }

                        if(toCreate != null)
                        {
                            Transform newObject = Instantiate(toCreate,
                            new Vector3(xPos, (level.Length - yPos),
                            0),
                            toCreate.rotation) as Transform;

                        // Set the object's parent to the DynamicObjects
                        // variable so it doesn't clutter our Hierachy
                        newObject.parent = dynamicParent.transform;
                        }

                }
            }
        }
```

Switch statements continued

As we described briefly previously in *Chapter 3, GUIs Part 2 – Clicker Game,*
a switch statement can be thought of as a nice way to compare a single variable
against a number of different values. As the case here, the switch statement could
be rewritten as:

```
    if(level[yPos][xPos] == 0)
    {

    }
    else if(level[yPos][xPos] == 1)
    {
    toCreate = wall;
    }
    else if(level[yPos][xPos] == 2)
    {
```

```
    toCreate = player;
    }
    else if(level[yPos][xPos] == 3)
    {
        toCreate = orb;
    }
    else
    {
        print("Invalid number: " +
        (level[yPos][xPos]).ToString());
    }
```

However, surely you can tell that writing it as a `switch` statement is much nicer to look at and requires less code duplication, which is something we want to reduce as much as possible:

1. After this, we need to modify our level array to actually have the collectibles and player in it. Replace one 0s in your level to a 2 to put the player there and add in some 3s for the player to collect. Mine looks like the following:

```
private int[][] level = new int[][]
{
    new int[]{1, 1, 1, 1, 1, 1, 1, 1, 1, 1, 1, 1, 1, 1, 1, 1, 1, 1, 1},
    new int[]{1, 0, 0, 0, 0, 0, 0, 0, 0, 0, 0, 0, 0, 0, 0, 0, 0, 0, 1},
    new int[]{1, 0, 0, 0, 0, 0, 0, 0, 0, 0, 0, 0, 0, 0, 0, 0, 0, 0, 1},
    new int[]{1, 3, 0, 0, 0, 0, 0, 0, 0, 0, 3, 3, 3, 0, 0, 0, 0, 0, 1},
    new int[]{1, 0, 0, 0, 0, 0, 0, 0, 0, 0, 0, 0, 0, 0, 0, 1, 1, 1, 1},
    new int[]{1, 0, 0, 0, 0, 0, 0, 0, 0, 0, 0, 0, 0, 0, 0, 1, 1, 1, 1},
    new int[]{1, 0, 0, 0, 0, 0, 0, 0, 1, 1, 1, 1, 1, 1, 1, 1, 1, 1, 1},
    new int[]{1, 1, 1, 1, 0, 0, 0, 0, 0, 0, 0, 0, 0, 0, 0, 0, 0, 0, 1},
    new int[]{1, 0, 0, 0, 0, 0, 0, 0, 0, 0, 0, 0, 0, 0, 0, 0, 0, 0, 1},
    new int[]{1, 0, 0, 0, 0, 0, 3, 0, 3, 0, 0, 0, 0, 0, 0, 0, 0, 0, 1},
    new int[]{1, 0, 0, 0, 0, 0, 0, 0, 0, 0, 0, 0, 0, 0, 0, 0, 0, 0, 1},
    new int[]{1, 1, 1, 1, 1, 1, 1, 0, 0, 0, 0, 0, 0, 0, 0, 0, 0, 0, 1},
    new int[]{1, 1, 1, 1, 1, 1, 1, 0, 0, 0, 1, 1, 1, 1, 0, 0, 0, 0, 1},
    new int[]{1, 0, 0, 0, 0, 0, 0, 0, 0, 0, 1, 1, 1, 1, 0, 0, 0, 3, 1},
    new int[]{1, 0, 0, 0, 0, 0, 0, 0, 0, 0, 0, 0, 0, 0, 0, 0, 0, 0, 1},
    new int[]{1, 0, 0, 0, 0, 0, 0, 0, 0, 0, 0, 0, 0, 0, 0, 0, 0, 1, 1},
    new int[]{1, 0, 0, 0, 0, 0, 0, 0, 0, 0, 0, 0, 0, 0, 0, 0, 1, 1, 1},
    new int[]{1, 0, 0, 0, 0, 0, 0, 0, 3, 0, 0, 0, 0, 0, 0, 1, 1, 1, 1},
    new int[]{1, 0, 0, 0, 0, 0, 0, 0, 0, 0, 0, 0, 0, 0, 1, 1, 1, 1, 1},
    new int[]{1, 0, 0, 0, 3, 0, 0, 1, 1, 1, 1, 0, 0, 1, 1, 1, 1, 1, 1},
    new int[]{1, 0, 0, 0, 0, 0, 0, 0, 0, 0, 0, 0, 0, 1, 1, 1, 1, 1, 1},
    new int[]{1, 0, 0, 0, 1, 1, 0, 0, 0, 0, 0, 0, 0, 1, 1, 1, 1, 1, 1},
    new int[]{1, 0, 0, 0, 1, 1, 0, 0, 0, 0, 0, 0, 0, 1, 1, 1, 1, 1, 1},
    new int[]{1, 0, 2, 0, 1, 1, 0, 0, 0, 0, 0, 0, 1, 1, 1, 1, 1, 1, 1},
    new int[]{1, 1, 1, 1, 1, 1, 1, 1, 1, 1, 1, 1, 1, 1, 1, 1, 1, 1, 1}
};
```

2. Save your script and exit back into the editor. Select your **Game Controller** and then assign the **Player** and **Orb** variables with the appropriate prefabs:

3. Finally, save your scene and run the game:

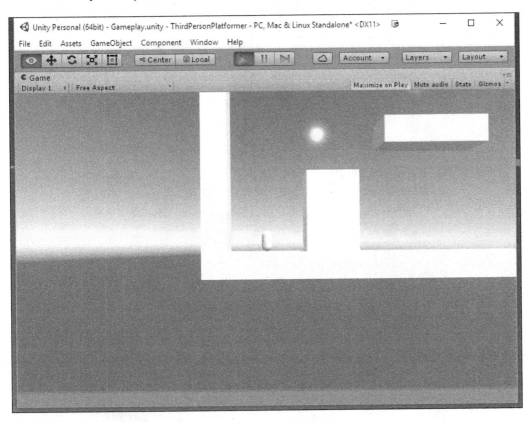

And there we go! Our player as well as collectibles are now spawning via our `BuildLevel` function. Finally, let's make it so we can actually collect these.

4. After we have the physical representation of the object done, let's now implement its functionality. Create a new script in our **Scripts** folder, which we will name `OrbBehaviour`. Open it up in `MonoDevelop` and fill it in with the following:

```
using UnityEngine;

public class OrbBehaviour : MonoBehaviour
{
    void OnTriggerEnter(Collider other)
    {
        Destroy(this.gameObject);
    }
}
```

5. Assign the **OrbBehaviour** component to the **Orb** prefab by going to the
   Project tab and opening the **Prefabs** folder and selecting the **Collectible**
   object. From there, scroll all the way down on the **Inspector** tab, click on **Add
   Component**, and start typing in **Orb** and then hitting the *Enter* key:

6. Save the scene and then play the game:

And with this, we can now collect orbs and they dissapear when we touch them!

Keeping score

We now want to make it so that when we collect all of the orbs in the level the goal will appear and then you will win the game when you touch it:

1. Go back into MonoDevelop and select the GameController class. Then, add the following variables:

```
public static GameController _instance;
private int orbsCollected;
private int orbsTotal;
```

Although it may make more sense English-wise to use totalOrbs and collectedOrbs programming-wise, putting the common word first means that when you start typing orbs, it will show both options for you when working with code completion in your own projects.

2. As normal, we will need to set these variables as well in the `Start` function:

    ```
    GameObject[] orbs;
    orbs = GameObject.FindGameObjectsWithTag("Orb");

    orbsCollected = 0;
    orbsTotal = orbs.Length;
    ```

    Make sure that you place this after the `BuildLevel` function or there will be no orbs for you to count!

3. We will also want to initialize the `_instance` variable, but instead of using `Start`, we will be using `Awake`:

    ```
    void Awake()
    {
        _instance = this;
    }
    ```

`Awake` gets called before `Start`, which is important because we have to initialize the `_instance` variable before you use it, this is known as a **Lazy Singleton**.

Singletons

As you work in Unity, you may find that you have certain managers such as our **Game Controller** that we will only have one of. Rather than having to have other objects store them as variables or find them at runtime, we can use a design pattern called the **singleton pattern**. The gist of it is that there is one and only one object of this class that can be created. The version that I am using is the quickest way to get singleton-like behavior going.

Never use the `GameController._instance` variable inside of another `Awake` function as you are not guaranteed the order in which they'll be called. However, if you use it in `Start` or any of the other functions we've talked about, you'll be okay.

As we collect orbs, we want to increase the value of our `orbsCollected` variable. Rather than just giving other things access to the variable, let's wrap this around a function so we can do other things, such as update the GUI later creating a function:

```
public void CollectedOrb()
{
    orbsCollected++;
}
```

In our `OrbBehaviour` script, we call the function:

```
void OnTriggerEnter(Collider other)
{
    GameController._instance.CollectedOrb();
    Destroy(this.gameObject);
}
```

When you access the `_instance` variable, you get access to the public functions and variables that exist in the class.

Now that we have this data stored, let's display it on the screen so players can see. Go to **GameObject | UI | Text**. Place it on the top left of the screen (a position of 0, 1, 0 with an Anchor of upper left and alignment of left) using the **Anchor Presets** menu we used in previous chapters. Next, give the object a name of **Score Text** and give it the **Pos X** of **10** and **Pos Y** of **-10**:

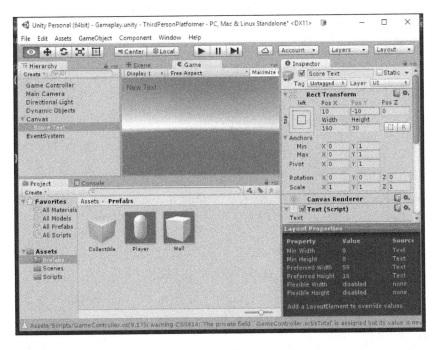

Now that we have the text object created, let's reference it inside code. To start off, we will need to add in the correct `using` line at the top of the **Game Controller** script:

```
using UnityEngine.UI; // Text
```

Then, we will need to add one last variable to our **Game Controller**:

```
public Text scoreText;
```

We need to initialize it in the `Start` function:

```
void Start()
{
    BuildLevel();

    GameObject[] orbs;
    orbs = GameObject.FindGameObjectsWithTag("Orb");

    orbsCollected = 0;
    orbsTotal = orbs.Length;

    scoreText.text = "Orbs: " + orbsCollected + "/" +
    orbsTotal;
}
```

And now because we have a text displaying the orbs, we can now update our text accordingly:

```
public void CollectedOrb()
{
    orbsCollected++;
    scoreText.text = "Orbs: " + orbsCollected + "/" +
    orbsTotal;
}
```

With this, save the script and then go back into the Unity editor. Once you reach here, set our newly created variable with the Text object we created and then click on the **Play** button:

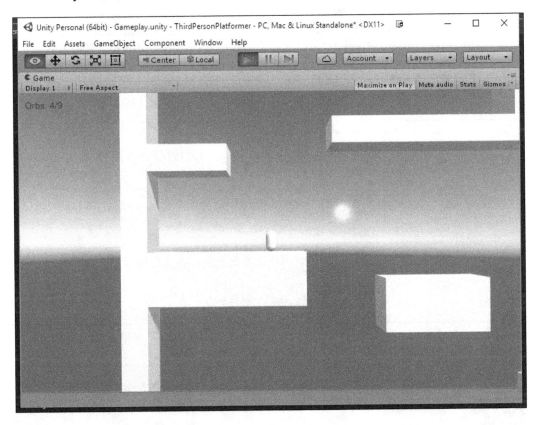

At this point, you can move around the level, and when you collect the orbs, they will now update the GUI letting us know how many coins you've collected and how many there are total in the level. We're making great progress and we almost have a full game, we just need one last thing, a way to win!

Winning the game

Now that we have the goals showing up, we now need some way in order to complete the project. With this in mind, let's create our final place, a goal, or the player to reach to go to the next level.

1. Create a new **Particle System** by going into **GameObject | Particle System**. Change the name of the object to Goal.

2. Under the **Shape** section, change the **Shape** variable to Box and change **Box X** to 1 and **Box Y** and **Box Z** to 0.

3. Click on the arrow on the right-hand side of **Start Lifetime** and change the values to be **Random Between Two Constants**. Change those values to 0 and 1. Do the same with **Start Speed** between 2 and 4. Make **Start Size** use random values between 0 and 0.5. Change the **Start Color** to a **Random Between Two Colors** using a green and purple color. Finally, uncheck the **Play On Awake** variable. Finally, we want the particles to fly up so change Rotation X to -90 or 270:

With this, you should have a nice stream of particles coming in for your new goal object!

4. Add in a **Box Collider** by selecting **Component | Physics | Box Collider**. Toggle the **Is Trigger** option to be true, set the **Center** to be (0,0,0) and the **Size** to be (1,1,1):

5. Now that we have the goal's object completed, let's now have it spawn within our `BuildLevel` function in our **Game Controller**. So, same as before, we drag and drop the object to our **Prefabs** folder and delete the original object. Then, we need to add two new variables for us to use:

```
public Transform goal;
private ParticleSystem goalPS;
```

6. After we add the new variables, add in the following in bold to `BuildLevel`:

```
void BuildLevel()
{
    // Get the DynamicObjects object so we can make it
    // our newly created objects' parent
    GameObject dynamicParent =
    GameObject.Find("DynamicObjects");


    //Go through each element inside our level variable
    for (int yPos = 0; yPos < level.Length; yPos++)
    {
        for (int xPos = 0; xPos < (level[yPos]).Length;
        xPos++)
        {
            Transform toCreate = null;
            switch(level[yPos][xPos])
            {
                case 0:
                //Do nothing because we don't want
                anything there.
                break;
                case 1:
                toCreate = wall;
                break;
                case 2:
                toCreate = player;
                break;
                case 3:
                toCreate = orb;
                break;
                case 4:
                toCreate = goal;
                break;
                default:
```

```
            print("Invalid number: " +
            (level[yPos][xPos]).ToString());
            break;
        }

        if(toCreate != null)
        {
            Transform newObject =
            Instantiate(toCreate,
        new Vector3(xPos,
        (level.Length - yPos),
        0),
        toCreate.rotation) as Transform;

            if(toCreate == goal)
            {
            goalPS =
            newObject.gameObject.GetComponent
            <ParticleSystem>();
            }
/*
Set the object's parent to the
DynamicObjects variable so it doesn't clutter our Hierarchy
*/
            newObject.parent =
            dynamicParent.transform;


        }
    }
}
```

7. We also need to add in a 4 somewhere inside of our level array:

```
private int[][] level = new int[][]
{
    new int[]{1, 1, 1, 1, 1, 1, 1, 1, 1, 1, 1, 1, 1, 1, 1, 1, 1, 1},
    new int[]{1, 0, 0, 0, 0, 0, 0, 0, 0, 0, 0, 0, 0, 0, 0, 0, 0, 1},
    new int[]{1, 0, 0, 0, 0, 0, 0, 0, 0, 0, 0, 0, 0, 0, 0, 0, 0, 1},
    new int[]{1, 3, 0, 0, 0, 0, 0, 0, 0, 0, 3, 3, 3, 0, 0, 0, 4, 0, 1},
    new int[]{1, 0, 0, 0, 0, 0, 0, 0, 0, 0, 0, 0, 0, 0, 0, 1, 1, 1, 1},
    new int[]{1, 0, 0, 0, 0, 0, 0, 0, 0, 0, 0, 0, 0, 0, 0, 1, 1, 1, 1},
    new int[]{1, 0, 0, 0, 0, 0, 0, 0, 1, 1, 1, 1, 1, 1, 1, 1, 1, 1, 1},
    new int[]{1, 1, 1, 1, 0, 0, 0, 0, 0, 0, 0, 0, 0, 0, 0, 0, 0, 1},
    new int[]{1, 0, 0, 0, 0, 0, 0, 0, 0, 0, 0, 0, 0, 0, 0, 0, 0, 1},
```

```
    new int[] {1, 0, 0, 0, 0, 0, 3, 0, 3, 0, 0, 0, 0, 0, 0, 0, 0, 0, 1},
    new int[] {1, 0, 0, 0, 0, 0, 0, 0, 0, 0, 0, 0, 0, 0, 0, 0, 0, 0, 1},
    new int[] {1, 1, 1, 1, 1, 1, 1, 0, 0, 0, 0, 0, 0, 0, 0, 0, 0, 0, 1},
    new int[] {1, 1, 1, 1, 1, 1, 1, 0, 0, 0, 1, 1, 1, 1, 0, 0, 0, 0, 1},
    new int[] {1, 0, 0, 0, 0, 0, 0, 0, 0, 0, 1, 1, 1, 1, 0, 0, 0, 3, 1},
    new int[] {1, 0, 0, 0, 0, 0, 0, 0, 0, 0, 0, 0, 0, 0, 0, 0, 0, 0, 1},
    new int[] {1, 0, 0, 0, 0, 0, 0, 0, 0, 0, 0, 0, 0, 0, 0, 0, 0, 1, 1},
    new int[] {1, 0, 0, 0, 0, 0, 0, 0, 0, 0, 0, 0, 0, 0, 0, 0, 1, 1, 1},
    new int[] {1, 0, 0, 0, 0, 0, 0, 0, 3, 0, 0, 0, 0, 0, 0, 1, 1, 1, 1},
    new int[] {1, 0, 0, 0, 0, 0, 0, 0, 0, 0, 0, 0, 0, 0, 1, 1, 1, 1, 1},
    new int[] {1, 0, 0, 0, 3, 0, 0, 1, 1, 1, 1, 0, 0, 1, 1, 1, 1, 1, 1},
    new int[] {1, 0, 0, 0, 0, 0, 0, 0, 0, 0, 0, 0, 0, 1, 1, 1, 1, 1, 1},
    new int[] {1, 0, 0, 0, 1, 1, 0, 0, 0, 0, 0, 0, 0, 1, 1, 1, 1, 1, 1},
    new int[] {1, 0, 0, 0, 1, 1, 0, 0, 0, 0, 0, 0, 0, 1, 1, 1, 1, 1, 1},
    new int[] {1, 0, 2, 0, 1, 1, 0, 0, 0, 0, 0, 0, 0, 1, 1, 1, 1, 1, 1},
    new int[] {1, 1, 1, 1, 1, 1, 1, 1, 1, 1, 1, 1, 1, 1, 1, 1, 1, 1, 1}
};
```

8. Next in the Unity Inspector, go in and assign the **Goal** object with your prefab of the same name.

9. With this done, we now need to go in and add in the ability to win. Go into the `CollectedOrb` function and start our **Particle System** when we get all of the orbs:

```
public void CollectedOrb()
{
    orbsCollected++;
    scoreText.text = "Orbs: " + orbsCollected + "/" +
    orbsTotal;

    if(orbsCollected >= orbsTotal)
    {
        goalPS.Play();
    }
}
```

10. After that we need to create the script for our goal. Create a new script in our **Scripts** folder that we will name `GoalBehaviour`. Open it up in `MonoDevelop` and fill it in with the following:

```
using UnityEngine;

public class GoalBehaviour : MonoBehaviour
{
    ParticleSystem ps;
    void Start()
    {
```

```
        ps = GetComponent<ParticleSystem>();
    }

    void OnTriggerEnter(Collider other)
    {
        if(ps.isPlaying)
        {
            print("You Win!");
        }
    }
}
```

11. Save the file and attach it do the **Goal** prefab. With this all done, save the scene and hit the **Play** button:

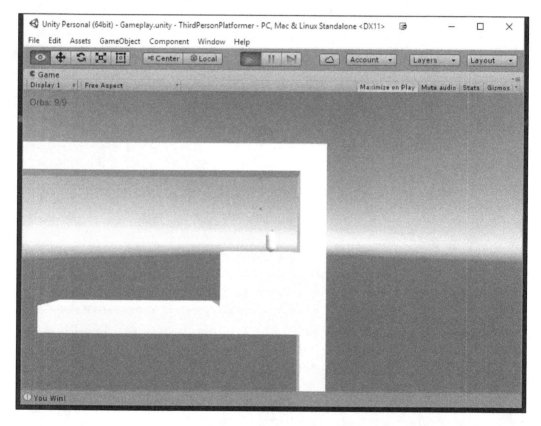

And with this, whenever we collect all of the coins that we've placed in our level, the goal will appear. Finally, when we touch it, the game will tell us that we have won!

Summary

We now have all you need to get started building a side-scrolling platformer game on your own adding in unique features and GUI, as we discussed in the previous chapter. While doing so, we've also gained an understanding of how working on 3D games is really not at all different than working with 2D. This will serve us greatly when we move on to the next chapter where we will get started on a new game project!

Challenges

For those of you who want to do more with this project, there are still plenty of things you can do, especially after finishing the rest of this book. Here are some ideas to get your mind thinking:

- Add in sounds and music to the game and customize the GUI in the ways we talked about earlier!

- Create levels of your own! Danny Calleri has created a really nice level editor called Toast Editor that you can run from your web browser to design levels graphically. To use it, go to `http://dannycalleri.github.io/toasteditor/index.html`. When exporting, use the C++ option and replace the top line with our levels line and add `new int []` to the beginning of every line in the array.

- Going one step further, instead of creating arrays for the levels, it is possible to load in text files in Unity, so you can load the levels from a file. For more information on **Text Assets**, see `http://docs.unity3d.com/Manual/class-TextAsset.html`.

- As it stands when the player hits one of the orbs, they can jump again, if you'd prefer to not have this happen, adding an additional parameter to the `Raycast` function with the **Tag** of the object would solve the issue.

7
First Person Shooter Part 1 – Creating Exterior Environments

Now that we have experience in working on all parts of the game in 2D and 3D, let's spend the next few chapters creating a full-featured game. We will be creating a first-person shooter; however, instead of shooting a gun to damage our enemies, we will be shooting a picture in a survival horror environment, similar to the *Fatal Frame* series of games and the recent indie title *DreadOut*. To get started on our project, we're first going to look at creating our level or, in this case, our environments starting with the exterior.

In the game industry, there are two main roles in level creation: an environment artist and a level designer.

An environment artist is a person who builds the assets that go into the environment. He/she uses tools such as 3Ds Max or Maya to create the model and then uses other tools such as Photoshop to create textures and normal maps.

The level designer is responsible for taking the assets that the environment artist created and assembling them in an environment for players to enjoy. He/she designs the gameplay elements, creates the scripted events, and tests the gameplay. Typically, a level designer will create environments through a combination of scripting and using a tool that may or may not be in development as the game is being made. In our case, that tool is Unity.

One important thing to note is that most companies have their own definition for different roles. In some companies, a level designer may need to create assets and an environment artist may need to create a level layout. There are also some places that hire someone to just do lighting or just to place meshes (called a mesher) because they're so good at it.

Project overview

In this chapter, we take on the role of an environment artist who has been tasked to create an outdoor environment. We will use assets that I've placed in the example code as well as assets already provided to us by Unity for mesh placement. In addition, you will also learn some tips and tricks when doing level design.

Your objectives

This project will be split into a number of tasks. It will be a simple step-by-step process from the beginning to end. Here is the outline of our tasks:

- Creating the exterior environment—terrain
- Beautifying the environment—adding water, trees, and grass
- Building the atmosphere
- Designing the level layout and background

Prerequisites

As in *Chapter 1, 2D Twin-stick Shooter,* you will need Unity installed on your computer, but we will be starting a new project from scratch.

This chapter uses graphical assets that can be downloaded from the example code provided for this book on Packt's website:

`https://www.packtpub.com/books/content/support`

In addition, the completed project and source files are located there for you if you have any questions or need clarification.

Project setup

At this point, I assume that you have a fresh installation of Unity and have started it. You can perform the following steps:

1. With Unity started, navigate to **File | New Project**.

2. Select a project location of your choice somewhere on your hard drive and ensure that you have **Setup defaults for** set to 3D. Then, put in a **Project name** (I used **First Person Shooter**):

3. Once completed, click on **Create project**. Here, if you see the **Welcome to Unity** popup, feel free to close it as we won't be using it.

Level design 101 – planning

Now just because we are going to be diving straight into Unity, I feel that it's important to talk a little more about how level design is done in the game industry. Although you may think a level designer will just jump into the editor and start playing, the truth is that you normally would need to do a ton of planning ahead of time before you even open up your tool.

In general, a level begins with an idea. This can come from anything; maybe you saw a really cool building, or a photo on the Internet gave you a certain feeling; maybe you want to teach the player a new mechanic. Turning this idea into a level is what a level designer does. Taking all of these ideas, the level designer will create a level design document, which will outline exactly what you're trying to achieve with the entire level from start to end.

A level design document will describe everything inside the level; listing all of the possible encounters, puzzles, so on and so forth, which the player will need to complete as well as any side quests that the player will be able to achieve. To prepare for this, you should include as many references as you can with maps, images, and movies similar to what you're trying to achieve. If you're working with a team, making this document available on a website or wiki will be a great asset so that you know exactly what is being done in the level, what the team can use in their levels, and how difficult their encounters can be. In general, you'll also want a top-down layout of your level done either on a computer or with a graph paper, with a line showing a player's general route for the level with encounters and missions planned out.

Of course, you don't want to be too tied down to your design document and it will change as you playtest and work on the level, but the documentation process will help solidify your ideas and give you a firm basis to work from.

For those of you interested in seeing some level design documents, feel free to check out *Adam Reynolds* (*Level Designer on Homefront* and *Call of Duty: World at War*) at `http://wiki.modsrepository.com/index.php?title=Level_Design:_Level_Design_Document_Example`.

If you want to learn more about level design, I'm a big fan of *Beginning Game Level Design, John Feil* (previously my teacher) *and Marc Scattergood, Cengage Learning PTR*. For more of an introduction to all of game design from scratch, check out *Level Up!: The Guide to Great Video Game Design, Scott Rogers, Wiley* and *The Art of Game Design, Jesse Schell, CRC Press.*

For some online resources, Scott has a neat GDC talk named *Everything I Learned About Level Design I Learned from Disneyland*, which can be found at `http://mrbossdesign.blogspot.com/2009/03/everything-i-learned-about-game-design.html`, and *World of Level Design* (`http://worldofleveldesign.com/`) is a good source for learning about of level design, though it does not talk about Unity specifically.

Introduction to terrain

Terrain is basically used for non-manmade ground; things such as hills, deserts, and mountains. Unity's way of dealing with terrain is different than what most engines use in the fact that there are two mays to make terrains, one being using a height map and the other sculpting from scratch.

Height maps

Height maps are a common way for game engines to support terrains. Rather than creating tools to build a terrain within the level, they use a piece of graphics software to create an image and then we can translate that image into a terrain using the grayscale colors provided to translate into different height levels, hence the name height map. The lighter in color the area is, the lower its height, so in this instance, black represents the terrain's lowest areas, whereas white represents the highest.

> The terrain's **Terrain Height** property sets how high white actually is compared with black.

In order to apply a height map to a terrain object, inside an object's `Terrain` component, click on the **Settings** button and scroll down to **Import Raw...**.

> For more information on Unity's Height tools, check out `http://docs.unity3d.com/Manual/terrain-Height.html`.
>
> If you want to learn more about creating your own HeightMaps using Photoshop while this tutorial is for UDK, the area in Photoshop is the same: `http://worldofleveldesign.com/categories/udk/udk-landscape-heightmaps-photoshop-clouds-filter.php`
>
> Others also use software such as Terragen to create HeightMaps. More information on that is at `http://planetside.co.uk/products/terragen3`.

Hand sculpting

The other way to create terrain is by hand. This allows us to have everything exactly as we want it and is the way that we will be doing it in this chapter.

Exterior environment – terrain

When creating exterior environments, we cannot use straight floors for the most part unless you're creating a highly urbanized area. Our game takes place in a haunted house in the middle of nowhere, so we're going to create a natural landscape. In Unity, the best tool to use to create a natural landscape is the **Terrain** tool. Unity's Terrain system lets us add landscapes, complete with bushes, trees, and fading materials to our game.

To show how easy it is to use the Terrain tool, let's get started.

The first thing that we're going to do is actually create the terrain we'll be placing for the world. Let's first create a Terrain by selecting **GameObject | 3D Object | Terrain**.

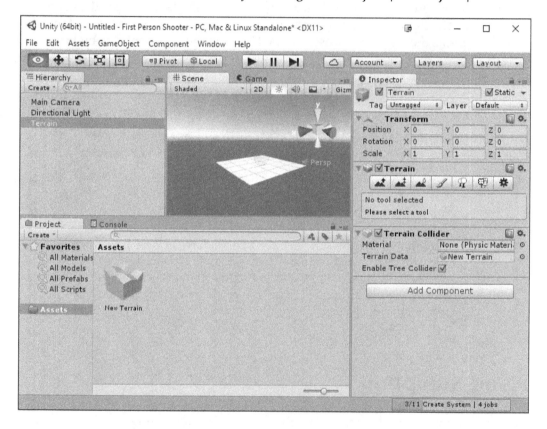

At this point, you should see the terrain on the screen.

If for some reason you have problems seeing the Terrain object, go to the **Hierarchy** tab and double-click on the Terrain object to focus your camera on it and move in as needed.

Right now, it's just a flat plane, but we'll be doing a lot to it to make it shine. If you look to the right with the Terrain object selected, you'll see the **Terrain** editing tools, which do the following (from left to right):

- **Raise/Lower Height** — This will allow us to raise or lower the height of our terrain in a certain radius to create hills, rivers, and more.

- **Paint Height** — If you already know exactly the height that a part of your terrain needs to be, this tool will allow you to paint a spot to that location.

- **Smooth Height** — This averages out the area that it is in, attempts to smooth out areas, and reduces the appearance of abrupt changes.

- **Paint Texture** — This allows us to add textures to the surface of our terrain. One of the nice features of this is the ability to lay multiple textures on top of each other.

- **Place Trees** — This allows us to paint objects in our environment that will appear on the surface. Unity attempts to optimize these objects by billboarding distant trees so we can have dense forests without having a horrible frame rate. By billboarding, I mean that the object will be simplified and its direction usually changes constantly as the object and camera move, so it always faces the camera direction.

- **Paint Details** — In addition to trees, you can also have small things like rocks or grass covering the surface of your environment, using 2D images to represent individual clumps with bits of randomization to make it appear more natural.

- **Terrain Settings** — Settings that will affect the overall properties of the particular Terrain, options such as the size of the terrain and wind can be found here.

By default, the entire Terrain is set to be at the bottom, but we want to have ground above us and below us so we can add in things like lakes.

1. With the Terrain object selected, click on the second button from the left on the Terrain component (Paint height mode). From there, set the **Height** value under **Settings** to 100 and then press the **Flatten** button. At this point, you should note the plane moving up, so now everything is above by default.

2. Next, we are going to create some interesting shapes to our world with some hills by "painting" on the surface. With the Terrain object selected, click on the first button on the left of our Terrain component (the **Raise/Lower Terrain** mode). Once this is completed, you should see a number of different brushes and shapes that you can select from.

Our use of terrain is to create hills in the background of our scene, so it does not seem like the world is completely flat.

1. Under the **Settings**, change the **Brush Size** and **Opacity** of your brush to 100 and left-click around the edges of the world to create some hills. You can increase the height of the current hills if you click on top of the previous hill.

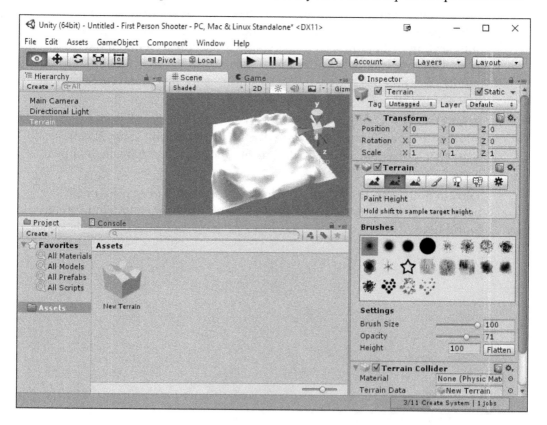

When creating hills, it's a good idea to look at multiple angles while you're building them, so you can make sure that none are too high or too low In general, you want to have taller hills as you go further back, or else you cannot see the smaller ones since they're blocked.

In the **Scene** view, to move your camera around, you can use the toolbar at the top-right corner or hold down the right mouse button and drag it in the direction you want the camera to move around in, pressing the *W*, *A*, *S*, and *D* keys to pan. In addition, you can hold down the middle mouse button and drag it to move the camera around. The mouse wheel can be scrolled to zoom in and out from where the camera is.

Even though you should plan out the level ahead of time on something like a piece of graph paper to plan out encounters, you will want to avoid making the level entirely from the preceding section, as the player will not actually see the game with a bird's eye view in the game at all (most likely). Referencing the map from the same perspective as your character will help ensure that the map looks great.

To see many different angles at one time, you can use a layout with multiple views of the scene, such as the 4 Split.

2. Once we have our land done, we now want to create some holes in the ground, which we will fill with water later. This will provide a natural barrier to our world that players will know they cannot pass, so we will create a moat by first changing the **Brush Size** value to **50** and then holding down the *Shift* key, and left-clicking around the middle of our texture.

In this case, it's okay to use the **Top** view; remember that this will eventually be water to fill in lakes, rivers, and so on, as shown in the following screenshot:

To make this easier to see, you can click on the sun-looking light icon from the **Scene** tab to disable lighting for the time being.

At this point, we have done what is referred to in the industry as "grayboxing," making the level in the engine in the simplest way possible but without artwork (also known as "whiteboxing" or "orangeboxing" depending on the company you're working for).

At this point in a traditional studio, you'd spend time playtesting the level and iterating on it before an artist or you will take the time to make it look great. However, for our purposes, we want to create a finished project as soon as possible. When doing your own games, be sure to play your level and have others play your level before you polish it.

For more information on grayboxing, check out `http://www.worldofleveldesign.com/categories/level_design_tutorials/art_of_blocking_in_your_map.php`.

For an example with images of a graybox to the final level, PC Gamer has a nice article available at `http://www.pcgamer.com/2014/03/18/building-crown-part-two-layout-design-textures-and-the-hammer-editor/`.

Adding color to our terrain – textures

This is interesting enough, but being in an all-white world would be quite boring. Thankfully, it's very easy to add textures to everything. However, first, we need to have some textures to paint onto the world. For this instance, we will make use of some of the free assets that Unity provides us with.

1. So, with that mindset, navigate to **Assets | Import Package | Environment.**

2. From there, uncheck all of the folders aside from the **Environment** one and then click on **Import**.

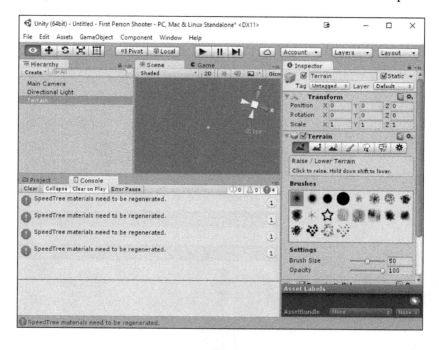

3. Once imported, you may see an error that says **SpeedTree materials need to be regenerated**. To check the error, click on the **Console** tab to open it up.

We aren't actually using the trees yet, but I don't like seeing errors so let's fix them now.

4. To fix this, switch back to the **Project** tab and open up the `Standard Assets\Environment\SpeedTree` folder. Inside the `Broadleaf` folder, you'll find two objects `Broadleaf_Desktop` and `Broadleaf_Mobile`, and from **Inspector,** click on the **Apply & Generate Materials** button. After this, use the `Conifer_Desktop` and the `Palm_Desktop` and do the same. And with that our errors are gone!

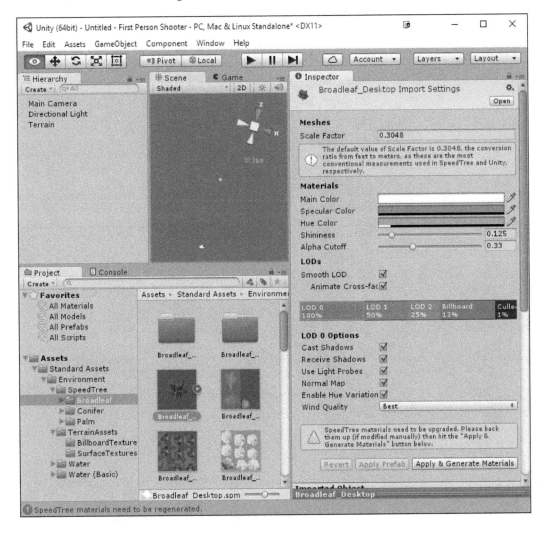

5. Go to the **Project** tab and open up the `Standard Assets\Environment\` `TerrainAssets\SurfaceTexture` folder. From here, you'll see the images that we are going to use to paint our terrain.

6. Select the **Terrain** object and then click on the fourth from the left button (that looks like a paint brush) to select the **Paint Texture** button. From here, you'll notice that it looks quite similar to the previous sections we've seen. However, now there is a **Textures** section as well, but as of now, there is the information for **No terrain textures defined**. So, let's fix that. Click on the **Edit Textures** button and then select **Add Texture**.

7. You'll see an **Add Terrain Texture** dialogue popup. Under the **Texture** variable, place the **GrassHillAlbedo** texture and then click on the **Add** button.

At this point, you should see the entire world change to green if you're far away. If you zoom in you'll see that now the entire terrain is now using the `GrassHillAlbedo` texture.

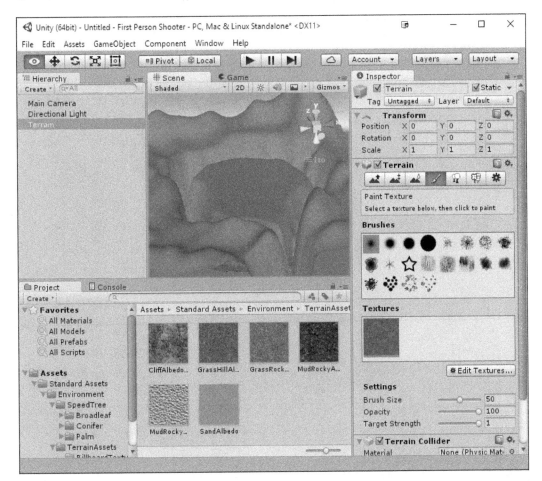

Adding multiple textures to a terrain

Now, we don't want the entire world to have grass. Next, we will add cliffs around the edges where the water is.

1. To do this, add an additional texture by navigating to **Edit Textures... | Add Texture**. Select **CliffAlbedoSpecular** as the texture and then select **Add**. Now if you select the terrain, you should see two textures. With the **CliffAlbedoSpecular** texture selected, paint the edges of the water by clicking and holding the mouse, modifying the **Brush Size** value as needed:

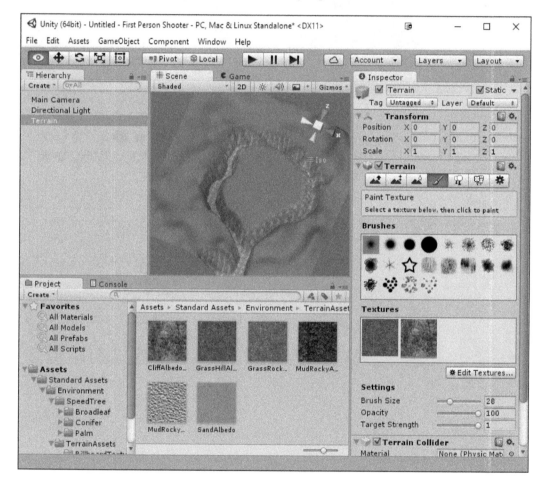

2. We now want to create a path for our player to follow, so we're going to create yet another texture this time using the **SandAlbedo** material. Since this is a path the player may take, I'm going to change the **Brush Size** value to **8** and the **Opacity** value to **30**, and use the second brush from the left, which is slightly less faded. Once finished, I'm going to paint in some trails that the player can follow. One thing that you will want to try to do is to make sure that the player shouldn't go too far before having to backtrack and reward the player for exploration. The following screenshot shows the path:

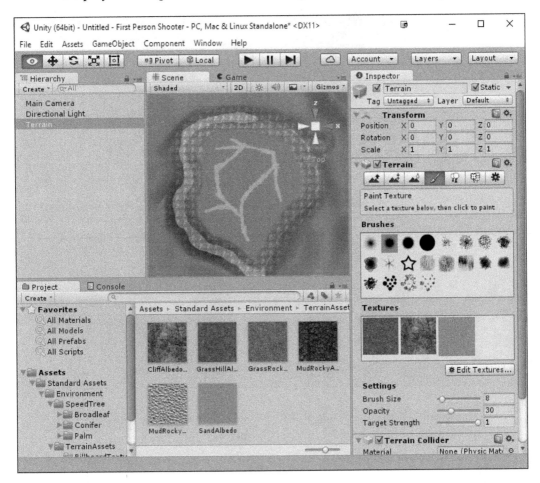

Now, it's starting to look really nice, but if we play the game and look at the floor or in the distance you can see some receptiveness in the textures, especially from the flat floor.

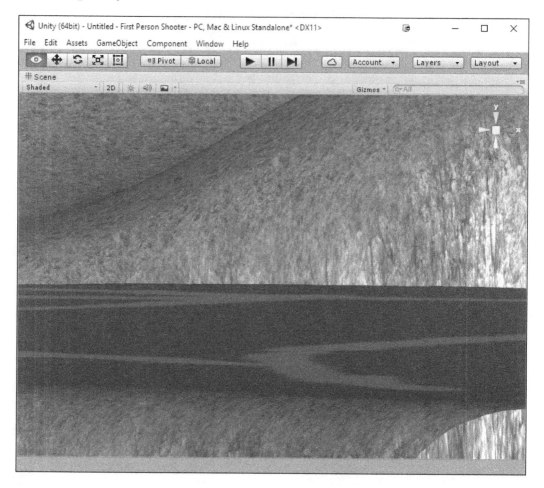

Thankfully, Unity has some things we can do in order to break up this monotony, namely that we can mix textures.

3. To reduce the appearance of texture duplication, we can introduce new materials with a very soft opacity, which we place in patches in areas where there is just plain ground. For example, let's create a new texture with the **GrassRockyAlbedo** texture. Change the **Brush Size** value to 16 and the **Opacity** value to something really low, such as 6, and then start painting the areas that look too repetitive. Feel free to select the first brush again to have a smoother touch up.

4. Now, if we zoom into the world as if we were a character there, I can tell that the first grass texture is way too big for the environment, but we can actually change that very easily. *Double-click* on the texture to change the **Size** value to (8,8). This will make the texture smaller before it duplicates. It's a good idea to have different textures with different sizes so that the seams of each texture aren't visible to others. The following screenshot shows the size options:

Edit Terrain Texture (Standard)	x

Albedo (RGB)
Smoothness (A)   Normal

None
(Texture2D)

Select   Select

Metallic ⊙━━━━ 0

Smoothness ⊙━━━ 0

Size	Offset
x	8	0
y	8	0

Apply

5. Do the same changes as in the preceding step for our sand texture as well, changing the **Size** option to (8,8):

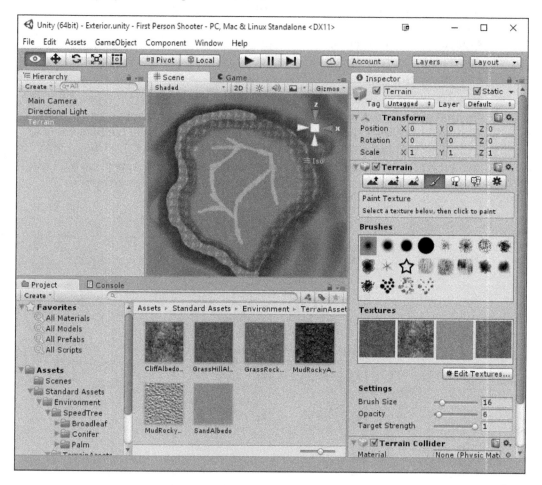

With this, we already have a level that looks pretty nice! However, that being said, it's just some hills. To really have a quality-looking title, we are going to need to do some additional work to beautify the environment.

Adding water

We created the lower section of our gameplay area to be the water level or where water will be. This can be a useful tool as a level designer to designate places that players can't go to if you can't swim. Thankfully, it's also quite easy to add to our level, and due to it being included with Unity, we won't need to go to the Asset Store to get it.

1. From the **Project** tab, go into the `Standard Assets/Environment/Water/Water/Prefabs` folder to then drag and drop the `WaterProNighttime` prefab into the scene.

2. Once in the scene, change the object's **Position** to `250, 90, 250` and give it a **Scale** of `250, 1, 250` so it covers the entire area. Next, in the **Water Script** component from the **Inspector** tab, change **Water Mode** to **Reflective**. This will make it so instead of seeing what's underneath the water it will instead reflect what's around us.

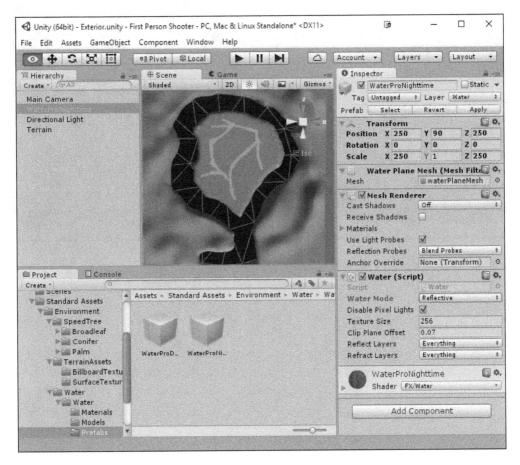

3. We've done a lot so let's save our scene by going to **File | Save Scene** and create a new folder named **Scenes**; from there, give it a name of **Exterior**.

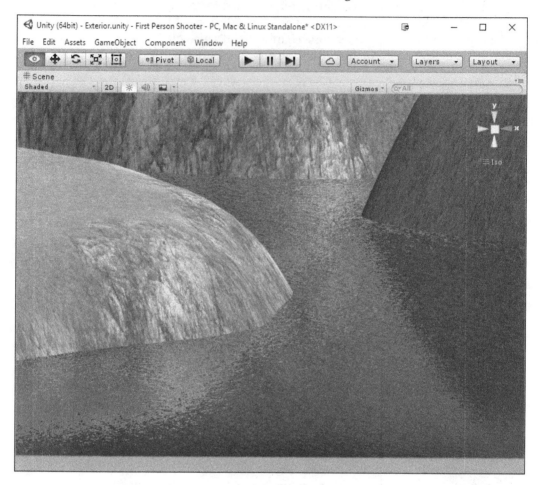

Adding trees

Hills typically aren't just grass, vegetation can be used to block player's visibility as well as give a better look for our environment:

1. With that finished, go back to our **Terrain** object and then click on the **Place Trees** mode button (the one that looks like two trees).

    [To check the names of each button, you can hold the mouse over the image for a second before it'll display what it is.]

2. Just like working with painting textures. There are no trees by default, so click on **Edit Trees... | Add Tree**.

3. From the window that pops up, set the **Tree Prefab** by going to the **Project** tab and then going to Standard Assets\Environment\SpeedTree\ Broadleaf and select **Broadleaf_Desktop** and then **Add**.

Add Tree		x
Tree Prefab	Broadleaf_Desktop	⊙
		Add

4. Next, under **Settings**, change **Tree Density** to 15 and then with our new tree selected, paint the areas where you'd like to see trees in the environment. One thing you could do is paint over all of the land areas and then remove the trees that are along your path.

    If you hold down *Shift* and paint, you will remove trees instead of placing them.

5. Save your level and play the game!

As you can see, the world is already much more nice to look at!

If you want to add even more detail to your levels, you can add additional trees and/or materials to the area as long as it makes sense to be there (not adding them in water for example).

You can also make trees of your own using Speed Tree within Unity. For more information on this, check out `http://docs.unity3d.com/Manual/tree-FirstTree.html`.

For more information on the Terrain engine that Unity has, please visit `http://docs.unity3d.com/Manual/script-Terrain.html`.

Adding in details – grass

Let's now see how we can use the Paint Details tool to add more detail to our maps.

1. The first thing we need to do is locate our grass images, which we can find by going to the **Project** tab and then open up the Standard Assets\ TerrainAssets\BillboardTextures folder. The two images there are what we are going to use, but right now, their edges are all green. From the **Inspector**, check the **Alpha Is Transparency** option and then hit the **Apply** button.

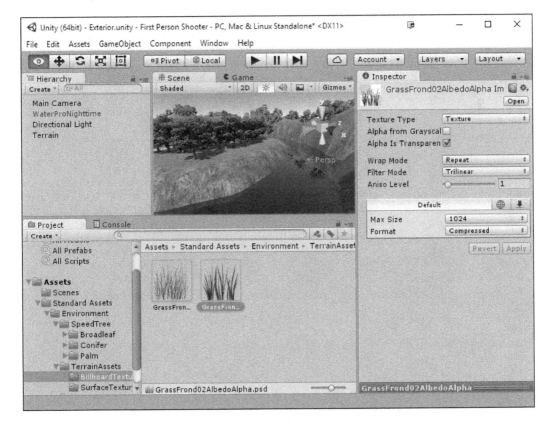

2. Go back to the **Hierarchy** tab and select out the **Terrain** object. The mode to the right of the **Plant Trees** mode is **Paint Details mode**.

3. Click on it and then click on the **Edit Details...** button and then select **Add Grass Texture**.

4. Select either of the `Grass` textures that we just changed for the **Detail Texture**. After this, set **Healthy Color** and **Dry Color** by using the eyedropper and choosing a color similar to our textures. Once you're done modifying the settings, then click on **Apply**.

Edit Grass Texture	x
Detail Texture	GrassFrond01AlbedoAlpha ⊙
Min Width	1
Max Width	2
Min Height	1
Max Height	2
Noise Spread	0.1
Healthy Color	
Dry Color	
Billboard	✓

Apply

5. Once created, paint the grass into the world in the same way we did textures. If you can't see it being placed, zoom in as you need to be close to see it.

Finally, our current island is very flat and while that's okay for cities, nature is random. Go back into the **Height Raise/Lower** tool and gently raise and lower some areas of the level to give the illusion of depth. Do note that your trees and grass will raise and fall with the changes that you make.

6. Once you're finished, save your level and play the game!

This aspect of level creation isn't very difficult, just time consuming. However, it's taking the time to put in these details that really sets a game apart from other titles. In general, you'll want to playtest and make sure that your level is fun before doing these actions; but I feel it's important to have an idea of how to do it for your future projects.

Building atmosphere

Now, the base of our world has been created; let's add some effects to make the game even more visually appealing and start to fit in with the survival horror feel that we're going to be giving the game.

In Unity 5, we are given a default skybox for 3D projects, but it's only for a bright sunny day, which is not ideal for a horror game. To fix this, we will be using a skybox. A **skybox** is a method to create backgrounds to make the area seems bigger than it really is. This is done by putting an image in the areas that are currently being filled with the light blue color, not moving in the same way that the sky doesn't move to us because it's so far away.

The reason why we call a skybox a skybox is because it is made up of six textures that will be the inside of the box (one for each side of a cube). Game engines such as Unreal have skydomes, which are the same thing; just that they are done with a hemisphere instead of a cube. We will perform the following steps to build the atmosphere for our horror title:

1. To add in our skybox, we are going to first go to our Example Code folder and open up the Art Assets\Skybox folder for this chapter. From there you'll see a number of images. Drag this folder into your project (the files will need to be unzipped for this to work).

2. Next, from the Project tab click on Create | Material and give it a name of Nightsky. Select the newly created material and from the Inspector tab under Shader, change the property to Skybox | 6 Sided. Next, fill in each of the 6 images in the Inspector with the appropriate image from our Skybox folder. When you're finished, it should look like this:

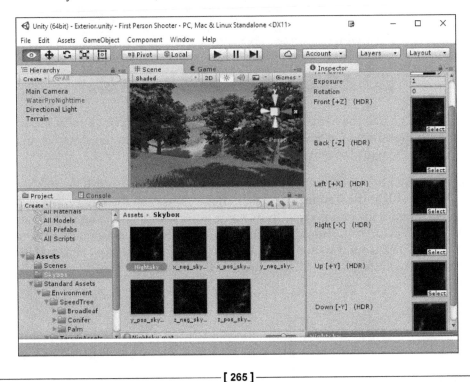

3. With this file imported, we need to navigate to **Window | Lighting** next. Once there, confirm you are in the **Scene** part and then set the **Skybox** option to the Nightsky skybox:

If you go into the game, you'll note the level starting to look nicer already with the addition of the skybox, except for the fact that the sky says night while the world says it's daytime. Let's fix that now.

4. Switch to the **Game** tab so that you can see the changes we'll be making next. While still at the **RenderSettings** menu, let's turn on the **Fog** property by clicking on the checkbox with its name and changing the **Fog Color** value to a black color. You should note that the surroundings are already turning very dark. Play around with the **Fog Density** value until you're comfortable with how much the player can see ahead of them; I used 0.005.

Fog obscures far away objects, which adds to the atmosphere and saves the rendering power. The denser the fog, the more the game will feel like a horror game. The first game of the Silent Hill franchise used fog to make the game run at an acceptable frame rate due to a large 3D environment it had on early PlayStation hardware. Due to how well it spooked players, it continued to be used in later games even though they could render larger areas with the current technology.

Let's add some lighting tweaks to make the environment the player is walking in seem more like night.

5. Go into the **DirectionalLight** properties section and change the **Intensity** value to 0.05. You'll see the value get darker, as shown in the following screenshot:

 If for some reason, you'd like to make the world pitch black, you'll need to modify the **Ambient Light** property to black inside the **RenderSettings** section. By default, it is dark gray, which will show up even if there are no lights placed in the world.

 In the preceding example, I increased the **Intensity** value to make it easier to see the world to make it easier for readers to follow, but in your project, you probably don't want the player to see so far out with such clarity.

With this, we now have a believable exterior area at night that will fit quite well for our horror game!

Summary

With this, we now have a great-looking exterior level for our game! In addition, we covered a lot of features that exist in Unity for you to be able to use in your own future projects. With this in mind, you will learn how to build an interior environment in the next chapter!

Challenges

For those of you who want to do more with this project, there are still plenty of things you can do, especially after finishing the rest of this book. Here are some ideas to get your mind thinking:

- Add additional trees and textures to make the level appear even more realistic.
- Another way to add in polish and add atmosphere to your level would be making use of Unity's Image Effect. You can read more about this at `http://blog.teamtreehouse.com/use-image-effects-unity`.
- Once you add a character, you have someone to play your game and see if they can navigate your environment to where you want to lead them.
- Once you learn how to create encounters, add some additional combat experiences in this level.
- Create collectibles that the player can collect in the level, in the same manner as the platformer project we did, to reward the player traveling the map.

8
First-person Shooter Part 2 – Creating Interior Environments

Because nature is very chaotic, it makes sense to use tools that you learned in the previous chapter such as terrain and placing objects with randomness to create a natural-looking environment. However, not all things are constructed like that. Man-made structures, such as office buildings, stone pillars, and floor tiles, are all made up of pieces that look similar to one another. Rather than modeling out every single wall in your building, can't you use one you made before?

As you might remember in *Chapter 6, Side-scrolling Platformer*, you learned how we can use tiles to build a level using only a couple of different objects, duplicating them as needed to create our environment. In this chapter, we will use the same line of thinking in a 3D environment using a method named modular level design.

Modular level design is a tool that **AAA** (pronounced triple A) developers (those working with the highest development budgets and promotion) have been using to create great-looking levels in the minimum amount of time possible. Breaking apart buildings into modules creates building blocks that can be placed next to one another, such as LEGO pieces, to create an entire structure. This makes it much easier to create levels than just trying to model everything from scratch and is a staple of large open-world games such as Bethesda's *Fallout 4*.

Project overview

Unlike the preceding chapter, where we worked as an environmental artist, here we take on the role of a level designer who has been tasked to create an interior environment using assets already provided to us by the environment artist. We will use already-provided assets as well as assets that are provided to us by Unity for mesh placement.

Your objectives

This project will be split into a number of tasks. It will be a simple step-by-step process from beginning to end. Here is the outline of our tasks:

- Importing assets
- Creating tiles
- Placing tiles with grid snapping
- Creating and placing props
- Light mapping quick start prerequisites

Prerequisites

In this chapter, we will continue from where the preceding chapter was left off using the same project. You can continue with your previous project or pick up a copy along with the assets for this chapter from the example code provided for this book on Packt Publishing's website.

```
https://www.packtpub.com/books/content/support
```

In addition, the completed project and source files are located there for you to check whether you have any questions or need clarification.

Project setup

At this point, I have assumed that you have Unity started up and have our project from the previous chapter loaded. Now, perform the following step:

With Unity started, open the project from the previous chapter and if you are on our previous level, create a new scene by selecting **File** | **New Scene**.

Creating architecture overview

As a level designer, one of the most time-consuming parts of your job will be creating environments. There are many different ways out there to create levels. By default, Unity gives us some default meshes, such as a **Box**, **Sphere**, and **Cylinder**, and while it's technically possible to build a level in that way, it could get really tedious really quickly. Next, I'm going to quickly go through the most popular options to build levels for games made in Unity before we jump into building a level of our own.

3D modelling software

A lot of times, opening a 3D modeling software package and building architecture that way is what professional games studios will often do. This gives you maximum freedom in creating your environment and allows you to do exactly what you'd like to do. However, this requires you to be proficient in that tool, whether that be Maya, 3Ds Max, Blender (which can be downloaded for free at blender.org), or some other tool. Then, you just need to export your models and import them into Unity.

Unity supports a lot of different formats for 3D models, but there are a lot of issues to consider. For some best practices, when it comes to creating art assets, please visit http://blogs.unity3d.com/2011/09/02/art-assets-best-practice-guide/.

Constructing geometry with brushes

Using **Constructive Solid Geometry (CSG)**, commonly referred to as brushes, has been a long-existing way for games to have in-game level editors, which has led to people creating levels for them. Tools such as Unreal Engine 4, Hammer, Radiant, and other professional game engines make use of this building structure, making it quite easy for people to create and iterate through levels quickly through a process named **whiteboxing**, as it's very easy to make changes to simple shapes. However, just like learning a modeling software tool, there can be a higher barrier to entry in using brushes to create your geometry, but for creating those certain types of games where you need to create a lot of different content, it can be a great tool.

Unity does not support building things like this by default, but there are several tools in the **Unity Asset Store** that allow you to do something like this. For example, **sixbyseven studio** has an extension named ProBuilder, which can add the ability to create world geometry using brushes within Unity, making it very easy to build levels (it's what I use normally when building environments for 3D games in Unity and I use it in one of my other titles, *Building an FPS Game with Unity*, also available from Packt Publishing). However, as an extension, you'll need to buy it either from the developer or through the Asset Store, as it is not free. You can find out more information about ProBuilder and the free version of their tool at `http://www.protoolsforunity3d.com/probuilder/`.

Modular tilesets

Another way to generate architecture is through the use of tiles that are created by an artist. You can use them to build your level. Similar to using LEGO pieces, we can use these tiles to snap together walls and other objects to create a building. With creative uses of tiles, you can create a large amount of content with just a minimal amount of assets. This is probably the easiest way to create a level at the expense of not being able to create unique-looking buildings since you only have a few pieces to work with.

Mix and match

Of course, it's also possible to use a mixture of the tools mentioned to get the advantages of certain ways of doing things. For example, you could use brushes to block out an area (which is why it is named **greyboxing**) and then use a group of tiles named a **tileset** to replace boxes with highly detailed models, which is what a lot of AAA studios do, using the boxes just for their collision. In addition, we could also place tiles initially and then add in props to break up the repetitiveness of levels, which is what we are going to do.

Importing assets

In this chapter, we are going to create an interior environment. This will be useful to know, because unlike a landscape, interiors are generally more structured than the outside world, with straight floors and walls where we can use 3D models modularly to build the environment!

To show how easy it is to use, let's get started. Perform the following steps:

1. From the **Project** tab, create a new folder named `Materials`. Then, enter the folder and create two new materials by selecting **Create | New Material**. Give one of the new materials the name `House` and the other, `Props`. Once you have created that go to your example code folder, and within the `Textures` folder, import the `2048_House_TEX.jpg` and `2048_Props_TEX.jpg` files from the `Example Code Assets` folder for this chapter. Once you've done that, apply that texture to the materials in the **Albedo** property via drag and drop. Once finished, it should look like the following screenshot:

2. Create a new folder from the **Project** tab named `Models`.

   John Espiritu has very kindly provided some models in modular pieces for us to work with. So, the next thing we will do is actually import those models.

 For more info on John's stuff or to commission him yourself, check out `http://raynehaize.tumblr.com/` or `http://raynehaize.deviantart.com/`.

3. With the `Models` folder selected, let's import the models by dragging and dropping the `Modular Pieces` and `Props` folders in it. Take a look at the following screenshot:

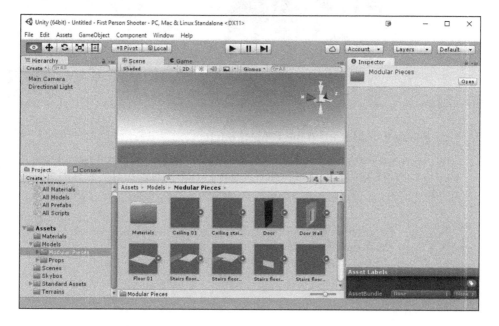

4. Back in Unity, move to the `Modular Pieces` folder in **Hierarchy**. At this point, it should look somewhat as follows:

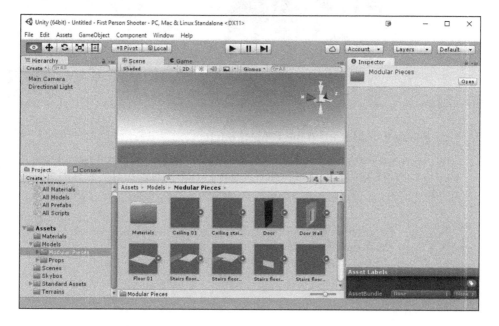

5. By default, Unity attempts to do some things automatically for us, which creates a lot of stuff we don't need for simple environment pieces like this. Select all the objects in this folder by selecting the `Ceiling 01` object, hold down the *Shift* key, and select the `Wall Plain` object at the bottom. This will bring you to **Model Importer**. Once you are in the **Inspector** tab, you will see the following three tabs:

   ° **Model**: This contains settings to import the model. For information, check out `http://docs.unity3d.com/Manual/FBXImporter-Model.html`.

   ° **Rig**: This has settings that will either allow the model to support animation or not. For more information, check out `http://docs.unity3d.com/Manual/FBXImporter-Rig.html`.

   ° **Animations**: This has settings to import different animations from the model file. For more information, check out `http://docs.unity3d.com/Manual/FBXImporter-Animations.html`.

6. Inside the **Model** tab, change **Scale Factor** to 2.5.

   The **Scale Factor** property allows you to apply a scalar to the model that you've imported. This is fine for this project, but generally, when working with animations, changing the scale factor may hurt your rig. So, be sure that you have your artist create art at the correct scale.

7. Next, uncheck the **Import Models** option from the **Materials** section. After this, click on the **Apply** button.

   If left checked, Unity will have each object use its own material, which is intended to have its own texture. All of our pieces use the same texture, so there's no need to have multiple textures.

8. Select the **Rig** tab, and confirm the **Animation Type** is None, and click on **Apply** if needed.

   If the object has animation, it will attempt to add an Avatar and more, which is unnecessary for this. Note that now the **Animations** tab will be grayed out because we have no animations.

9. Delete the `Materials` folder inside the `Modular Pieces` folder.

When exporting an FBX file, it exports your model with UV coordinates but doesn't include the textures in the FBX file. You have to import your textures separately into Unity and add it to the material generated or assign it on your own.

As of this version of Unity, there is no way to have models not generate a material by default, hence we need to delete them. We will add materials to these models when we create their prefabs.

10. Repeat steps 5–8 with the `Props` folder as well. Once you finish, the folder should look like the following screenshot:

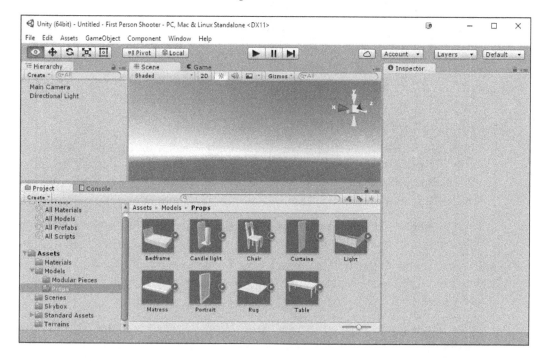

Now, we have our models in the project! This is a great first step, but it's useless unless the models are actually in the game world. Let's get started with that now.

Creating tiles

Before we get started, it's a good idea to see how the object looks to us, so let's add in a temporary controller to give us an idea of what it looks like. Therefore, let's follow the these steps:

1. Now, in the upper-right corner of the scene view is the scene gizmo. This will display our current camera orientation, allow us to quickly modify the viewing angle, and switch from the **Perspective** to **Isometric** mode easily, which will help us when placing objects in the world. (Note that in 2D mode, this gizmo won't be shown, so untoggle the 2D button on the **Scene** toolbar if that is the case.)

2. Click on the **Y** axis on the scene gizmo to switch our camera to an overhead view. Once there, go to the **Modular Pieces** folder and then drag and drop the **Floor 01** object into our world, and change **Position** to (0, 0, 0) from the **Transform** section. Then, you can double-click on the object in the **Hierarchy** tab to zoom to its position.

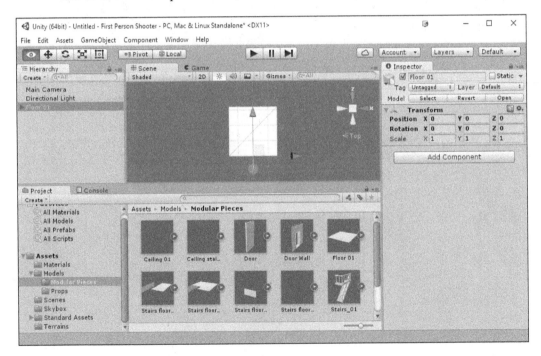

You'll note that instead of the floor tile being in the center of the world when the position is reset, the pivot is off on the Z axis. This is because the art files that the artist provided to us placed the pivot there, which you will see if the **Gizmo Display Toggles** are set to **Pivot** (the button to the right of the Transform widgets in the toolbar). Now, since we're going to be placing these objects as tiles, we want them to snap together as easily as possible. In general, we want to place these pivots along one of the edges of the object. Some people prefer to place it on the center of the mesh, which you can easily do by changing the pivot toggle to **Center** by clicking on the button that currently says **Pivot** to change it to the **Center** move, but I don't like it, as it makes rotations and scaling more of a pain. For more information on the Gizmo Display Toggles, check out `http://docs.unity3d.com/410/Documentation/Manual/PositioningGameObjects.html`.

3. After this, open the **Floor 01** object to see the `Floor_01_Modular_pieces_grp` object and select it. This is the actual mesh we want to work with. With it selected, go to the **Mesh Renderer** component and expand the **Materials** section. Then, change **Element 0** to our house material either by dragging and dropping or clicking on the right-hand side circle button and then selecting it from the list shown. Finally, let's add in a box collider by going to **Component | Physics | Box Collider**.

   This collider is what the player will collide with in the world, so what you see will be what they will be walking into.

4. Now that we have created the revised version created, rename the **Floor_01_Modular_pieces_grp** game object to `Floor`, and from the **Project** tab, create a new folder named `Prefabs`. Drag and drop just the `Floor` object as a prefab in the `Prefabs` folder; optionally, you can place the object in a new folder named `Modular Pieces`.

5. Now repeat steps 3 to 5 for the **Wall Plain** object:

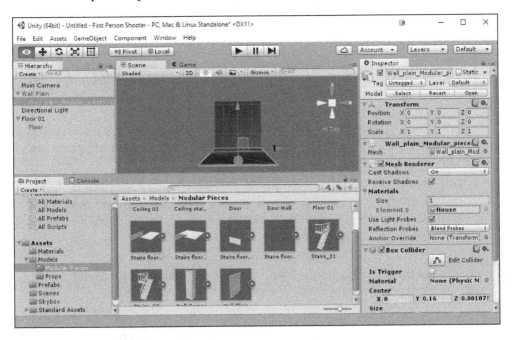

As you can see if we move the camera, the two pieces together are already starting to look like a room. Not too hard, right?

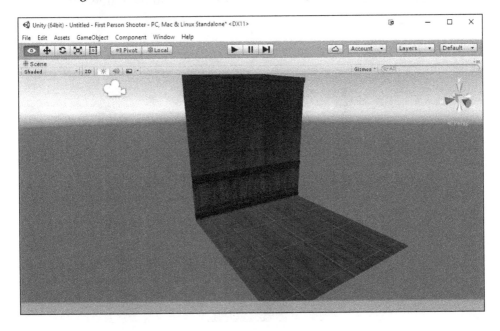

6. Delete those two prefabs, and now do the same steps for the other models in the `Modular Pieces` folders, thereby deleting them as they go on, using **Mesh Colliders** on the **Door Wall** and **Stairs** objects.

 Everything besides the renaming and moving to the `Prefabs` folder can be done to all the objects by shift-clicking on them all to do each of the steps.

7. Now that we have the models for our environment fixed, let's assemble them into some tiles that we can place in the world. Create an empty game object, name it `Hallway` and reset its position.

   The pivot of an object is extremely important when doing modular level design. We want to make it extremely easy for us to duplicate objects and snap them together, so picking a part of the object that will tile well can save you a lot of time in the future.

 For those interested in learning more about creating good modular game art, check out http://www.gamasutra.com/view/ feature/130885/creating_modular_game_art_for_fast_.php.

8. Add a **Floor**, **Ceiling**, and **Wall** prefab to the object as children.

9. Duplicate the wall by pressing *Ctrl + D*, and then change **Position** of **Z** axis to 3.2 and **Rotation** of **Y** axis to 180. Take a look at the following screenshot:

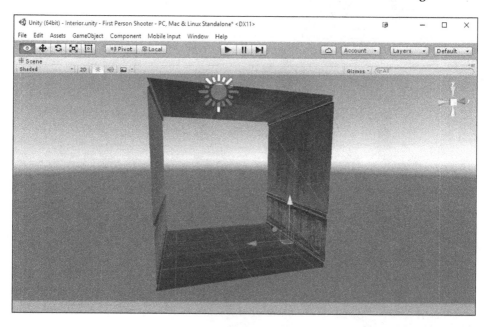

This will act as our first building block, which we can use to create hallways by merely duplicating these **Hallway** objects.

10. Now, inside the project, add a folder to the `Prefabs` folder named `Tiles`. Make **Hallway** a prefab by dragging and dropping it in the `Tiles` folder. Take a look at the following screenshot:

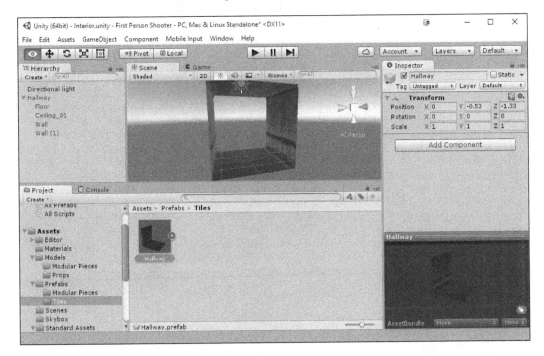

11. Delete one of the wall objects, (click on **Continue** at the notification) and you'll note that the object is no longer a prefab, as it's no longer colored blue. This is fine because now we're going to create a doorway. Rename **Hallway** to `Hall Door`. Then, add a **Door** object and a **Door Wall** object as children to the new **Hall Door** on the side that your wall object was previously at. Then, add **Hall Door** as a prefab in the `Tiles` folder.

You can make these doors functional later on, but for now, we are just building the environment.

12. Apart from these very simple tiles that we have just made, we also want to create some rooms that are larger than one big tile, so next, we need to create nine additional prefab tiles that will look like the following screenshot:

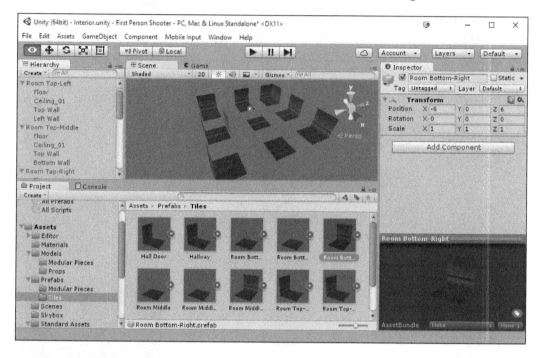

To name the objects, I went with the following convention:
- Room Top-Left
- Room Top-Middle
- Room Top-Right
- Room Middle-Left
- Room Middle
- Room Middle-Right
- Room Bottom-Left
- Room Bottom-Middle
- Room Bottom-Right

13. With these pieces, we can make rooms of whatever size we want! Delete the newly created prefabs from the hierarchy.

14. Finally, let's get the staircase built! Create an empty game object and give it a name of `Left Stairs`. Go back to our **Modular Pieces** prefabs and then place two floors next to each other, one at **Position** (0, 0, 0) and the other at (-3.2, 0, 0). Next, add **Stairs 1**, **Stairs Floor 1**, and objects together, all at **Position** (0, 0, 0). Add **Stairs Floor 2** at **Position** (-3.2, 0, 0). Finally, add two walls on the first floor (one with 0.0 on **X** and one with -3.2) and two on the second floor (**Y** at 4). Once completed, you should have a staircase built, as shown in the following screenshot:

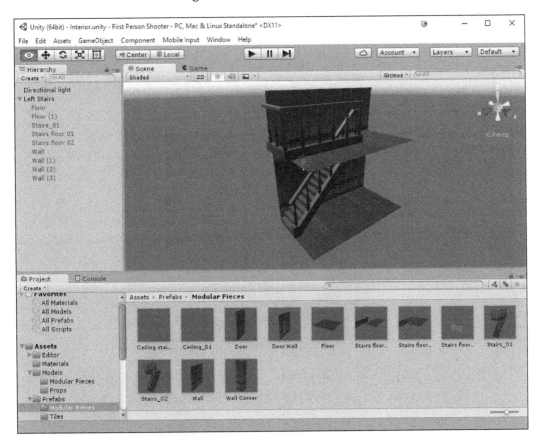

15. Then, make our **Left Stairs** object a prefab inside of the `Prefabs\Tiles` folder. Be sure to reset the position of **GameObject** by right-clicking on its **Transform** component and by selecting **Reset Position**.

16. Afterwards, go ahead and delete the **Left Stairs** prefab. And with this, we now have our tiles all set!

Placing tiles with grid snapping

Now that we have all of our tiles created, let's start building out our area:

1. Put a tile prefab in the world of your choice. Hold down the *Ctrl* key, and pull it in an axis' direction. You may have noted a little snap that you wouldn't see when moving normally. This is due to unit snapping.

2. **Grid snapping** is a really useful tool when it comes to building stuff inside Unity. Instead of punching in numbers all the time when trying to set the positions of all of these tiles, we can just set our **Snap** size to be the size of our tiles 3.2 x 3.2 x 3.2.

[In addition to movement, we can also snap rotations and scaling.]

3. Go to **Edit | Snap Settings**; we can change the value to snap easily by changing **Move** to 3.2 and **Move Z** to 3.561, taking into account the wall thickness.

Snap settings				x
Move X		3.2		
Move Y		1		
Move Z		3.561|		
Scale		0.1		
Rotation		15		
Snap All Axes	X	Y	Z	

4. Now that we have the snap settings working correctly, we will place a hallway to start our level and reset its **Position** property to (0, 0, 0).

5. Next, duplicate the mesh by hitting *Ctrl + D*, and then, holding *Ctrl*, drag the tile over to the right-hand side to continue the hallway.

6. After this, I'm going to create a couple of other hallways and then place two **Hall Door** prefabs to fill out the area, as shown in the following screenshot:

7. Now, we need to create a few rooms. Open your rooms prefab and from the top viewport, place your middle piece in front of each doorway by first dragging it out, resetting its position, then holding down *Ctrl* and snapping it there.

> Another way of placing assets in this way would be to place floors first wherever you want to create your layout and then spawning walls around the edges.

Next, use the correct **Room** tiles to fill out your rooms as you want them to look. Start with using your **Top Left**, **Top**, and **Right** prefabs.

> Remember that once you place the object for the first time, all you need to do is duplicate, which should make it extremely quick to build (or prototype) levels.

Once we get over the wall, you'll remember that normal tiles are still 3.2, so modify **Move** of **Z** as needed to 3.2 or 3.561 accordingly. You can also assemble tiles by making use of the vertex snapping tool. Basically, you can take any vertex of a mesh, and with your mouse, place that vertex in the same position as a vertex from any other mesh.

8. Select the mesh you want to manipulate, and make sure that the **Transform** tool is active. Press and hold *V* to enter the vertex snapping mode. Move your cursor over the vertex on the mesh you want to use as the pivot point. Hold down the left button once your cursor is over the desired vertex and drag your mesh next to any other vertex on another mesh. You should see the object moving around via your input.

9. Release your mouse button and the *V* key when you are happy with the results. This should make it really easy to build out the rest of the rooms, but make sure that you check at multiple angles to make sure the part is placed in the right area.

10. For the sake of trying it out, go to the **Hall Door** prefab inside the **Project** tab, and you should see a little button to the right of the image of the prefab. Once there, click on it to have all the children objects show up so that we can modify them. From there, select the **Door** object and uncheck the **Box Collider** component. This way, you can walk through the doors to see the rooms. Take a look at the following screenshot:

11. Using these same tools and a little trial and error, you can create a large amount of variety in your environments, such as the following:

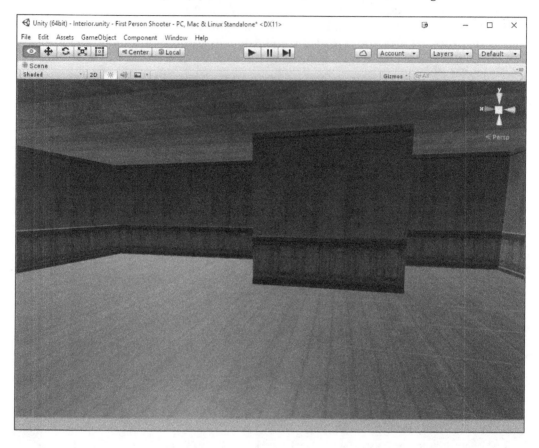

12. Finally, create an empty game object, name it `Level 01`, and assign all the rooms to it as children.

Save your level if you haven't already in the **Scenes** folder.

And there we go! We now know how to build out rooms using tiles and vertex snapping!

Creating and placing props

Now, it's great that we have a layout, but just a floor plan would get really boring really quickly in a first-person game. Luckily, we have a number of props that we can use to spice up the level a bit and add additional detail to our world. Perform the following steps:

1. First, let's move our **Level 1** object out of the way for now by making it a prefab and then deleting it from the **Hierarchy** tab.

2. Next, go to the `Models/Props` folder and select all of your models. Under the **Model** tab, check the **Generate Colliders** option, and click on **Apply**.

    This will create collisions for all the objects that we want to use. We didn't choose to generate colliders for the modular pieces because we will generate them from scratch for our rooms.

3. Move the **Bedframe** object to your scene, and change the **Position** property of the object to (0, 0, 0) from the **Transform** section. To focus on the object, select it in **Hierarchy** and then press the *F* key (this only works if the scene is selected). Alternatively, you can also double-click on it. You'll note that in spite of being in the center of the world when the position is reset, the bed is off on the **X** axis, and that's again because of the art that we were provided with.

4. The first thing that we want to do is assign the **Props** material to all of these objects. We could do the same as before, but instead, I'm going to place each of the objects at (0, 0, 0), then select the actual mesh for all of them by holding down the *Ctrl* key (*Command* on Mac), selecting them, and then setting the material.

    You'll note that the material fits really nicely with the models that were created. This is because the artist who created this used a UV map to tell the engine how to cut up the material and place it onto the faces that make up the object (the vertices). The texture that we have on the material is drawn in such a way that it has the appropriate part of the image at the right place. Setting up the UVs of an object is something that is done in a 3D modeling program, but when we load the model file, it contains this information.

Take a look at the screenshot following the next information box.

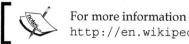

For more information on UV mapping, check out
http://en.wikipedia.org/wiki/UV_mapping.

5. Just as we did with each of the modular pieces, make each of these a prefab inside a new `Props` folder, as shown in the following screenshot:

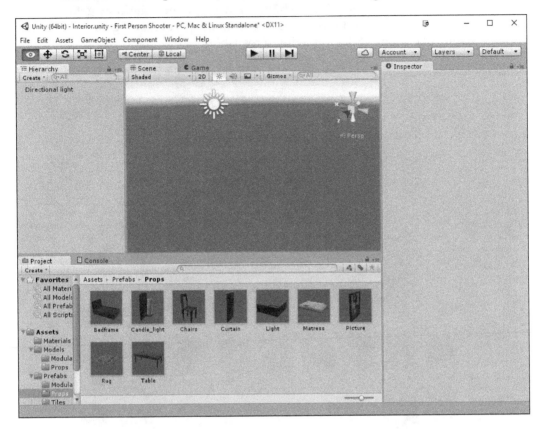

6. Now with this in mind, let's bring the **Level 01** prefab back to the level. Let's start off by adding the simplest of props to add, the chair. Drag and drop a chair object in your level; you should note that it automatically gets placed on the floor at the right position, aside from the pivot looking quite out of place. Take a look at the following screenshot:

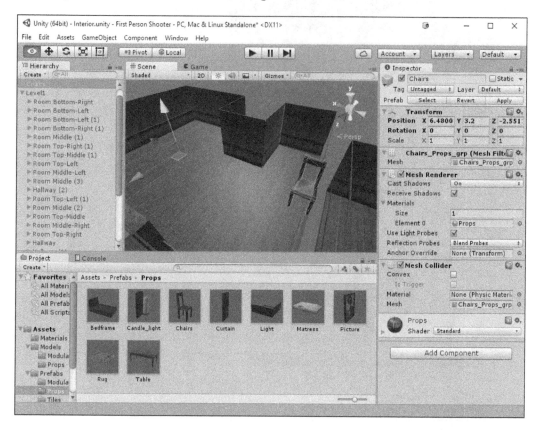

7. We could go back to our 3D modeling software to fix this problem, but perhaps you don't have access to the software, so let's fix the problem in Unity. Create a cube by going to **GameObject | 3D Objects | Cube**). Change the cube's **Position** property to (0, 0, 0) and **Scale** to (0, 0, 0). Then, we'll use **Vertex Snapping** to move the bottom of the chair's leg to be at (0, 0, 0), so it looks like it does in the following image. Feel free to hide other objects in the scene to make it easier to see by selecting them in **Hierarchy** and then toggling the check by their name in the **Inspector**:

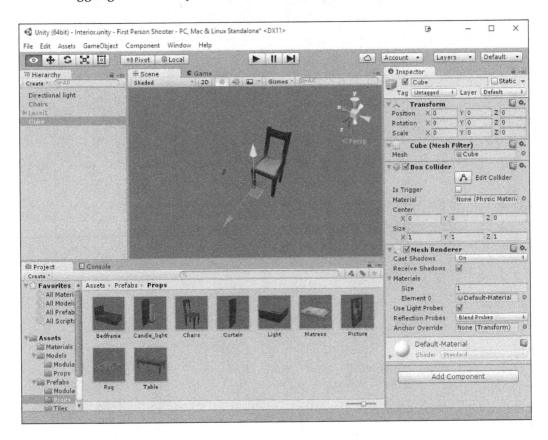

8. Once this is done, delete the **Cube** object, create an **Empty GameObject** (**GameObject | Create Empty**) with the name of `FixedChair`, and have the previous **Chairs** be the child of our new one. After this, create a prefab named `Fixed Chair` in our `Prefabs\Props` folder and then delete it from **Hierarchy**.

9. After this, bring back our **Level 01** prefab and now drop a `chair` in. As I'm sure that you can see, it's much easier to place them now. Take a look at the following screenshot:

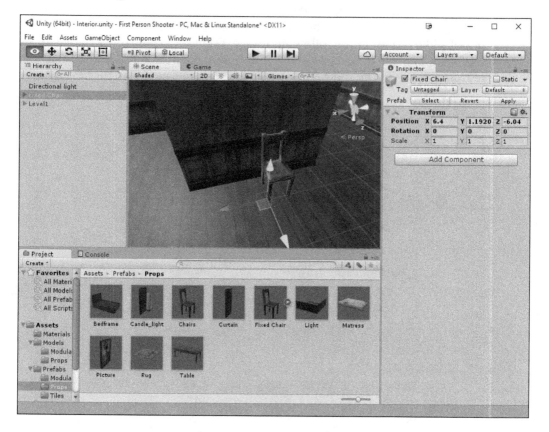

10. With this in mind, we can also use the **Rotation** tool to rotate the **Chairs** a little bit and create some duplicates by pressing *Ctrl + D*, moving them and then rotating them to break up the symmetry:

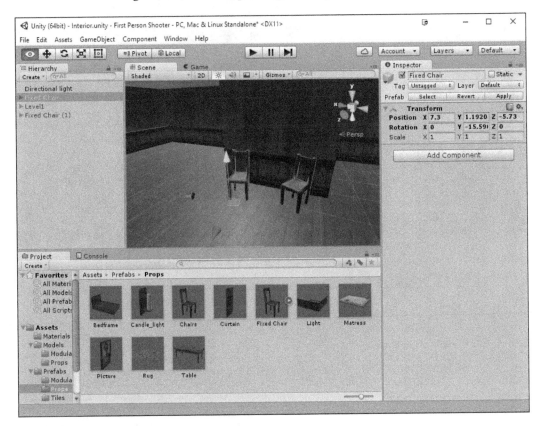

11. Now, we can continue with this with the other props as well, placing them how you feel would make the environment look more realistic.

12. Next, make sure that all the newly added props are added to the **Level 01** prefab, and click on the **Apply** button to save all the changes we made.

    We now have the first story all fixed; let's now show how simple it is to create a second level.

13. Find a spot in your level that has an open space, and add in the **LeftStairs** object, adding in walls if needed to finish the space. After this, start placing tiles just as we did with Level 01.

14. A nice thing to keep in mind if you want to only focus on one level at a time, you can select the **Level 01** game object and click on the checkbox next to its name to disable everything about it, which will let you focus on just what you are doing with this level. In addition, we can use this in the future to also turn off and turn on levels to help with the frame rate if we have too many objects on the screen. Take a look at the following screenshot:

Lightmapping quickstart

Lightmapping is the process of baking or precalculating the lighting on a texture of static objects to make the game run faster and allow us to get the most out of our projects.

This generally isn't done as an optimization until you have finished building your entire level, but I think this is probably the best place to talk about it. If you prefer to wait, come back to this section when you are done with your level, as doing a lightmapping pass can take a long time:

1. Go into **Window | Lighting**. From there, select the **Scene** tab and then change **Ambient Intensity** to 0 as we want to have all of the light in the level to be from our lighting. Also select the **Skybox** property and select our **Nightsky** and you should note the world get a lot darker. To also do this, go to the **House** and **Props** materials and change the **Metallic** property to 0 .75 and **Smoothness** to 0.

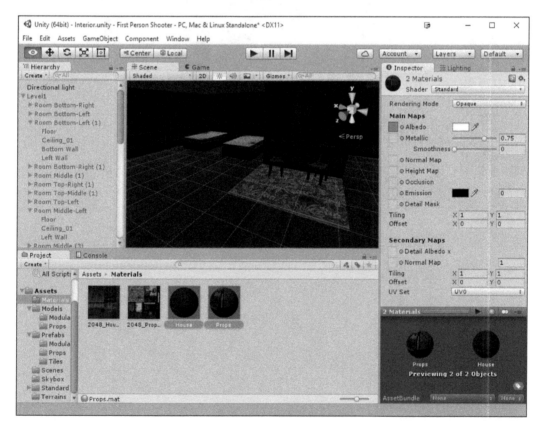

2. Next, we will need to select all of our model files in the `Models/Props` and `Models/Modular Pieces` folders (not the prefabs). From there, check **Generate Lightmap UVs** from the **Model** tab and then click on the **Apply** button.

3. Lightmapping is most efficient when dealing with static objects, that is, objects that will not be moving. That's our level stuff for sure, so select our **Level 01** parent object, and click on the **Static** option. It will ask if you want the change for the children as well, and you should click on **Yes, change children**. Take a look at the following screenshot:

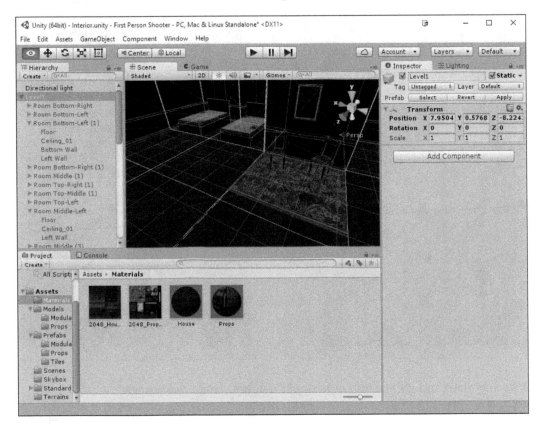

4. Next, go to **Window | Lighting**. Then, select the **Lightmap** tab. This opens **Lightmapping Editor**, which we can use to bake our object, and more. By default, this should be set to **Auto**, which means that it will automatically do it but if not click on the **Bake** option. This may take a while on your larger projects. Once the process is completed, your scene will be lit correctly. Take a look at the following screenshot:

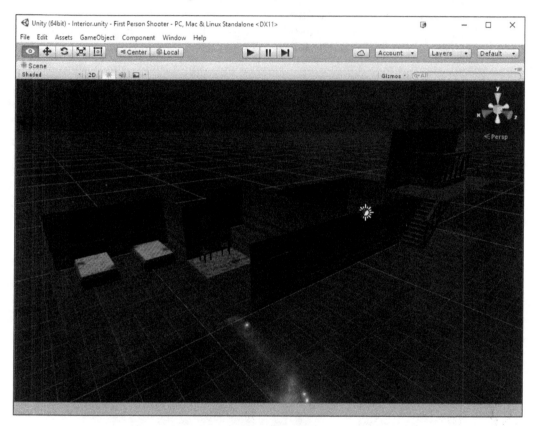

Looking great and it's starting to look like a spooky haunted house!

 For more information on lightmapping with Unity's new Global Illumination system, check out:

`http://docs.unity3d.com/Manual/GIIntro.html`.

Summary

And with this, we now have a great-looking interior level for our game! In addition, we covered a lot of features that exist in Unity for you to be able to use in your own future projects. With this in mind in the next chapter, we actually implement the mechanics we need to create a fully featured project!

Challenges

For those of you who want to do more with this project, there are still plenty of things you can do, especially after finishing the rest of this book. Here are some ideas to get your mind thinking:

- Create the layout for your game project. Try to create interesting areas, which you can use for encounters later on in the game.

- Place the props in interesting ways to break up repetition.

- Instead of having box colliders for every tile in our game, it would be much more efficient to just create box colliders for all the walls that are together.

- One of the major tools that level designers have is lighting. With it, we can create a mood or feeling in a place using the color, intensity, or even the lack of light. Players, in general, tend to follow lights, and you can use that as a level designer to help lead players along. Try using this in your level to lead players to the end of your level!

- Currently, the doors do not do anything. Add a trigger to the door (box collider with **Is Trigger** toggled), so when the player gets near a door, it will disappear. Once the player leaves the trigger, make it visible again. In addition, you can have a sound play when the door disappears to signify that the door has opened.

9
First Person Shooter Part 3 – Implementing Gameplay and AI

When I start teaching my game design students, one of the questions that I'll often hear is "What is a game?" Now, to some people, the card game *War* (`http://en.wikipedia.org/wiki/War_(card_game)`) is a game; however, the game is already determined before anyone actually plays the game because players have absolutely no interactions besides flipping cards.

Renowned game programmer and designer Sid Meier says that a game is "a series of interesting choices," and I really like that definition. At my alma mater and current employer DigiPen, we were taught that a video game was a real-time interactive simulation.

Having an environment is an excellent first step towards creating your game project, but this is a real-time simulation though it's not very interactive.

Project overview

In this chapter, we are going to be adding that interactivity in the form of adding enemies, shooting behaviors, and the gameplay to make our game truly shine. In addition, we'll also learn how to use an Xbox 360 Controller to accept input in our game as well.

Your objectives

This project will be split into a number of tasks. It will be a simple step-by-step process from beginning to end. Here is the outline of our tasks:

- Creating our player
- Adding shooting behavior
- Creating an enemy
- Enemy movement
- Shooting/killing enemies
- Using Xbox 360 Controller Input
- Moving to other levels

In this chapter, we will continue where the last chapter left off using the same project. You may continue with your previous project or pick up a copy along with the assets for this chapter from the example code provided for this book on Packt's website at https://www.packtpub.com/books/content/support.

In addition, the completed project and source files are located there for you to check whether you have any questions or need clarification.

Setting up the project

At this point, I assume that you have Unity started up and have our project from the previous chapter loaded. You can perform the following steps:

1. With Unity started, open the project from the previous chapter.
2. With this done, open our exterior environment from *Chapter 7, First-person Shooter Part 1 – Creating Exterior Environments*, by double-clicking on it in the **Scenes** folder.

Creating our player

To begin with, let's add in our player so we can see what the world itself looks like. Thankfully, Unity has created some of these behaviors for us that are included in the engine.

1. Open up our Exterior level if it isn't open already and to make it easier to see, go to the **Lighting** tab and in the **Scene** section uncheck the **Fog** property.

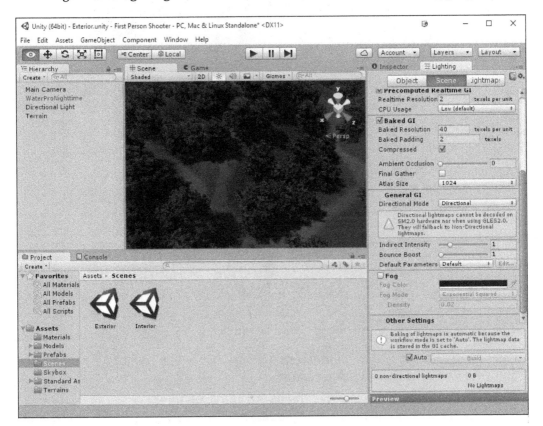

2. Next, go to **Assets | Import Package | Characters**. This will open up a window with a lot of different assets included. In this case, we will not need the PhysicsMaterials and Characters folder aside from the FirstPersonCharacter so uncheck them. Closing all the folders should show something similar to this:

3. Once finished selecting the correct actions, *click* on the **Import** button and wait for everything to be imported.

4. Once imported, move to the **Project** tab and open up the Standard Assets/Characters/FirstPersonCharacter/Prefabs folder. From there, drag and drop the FPSController object into our scene.

5. *Double-click* on the object to zoom into it on the **Scene** tab and from there drag it up in the Y axis until it's onto of the surface.

6. The prefab object already contains a camera so we don't need the default one anymore. With this in mind, go to the **Hierarchy** tab and delete the **Main Camera** object.

7. Finally, go back to the **Lighting** tab and then recheck the **Fog** option.

8. Save your level and then play the game!

As you can see, we now have a character that exists and will walk around when we press the *WASD* keys. It also traps (or captures) mouse input until we press the *Esc* key, and if we hold down *Shift*, we will move quickly running. This is a great starting point from which we can build our own character.

Adding a flashlight

Now that we have a player, we can start creating some custom behaviors for them.
Our level currently looks like a dark night, but we still want to give our players the
ability to see what's in front of them with a flashlight. We will customize the **FPS
Controller** object to fit our needs:

1. Create a spotlight by navigating to **GameObject | Light | Spotlight**. Once
   created, we are going to make the spotlight a child of the **FPSController**
   object's **FirstPersonCharacter** object by dragging and dropping it on top of it.

2. Once this is done, change the **Transform Position** value to (0, -.95, 0). Because positions are relative to your components position, this places the light slightly lower than the camera's center, just like a hand holding a flashlight. Now change the **Rotation** value to (0,0,0) or give it a slight diagonal effect across the scene if you don't want it to look like it's coming straight out:

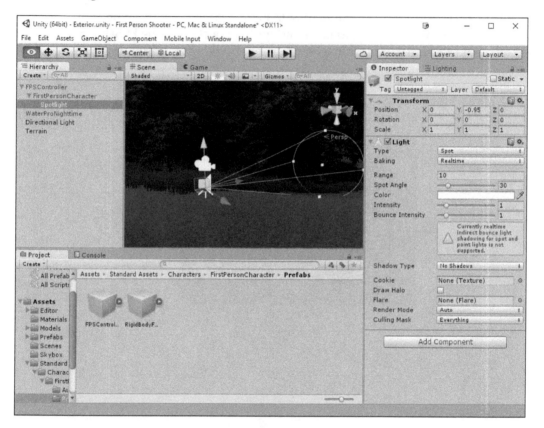

3. Now, we want the flashlight to reach out the distance. So we will change the **Range** value to 1000, and to make the light wider, we will change the **Spot Angle** value to 45. Finally, we can change the **Shadow Type** to **Hard Shadows** so the light will cause shadows behind objects that it hits. The effects are shown in the following screenshot:

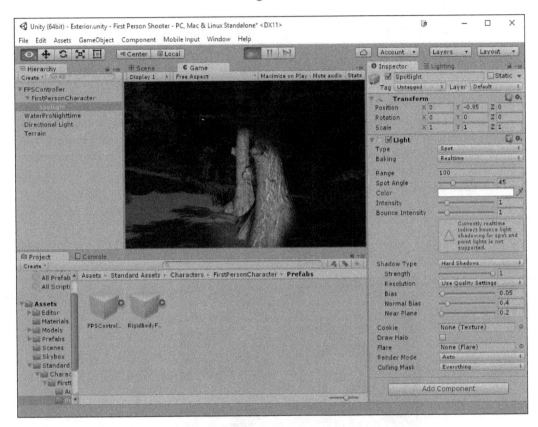

We now have a flashlight, so the player can focus on a particular area and relax.

Creating our weapon

Now, with a traditional first-person shooter, we shoot a bullet from a gun to damage enemies. However, we will create a camera that will take pictures to damage enemies.

Creating our camera

Now before we can shoot anything, we need to make our camera, and to do this, we are going to create another camera object that is zoomed in and then give it a border to look more realistic. To show how easy it is to do, let's get started! Perform the following steps:

1. The first thing we need to do is go to the flashlight **Spotlight** object we created earlier. So, with it selected, double-click on it to center the camera on it.

2. Our camera weapon is going to be another object, which will be a child of the **FirstPersonCharacter** object. To do this, first select the **FirstPersonCharacter** object that is located on our **FPSController** object and then right-click on it from the **Hierarchy** and then select **Create Empty**. Also, in the **Inspector** section for this newly created object, confirm whether the object's position is 0, 0, 0. If it isn't, set it at that position. Finally, name the object Photo Camera. Take a look at the following screenshot:

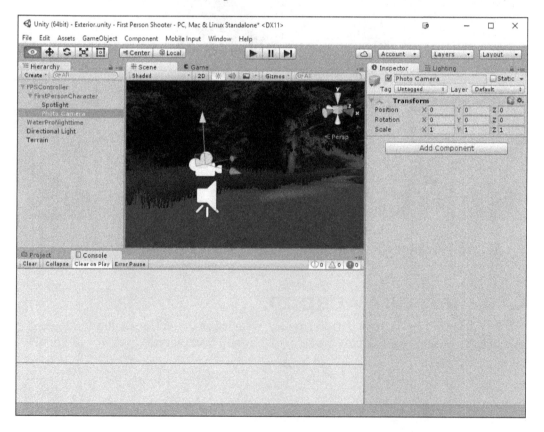

3. Next, add a camera component by clicking on the **Add Component** button at the bottom of the **Inspector** tab and then putting in the text Camera in the search bar before selecting it.

 Alternatively, you can just navigate to **Component | Add...** from the top bar to bring up the menu.

4. This camera will be zoomed in from the normal camera, so I'm going to change the **Field of View** value to 30. Now, switch the **Scene** tab over the **Game** tab so you can see what we will be doing. This will aid in understanding what each of these properties do.

5. We also want this camera to be on top of the previously created one, so we are going to change the **Depth** value to 1 (higher numbers put things in front of the other cameras).

6. This being said, we still want to see our previous camera as well in the background, so we're going to set the **Viewport Rect** values to put our new camera in the center of the screen at 75% of the size of the previous one. To do this, set the **X** and **Y** properties in the **Viewport Rect** option to .125 and the **W** and **H** properties to .75.

7. Now, in our game, this camera isn't just going to be a camera; it's also going to have a border around it. In this case, it'll be a cell phone. From the `Chapter 9/Art Assets` folder included in the example code, grab the `phone.png` file and move it into the `Materials` folder inside your project browser.

8. Once it's imported, select it to bring up the properties in the **Inspector** tab. By default, in a 3D project, `.png` files will be imported with a **Texture Type** value of `Texture`. We want to change it to `Sprite (2D and UI)`, so click on **Apply**.

9. Next, we need to add this texture to our inner camera. To do this, let's create a **Panel** object by going to **GameObject | UI | Panel**. As you recall, panels resize themselves to fit their canvas.

10. Next go to the **Panel** object and then drag and drop our phone image into the **Source Image** slot. The image shows up, but it's semi-transparent. To fix this, go to the **Color** property and change the color to be fully white.

11. The phone is not sized really well and doesn't match a phone's normal size, so let's check **Preserve Aspect** and you'll see the image now looks correct, but is also somewhat zoomed in. Let's click on **Set Native Size** next and you'll see the image resize it once more. Then, go to the **Anchors Preset** menu, hold down *Shift + Alt* and then *click* on the middle-middle option to center the camera to the world.

12. One of the things you may note now is that the camera stays the same size, no matter where the screen is. To fix this, select the **Canvas** object and then under the **Canvas Scaler** component, change the **UI Scale Mode** to **Scale with Screen Size**.

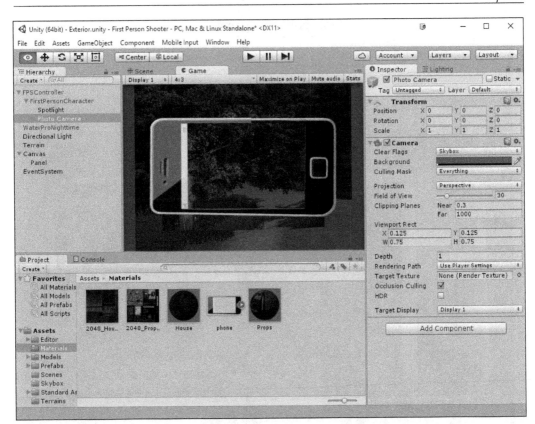

13. Right now, I have the aspect ratio set to **4:3**, which we can see in the **Game** tab in the top-left corner just below the tab. This ratio is of the same size as old television sets and monitors, but the code we just created also works with widescreen monitors and makes the camera look much better. So, let's make the game use an aspect ratio of **16:9**. We can do this by clicking on the drop-down list beside **4:3** and then selecting **16:9**.

If you play the game at this point, the game should look something like the following screenshot:

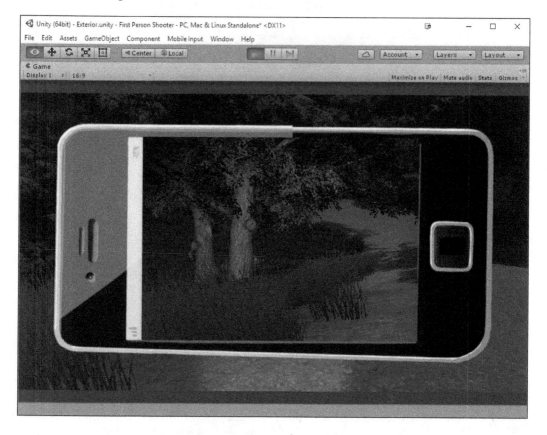

Looks pretty good! But right now, the camera is always up there, and I only want to see it if the player right-clicks to zoom in.

14. So, with this in mind, let's create another C# script named `PhoneBehaviour` and open it inside of your IDE.

15. Place the following code into the `PhoneBehaviour` class as follows:

```
using UnityEngine;
using System.Collections.Generic; // List

public class PhoneBehaviour : MonoBehaviour
{

    public List<GameObject> phoneObjects;
```

```
private bool cameraActive = false;

void Start()
{
    SetCameraActive(false);
}

// Update is called once per frame
void Update () {
    // Are we holding down the right mouse button
    if (Input.GetMouseButton(1) && !cameraActive)
    {
        SetCameraActive(true);
    }
    else if(cameraActive && !Input.GetMouseButton(1))
    {
        SetCameraActive(false);
    }

}

void SetCameraActive(bool active)
{
    cameraActive = active;

    foreach (var obj in phoneObjects)
    {
        obj.SetActive(active);
    }
}
}
```

This script basically makes it so when the player holds down the right mouse button, we will turn on all of the objects that we placed in phoneObjects and then when we release, we turn them off. We only want to do this on frames when it changes from one state to another (turning it on every frame would be inefficient), so we added in a Boolean to keep track where we were in the last frame.

Go in and add the **PhoneBehaviour** component to the **FirstPersonCharacter** object. From there change the **Size** of **Phone Objects** to 2 and assign **Photo Camera** and our **Canvas' Panel** to the property.

Save our project, level, and play the game!

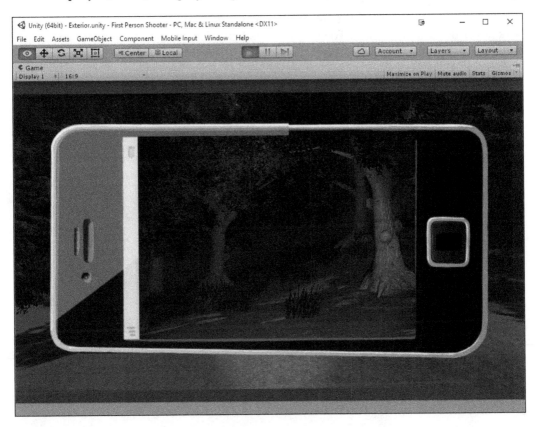

Now, the camera will only come up whenever we hold down the right mouse button! Awesome! It's just like a sniper rifle in most FPS games.

Shooting our camera

Next, we want to add the ability to shoot our weapon and flash it on the screen whenever the camera is shot. To simulate this behavior, we will first create an image to be placed over our entire screen. We perform the following steps:

1. Just to make it easier to see things, let's first go to the **Photo Camera** object and disable it by unchecking the checkbox by the object's name from the **Inspector** menu. Afterwards, do the same thing for the **Panel** object, and while we are here, let's rename it to `Phone Border`.

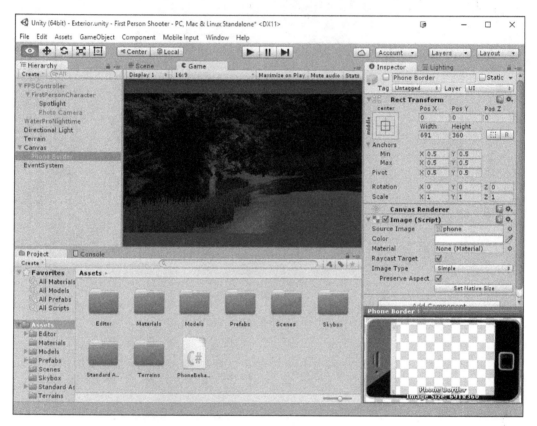

2. Now that we are back to a normal screen, let's add in a panel to act as our flash. To do this, go to the **Hierarchy** tab and right-click on our **Canvas** object. From there, select **UI | Panel**. Rename our panel's name to **Camera Flash** and change the color to be fully transparent because we will be changing its color via code.

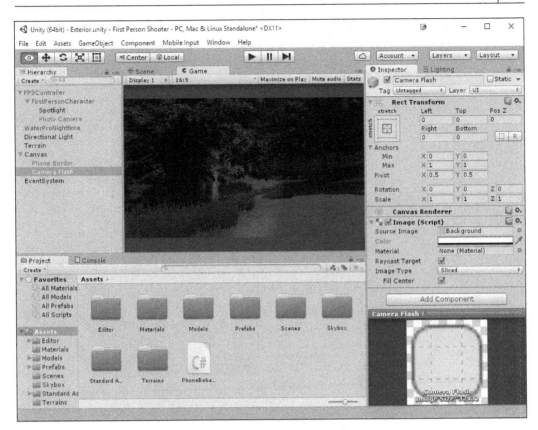

3. Next, go back to the `PhoneBehaviour` file, and add in the following `using` statement:

   ```
   using UnityEngine.UI; // Image
   ```

4. Then, add the following variable:

   ```
   public Image cameraFlash;
   ```

5. Now, a flash contains two parts: fading to white and then fading to a transparent color. The pieces of code doing both of these things are very similar, so we will create a helper function to do this for us, named `Fade`.

6. To do this, first, we will need to add in the following `using` statement:

   ```
   using System.Collections; // IEnumerator
   ```

7. Take a look at the following code:

```
IEnumerator Fade(float start, float end, float length,
        Image currentObject)
{
    if (currentObject.color.a == start)
    {
        Color curColor;
        for (float i = 0.0f; i < 1.0f;
            i += Time.deltaTime * (1 / length))
        {
/*
Cannot modify the color property
directly, so we need to create a copy
*/
            curColor = currentObject.color;


/*
Do a linear interpolation of the value
of the transparency from the start value to the end value in equal
increments
*/
            curColor.a = Mathf.Lerp(start, end, i);

            // Then we assign the copy to the original
            // object
            currentObject.color = curColor;

            yield return null;
        }
        curColor = currentObject.color;


/*
ensure the fade is completely finished
(because lerp doesn't always end on the exact value due to
rounding errors)
*/
        curColor.a = end;
        currentObject.color = curColor;
    }
}
```

As you may recall from *Chapter 1, 2D Twin-Stick Shooter*, we can use coroutines to pause functionality, yielding for a time and then resuming functionality. The `IEnumerator` class holds the current state of the program and tells us where to continue. The yield return here is asking us to stop the function now and resume after a period.

Because coroutines are just functions, we can also have parameters in them, just as in the preceding function. With this in mind, we can also nest them together in order to have complex interactions and use our abstracted functions in multiple ways to create interesting behaviors.

8. Then, we will call this function twice with our main function, `CameraFlash`, as follows:

```
IEnumerator CameraFlash()
{
    yield return StartCoroutine(Fade(0.0f, 0.8f, 0.2f,
    cameraFlash));
    yield return StartCoroutine(Fade(0.8f, 0.0f, 0.2f,
    cameraFlash));
    StopCoroutine ("CameraFlash");
}
```

 For more examples on how coroutines can be used, check out http://unitypatterns.com/introduction-to-coroutines/ and http://unitypatterns.com/scripting-with-coroutines/.

9. Finally, this function will never be called if we don't call it, so add the following code to the end of the `PhoneBehaviour` scripts' `Update` function:

```
if (cameraActive && Input.GetMouseButton(0))
{
    StartCoroutine(CameraFlash());

}
```

10. Save the file and go back to the Unity Editor. Finally, back at the `Photo Camera` object, assign the `Camera Flash` object to the `Camera Flash` variable.

11. Save the scene (*Ctrl + S*), click on the **Play** button, and try out your new camera. Take a look at the following screenshot:

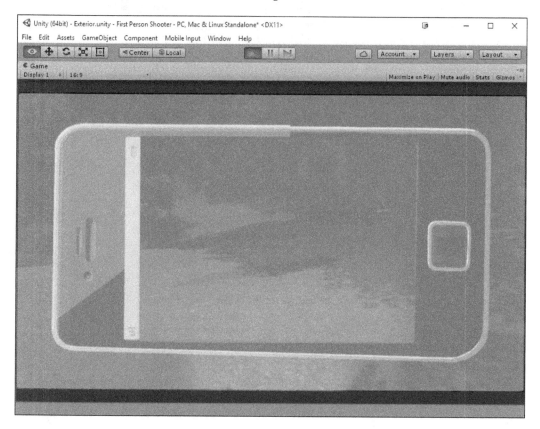

Looks like everything is in working order! We can look around with our camera, zoom in and out, and shoot pictures.

Creating an enemy

Now that we can take pictures, let's create an enemy to take pictures of! We will perform the following steps:

1. The first step to adding in an enemy is to import the assets required to use it. Inside our `Chapter 9\Art Assets\Ghost Model` location, you'll find a series of files. Go ahead and drag and drop the folder into your project.

2. Open up the **Ghost Model** object from the **Project** tab and then select the Ghost_mesh object. Now, select the object to bring up its properties in the **Inspector** tab. Under **Scale Factor** in the **Model** tab, change the value to .10 to scale the object to 1/10th of its starting size. Then, check **Generate Colliders**, making sure to hit **Apply**.

3. Under the **Rig** tab, confirm the **Animation Type** value to **None**, as this model doesn't have any animations and then click on **Apply** if needed.

4. Now, go somewhere in your world in the **Scene** view, and drag and drop the character onto the screen near your player and terrain. Take a look at the following screenshot:

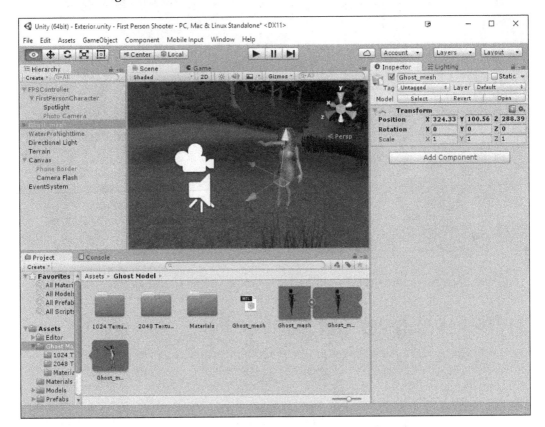

Now, save the project, level and start up the game.

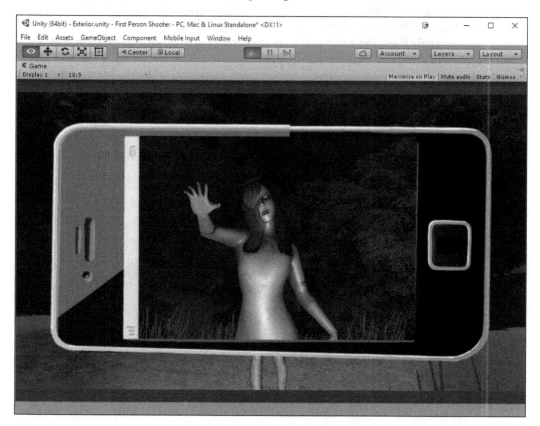

And now, the character is displayed and we can see them in the game. Spooky!

State machines 101

We oftentimes write code to provide the reactive or interactive parts within our simulation (or game world) – things such as when you're pressing a button or if you're walking or jumping. If you look at real life, you should note that a lot of things are reactive systems in that same way, such as your mobile phone and toaster. Depending on the stimuli provided to these objects, the state of these objects may change. We describe something that can be in one of the multiple states at a time as a state machine.

Almost every program that we write is or can be a state machine of some sort because technically, the moment you write an `if` statement, you've created code that can be in one of at least two states. However, having a number of `switch` and `if` statements can quickly get out of hand, making it very hard for people to understand what your code is actually doing. As a programmer, we want to isolate problems and break them down into their simplest parts before jumping in to solve them.

There are different kinds of state machines, but for this first example, we are going to create a simple **Finite State Machine (FSM)**. When I say finite, it means that each of the states is already defined ahead of time. With a finite state machine, we can have different states in which we can process input differently depending on the state.

For example, if you are on a ladder, you can only move up and down and not to the sides.

Enemy movement

As spooky as the character is, right now, it is just a static mesh. It will not come to us to damage us, and we cannot damage it. Let's fix that next using the state machines you've just learned about! Perform the following steps:

1. Create a new script named `EnemyBehaviour`.

   We want our enemy to follow the player if they get too close to them; however, they will stay where they are if the player gets far enough away. Finally, if, for some reason, we defeat the enemy, they should no longer run this behavior, and we should kill them. The first step to creating a state machine is to extract the states that the object can be in. In this case, we have three states: `Idle`, `Following`, and `Death`. Just as we discussed in *Chapter 2*, *Creating GUIs*, using an enumeration is the best tool for the job here as well.

2. Add the following code to the top of the `EnemyBehaviour` class:

   ```
   public enum State
   {
       Idle,
       Follow,
       Die,
   }

   // The current state the player is in
   public State state;
   ```

Now, depending on the value that the state is currently in, we can do different things. We could use something like the following code:

```
void Update()
{
    if(state == State.Idle)
    {
        //And so on
    }
    else if(state == State.Follow)
    {
        //And so on
    }
    //etc...
}
```

But, as I'm sure you can already see, this is incredibly messy. Also, what if we want to do something when we first enter the state? What about when you leave? To fix this issue, let's use a tool we covered earlier, the coroutine function, which will contain the contents for each of our states.

3. Next, we need to add in some additional variables we will use. Take a look at the following code:

```
// The object the enemy wants to follow
public Transform target;

// How fast should the enemy move?
public float moveSpeed = 3.0f;
public float rotateSpeed = 3.0f;

// How close should the enemy be before they follow?
public float followRange = 10.0f;

// How far should the target be before the enemy gives up
// following?
// Note: Needs to be >= followRange
public float idleRange = 10.0f;
```

4. Now, we need to add in a coroutine function for each of the possible states, starting with the `Idle` state. Take a look at the following code:

```
IEnumerator IdleState()
{
    //OnEnter
    Debug.Log("Idle: Enter");
    while (state == State.Idle)
```

```
  {
    //OnUpdate
    if(GetDistance() < followRange)
    {
      state = State.Follow;
    }

    yield return 0;
  }
  //OnEnd
  Debug.Log("Idle: Exit");
  GoToNextState();
}
```

This state will continuously check whether the players are close enough to the target to start following it until its state is no longer State.Idle. You'll note the two functions we'll need to create later, GetDistance and GoToNextState, which we will implement after we finish the other states.

5. Continue with the Following state, as follows:

```
IEnumerator FollowState ()
{
  Debug.Log("Follow: Enter");
  while (state == State.Follow)
  {
    transform.position =
    Vector3.MoveTowards(transform.position,
                target.position,
                Time.deltaTime * moveSpeed);

    RotateTowardsTarget();

    if(GetDistance() > idleRange)
    {
      state = State.Idle;
    }

    yield return 0;
  }
  Debug.Log("Follow: Exit");
  GoToNextState();
}
```

This state will move the enemy closer to the player while continuously checking if the target is far enough to go back to `Idle`. In addition to the other functions we talked about earlier, we also have a new function named `RotateTowardsTarget`, which we will also need to add in.

6. Finish off by adding in the `Die` state, as follows:

```
IEnumerator DieState ()
{
    Debug.Log("Die: Enter");

    Destroy (this.gameObject);
    yield return 0;
}
```

This state just destroys the object attached to it. Right now, there is no way to get here aside from us setting it in the **Inspector** tab, but it will be useful when we add in damage.

7. Now, we need to add in those functions we talked about earlier. First, let's add in `GetDistance` and `RotateTowardsTarget`, which are self-explanatory in terms of what they do. Take a look at the following code:

```
public float GetDistance()
{
    return (transform.position -
target.transform.position).magnitude;
}

private void RotateTowardsTarget()
{
    transform.rotation =
    Quaternion.Slerp(transform.rotation,
    Quaternion.LookRotation
    (target.position -
                    transform.position),
                    rotateSpeed * Time.deltaTime);
}
```

> The `Vector3` class also has a `Distance` function you can use. `Vector3.Distance(transform.position, target.transform.position);` will do the same thing as our `GetDistance` function does, but knowing the math behind things can be extremely helpful!

8. Now, we need to add in the ability to go to another state, as follows:

```
void GoToNextState ()
{
    // Find out the name of the function we want to call
    string methodName = state.ToString() + "State";

    // Searches this class for a function with the name of
    // state + State (for example: idleState)
    System.Reflection.MethodInfo info =
    GetType().GetMethod(methodName,
    System.Reflection.BindingFlags.NonPublic |
    System.Reflection.BindingFlags.Instance);
    StartCoroutine((IEnumerator)info.Invoke(this, null));
}
```

The preceding code is fairly advanced stuff, so it's okay if you do not fully understand it at a glance. For the preceding code, I could have written something like the Update example I wrote previously, calling the appropriate coroutine based on the state to go to.

Instead, this code will call the appropriate function with the name of the state plus the word State. The nice thing about this is that you can now write as many additional states as you want without having to modify this function. All you have to do is add an item to the State enumerator and then write a function for it with a proper name!

For information on the GetMethod function and the different kinds of BindingFlags, you can visit http://msdn.microsoft.com/en-us/library/05eey4y9(v=vs.110).aspx.

9. Then, we need to start this whole state machine up with the following code:

```
void Start ()
{
    GoToNextState();
}
```

10. Finally, we need to save our file and exit back to the Unity Editor. Attach the **Enemy Behaviour** script to our **Ghost_mesh** object and set the **Target** property to our **FPSController** object. Take a look at the following screenshot:

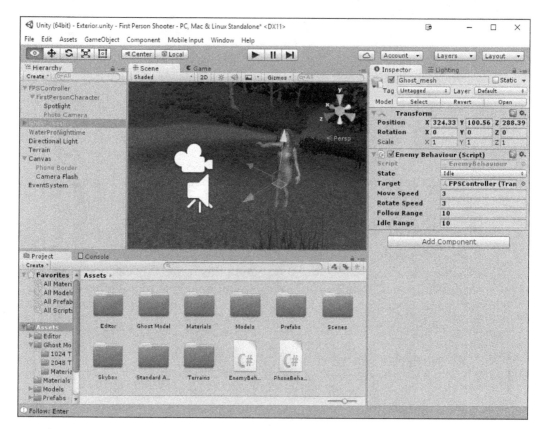

11. Save the scene and play the game. Take a look at the following screenshot:

As you can see now, you can follow the enemy's current state in the **Inspector** tab, and they will turn and move towards you whenever you get too close!

Advanced FSMs

This is a good introduction to state machines and what you can use them for, but there is a lot of additional information out there on their uses, such as an abstract version of a state machine at `http://playmedusa.com/blog/a-finite-state-machine-in-c-for-unity3d/`.

The **Asset Store** also features Playmaker, which is a fairly popular commercial add-on that creates state machines with a visual editor, making it very easy to add in states. For more information on Playmaker, check out `http://www.hutonggames.com/`.

Damaging and killing enemies

Now that we have enemies moving towards us, we need some way for them to be damaged and killed! Let's do that now by performing the following steps:

1. The first thing we need to do is make it easy to get a reference to all of our enemies, so let's add a tag by going to the **Inspector** tab and navigating to **Tag | Add Tag…**. Once the **Tag** and **Layer** menus come up, type in Enemy into **Element 0**.

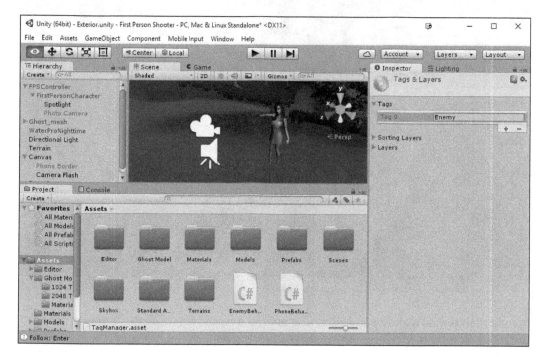

2. Then, go back to the **Ghost_mesh** child object, add the **Enemy** tag to it, and rename the parent object to `Ghost`:

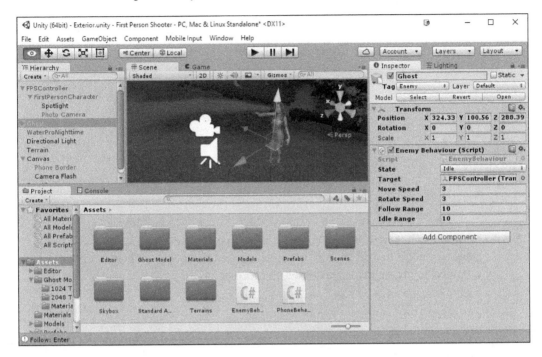

3. Next, let's dive back into MonoDevelop, edit our `PhoneBehaviour` script and add the following code in bold to its `Update` function:

```
// Update is called once per frame
void Update () {
    // Are we holding down the right mouse button
    if (Input.GetMouseButton(1) && !cameraActive)
    {
        SetCameraActive(true);
    }
    else if(cameraActive && !Input.GetMouseButton(1))
    {
        SetCameraActive(false);
    }

    if (cameraActive && Input.GetMouseButton(0))
    {
```

```
            StartCoroutine(CameraFlash());

            GameObject[] enemyList =
            GameObject.FindGameObjectsWithTag("Enemy");

            foreach (GameObject enemy in enemyList)
            {
                if (enemy.activeInHierarchy)
                {
                    EnemyBehaviour behaviour =
                    enemy.GetComponent<EnemyBehaviour>();
                    behaviour.TakeDamage();
                }
            }

        }
```

Now that we say there is a `TakeDamage` function in our `EnemyBehaviour` class, we need to add that in. Open the `EnemyBehaviour` class, and first, we need to create some variables as follows:

```
public float health = 100.0f;
private float currentHealth;
```

4. Next, we need to initialize `currentHealth`, so add the following code in bold to the `Start` function:

```
void Start ()
{
  GoToNextState();
  currentHealth = health;
}
```

5. Now, let's add in the `TakeDamage` function, as follows:

```
public void TakeDamage()
    {
        // The closer I am, the more damage I do
        float damageToDo = 100.0f - (GetDistance () * 5);

        if (damageToDo < 0)
          damageToDo = 0;
        if (damageToDo > health)
```

```
        damageToDo = health;

    currentHealth -= damageToDo;

    if(currentHealth <= 0)
    {
      state = State.Die;
    }
    else
    {
      // If we're not dead, now that we took a picture the
      // enemy
          // knows where we are
      followRange = Mathf.Max(GetDistance(), followRange);
      state = State.Follow;
    }

    print ("Ow! - Current Health: " +
    currentHealth.ToString());


  }
```

6. Now, save your scene and all the script files, and play the game! The
   following screenshot depicts the game screen:

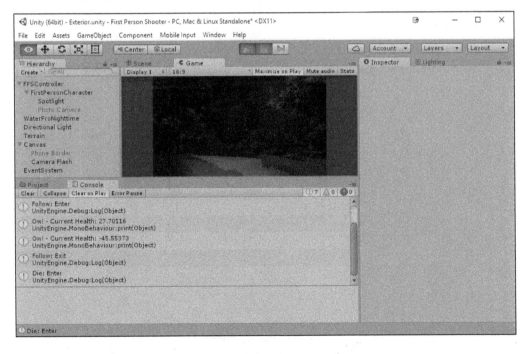

Now, the enemy will follow you when you take its picture and the closer you are to it, the more it will get damaged, which you can see by looking at the console!

Using controller input

One of the biggest advantages of using Unity as a game engine is the fact that you can support multiple platforms with minimal changes to your base game. In fact, right now, if you plug in an Xbox 360 Controller into your computer, restart Unity, and try to play the game, you'll note that the left-hand side joystick already moves the player, and if you press the Y button, you will jump into the air. However, some of the aspects don't work, so let's get them implemented.

Let's get started by performing the following steps:

1. The first thing that we're going to need to do is let Unity know that we want to work with some new input. So, to do this, we will need to navigate to **Edit | Project Settings | Input**.

2. Once there, we need to add four new axes to our project, the first being a new horizontal axis, so right-click on the **Mouse X** axis and select **Duplicate Array Element**.

3. Extend the newly created **Mouse X** axes and rename it to `360 Right Horizontal`. The controller output is never 100% correct, so we want to change the **Dead** value to `.05` so that any value between `-.05` and `.05` won't be counted.

4. Change the **Type** value to **Joystick Axis** and the **Axis** value to **4th axis (Joysticks)**.

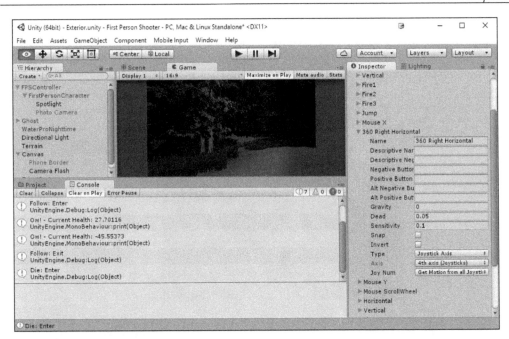

5. Do the same for the **Mouse Y** axis with the name `360 Right Vertical` using the **5th axis (Joysticks)** option. Take a look at the following screenshot:

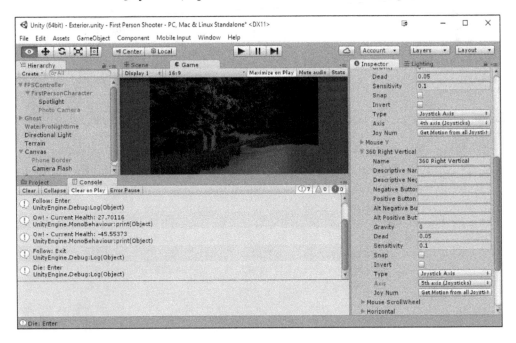

6. We will also want to have triggers work, so add in `360 Left Trigger` and `360 Right Trigger` by changing the **Size** of the **Axes** to 22 and renaming the last 2. Removing the positive and negative buttons. Changing the **Type** to **Joystick Axis** and then the **Axis** to 9 and 10, respectively.

7. Now, we will need to alter the character controller's `MouseLook` script file, so double-click on it to open MonoDevelop. Once opened, add the following bolded code to its `LookRotation` function:

```
public void LookRotation(Transform character, Transform
camera)
{
    float yRot =
    CrossPlatformInputManager.GetAxis("Mouse X") *
    XSensitivity;
```

```
float xRot =
CrossPlatformInputManager.GetAxis("Mouse Y") *
YSensitivity;


float xRot360 = Input.GetAxis("360 Right
Horizontal") * 15 * XSensitivity;
float yRot360 = Input.GetAxis("360 Right
Vertical") * 15 * YSensitivity;

yRot += xRot360;
xRot -= yRot360;

m_CharacterTargetRot *= Quaternion.Euler (0f,
yRot, 0f);
m_CameraTargetRot *= Quaternion.Euler (-xRot,
0f, 0f);

if(clampVerticalRotation)
    m_CameraTargetRot =
    ClampRotationAroundXAxis
    (m_CameraTargetRot);

if(smooth)
{
    character.localRotation = Quaternion.Slerp
    (character.localRotation,
    m_CharacterTargetRot,
        smoothTime * Time.deltaTime);
    camera.localRotation = Quaternion.Slerp
    (camera.localRotation, m_CameraTargetRot,
        smoothTime * Time.deltaTime);
}
else
{
    character.localRotation =
    m_CharacterTargetRot;
    camera.localRotation = m_CameraTargetRot;
}

UpdateCursorLock();
}
```

This code will make the right joystick rotate the player's camera.

8. Now that we have that done, let's get the camera and shoot to work. To do that, we need to now open the `PhoneBehaviour` script. First of all, we're going to need to introduce a new variable to account for the fact that we want the player to have to release the right trigger before they can shoot again:

```
private bool shotStarted = false;
```

9. Now, we will update the `Update` function to the following code. Note the changes set in bold:

```
void Update () {
    // Are we holding down the right mouse button
    if ((Input.GetMouseButton(1) || (Input.GetAxis("360
    Left Trigger") > 0)) && !cameraActive)
    {
        SetCameraActive(true);
    }
    else if(cameraActive && !(Input.GetMouseButton(1)
    || (Input.GetAxis("360 Left Trigger") > 0)))
    {
        SetCameraActive(false);
    }

    if (cameraActive && (Input.GetMouseButton(0) ||
    (Input.GetAxis("360 Right Trigger") > 0)))
    {
        shotStarted = true;

        StartCoroutine(CameraFlash());

        GameObject[] enemyList =
        GameObject.FindGameObjectsWithTag("Enemy");

        foreach (GameObject enemy in enemyList)
        {
            if (enemy.activeInHierarchy)
            {
                EnemyBehaviour behaviour =
                enemy.GetComponent<EnemyBehaviour>();
                behaviour.TakeDamage();
            }
        }
    }

    if (Input.GetAxis("360 Right Trigger") == 0)
```

```
    {
        shotStarted = false;
    }


}
```

10. Save your scripts and start the game. Take a look at the following screenshot:

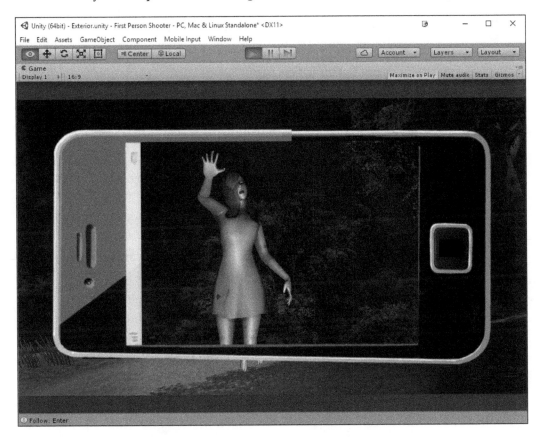

At this point, you should be able to play the project using an Xbox 360 Controller!

Now, depending on what platform you're running Unity, there may be special things to take into consideration. For more information about using the Xbox 360 Controller, visit http://wiki.unity3d.com/index.php?title=Xbox360Controller.

For those who don't want to deal with input too much and just want something that will standardize your input for common controllers, I hear good things about Gallant Games' InControl input manager. You can find out more about from `http://www.gallantgames.com/incontrol`.

While not all the features are included, they have an open source version of most of the content at `http://github.com/pbhogan/InControl`, but if you use their tool and find it useful, I recommend that you buy it to support further development.

Moving to other levels

Finally, let's see what we can do to make the changes we've made in this chapter show up in all of our levels. We perform the following steps:

1. We've been modifying a series of prefabs, so thankfully, it's quite easy to update them for other levels. Select the **FPSController** object and in the **Prefab** section, click on the **Apply** button to save our changes to the prefab.

2. The **Ghost** object, however, is just a model, so let's open the **Prefabs** folder in our project browser and drag and drop the object in there.

3. Finally, we will also need to bring over our **Camera Canvas**, so to make it easier, we will rename it to **Camera Canvas** and make it a prefab as well.

4. Now that we have everything set up, let's open our interior level.

5. First of all, let's bring in the **Camera Canvas** since its position doesn't matter.

6. Next, add in our player by going to the **FPSController** prefab and then dragging and dropping it into our world. From there, open up the **FPSController** and select the **FirstPersonCharacter** prefab and then assign the **Phone Border** and **Camera Flash** variables within the **Phone Behaviour** component.

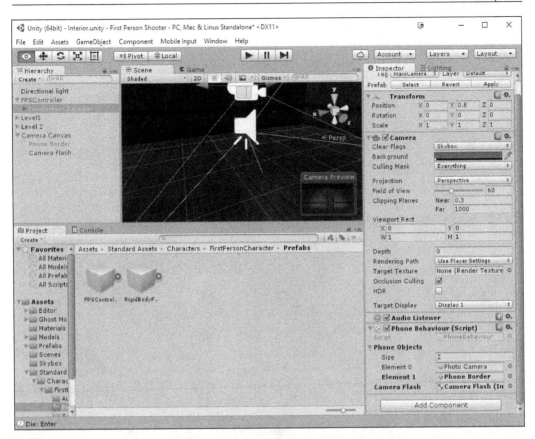

7. Then, you can drag and drop a **Ghost** prefab into the scene at a place of your choice and set the **Enemy Behaviour** object's **Target** property to the **FPSController** object.

8. After this, save the project and play the game. Take a look at the following screenshot:

Summary

At this point we now have our game completed! Over the course of the chapter, we learned about how to create characters, enemies, and even a bit about how to support other types of input via the 360 controller. Now that we have our game finished, let's learn about some more advanced coding in the next chapter by creating our own level editor!

Challenges

For those of you who want to do more with this project, there are still plenty of things you can do, especially after finishing the rest of this book. Here are some ideas to get you thinking:

- Right now, the enemy will continue following you even if you're through a tree or a wall. Use the `Raycast` function we talked about in *Chapter 3, Side-Scrolling Platformer*, to check a line from the player when the enemy collides with something. If it does, then set the enemy's state to `Idle`.

- Add sound effects to the ghost character so that the player knows when they are coming closer to the player and add some tension to the game. Adding in other sound effects, such as those for taking a picture and walking around, can help create ambience as well. A good website to visit for sound effects is `https://www.freesound.org/`. However, you may need to edit them a bit to help make them fit the game better. To do this, I suggest Audacity, which you can download from `http://audacity.sourceforge.net/`.

- Add in multiple ghosts in the level to create interesting encounters for the player to work with.

- In addition, you could create additional ghosts, which can be faster and/or more aggressive. You could also use Unity's Culling Mask system to make the ghosts only visible if you have the camera out by putting the object on different layers (`http://docs.unity3d.com/Documentation/Components/Layers.html`). Then, you can set the culling mask for each camera to only display the layers that you want (`http://docs.unity3d.com/Documentation/Components/class-Camera.html`).

- In the last section, you saw that we set a couple of different objects to make sure that the game worked correctly. This's the most efficient way performance-wise, but for convenience, you may want to get the objects through code with the `GameObject.Find` function. For more information about it, check out `http://docs.unity3d.com/ScriptReference/GameObject.Find.html`.

10
Building an In-Game Level Editor

Once you have your game mechanics finished up, you will need to fill up your game with content. You could use the Unity Editor to place things by hand, but as you may have seen earlier, it takes a really long time. It's also possible for us to create an array as we did earlier in *Chapter 6, Side-Scrolling Platformer*, but in that case, your levels need to be defined in a script and you'll need to either use an external tool or type in numbers individually for it to work correctly.

Another option is to save and load level files inside the game, and that way you can playtest your levels and make changes on the fly and save them when you're ready. We also have the advantage of being able to see exactly what the level looks like when you're making it.

Project overview

In this chapter, we are going to add in functionality to our previously created side-scrolling platformer game, adding in an in-game level editor, which can be used for future projects.

In addition, we will also gain exposure to the **Immediate Mode GUI system (IMGUI)**, which is a code-driven GUI system that was the only way to create GUIs before Unity 4.6, and is currently a tool primarily used by programmers for tools development and custom inspectors for scripts or new editors to extend Unity itself.

One of the nice things of working with this system is that you do not need to have any art assets to create and can make your menus entirely through code, so it's still worthwhile to touch and then decide which you'd like to use for your own future projects.

Your objectives

This project will be split into a number of tasks. It will be a simple step-by-step process from beginning to end. Here is the outline of our tasks:

- Level editor – introduction
- Adding/removing walls at runtime
- Toggling editor, GUI, and selecting additional tiles
- Saving/loading levels to file

Prerequisites

In this chapter, we will use projects that we created in the earlier chapters, specifically the project from *Chapter 6, Side-Scrolling Platformer*. You may continue with your previous projects or pick up a copy along with the assets for this chapter from the example code provided for this book on Packt Publishing's website (https://www.packtpub.com/books/content/support).

In addition, the completed project and source files are located there for you to check whether you have any questions or need clarification.

Level editor – introduction

To create something that can save files, we'll need to cover new territory. We've already discussed working with `PlayerPrefs` back in *Chapter 5, Shooting Gallery – Working with Animations and Tweens*, but there can be a time when you want to save things other than just `string`, `int`, or `float` variables. To deal with complex data types, there are more things that we can do. Perform the following steps:

1. We are going to first open up our **3D Platformer** project we created back in *Chapter 6, Side-Scrolling Platformer*. Open your gameplay scene (in the example code saved as `Gameplay`) from the link described in the project setup.

2. As it currently stands, the ability to create our levels is inside our **GameController** script. For this project, however, we're going to extract that functionality and move it over to a new class. In **Project Browser**, go to the `Scripts` folder and create a new C# script named `LevelEditor`. With this finished, open your IDE.

3. Once there, click on the `GameController.cs` file and highlight the `level` variable. Cut it (*Ctrl + X*) and paste it (*Ctrl + V*) as a declaration in the `LevelEditor` class.

4. After this, remove the `BuildLevel` function from the file and stop it from being called in our `GameController` script's `Start` function. Instead of calling it here, we will be writing a new version for our new `LevelEditor` script.

Next, we want access to our `goalPS` variable inside the `LevelEditor` class so that we have a reference to the particle system to turn to when we collect all the orbs, but right now, it's private. Now, I could set this variable as being `public` and be done with it, but instead, we're going to use another aspect of programming in C# named **properties**.

> If you decide to make something public but don't want to see it in **Inspector**, you can write code as the following:
>
> ```
> [HideInInspector]
> public ParticleSystem goalPS;
> ```

5. Add the following code after your `goalPS` variable declaration:

```
public ParticleSystem GoalPS
{
  get
  {
    return goalPS;
  }

  set
  {
    goalPS = value;
  }
}
```

This will allow us to access this newly created `GoalPS` variable to modify `goalPS` (our original one). The value that you see in the `set` function is a keyword that will be assigned.

Now, you may be asking why you should do this instead of making it `public`. There are two main reasons. First, we are allowed to use `get` and `set` just like a normal function. This will allow us to check the value of the variable before we actually assign something, which can be really useful if you want to make sure that a variable is within a certain range. Take a look at the following code:

```
private int health;
public int Health
{
  get
```

```
  {
    return health;
  }

  set
  {
    // Value can only be up to 100
    health = value % 100;
    if(health <= 0)
    print ("I'm dead");
  }
}
```

Also, by omitting either set or get, we can say that the variable cannot be changed outside of the class or accessed outside of the class.

For more information on properties, check out http://unity3d.com/learn/ tutorials/modules/intermediate/scripting/properties.

We will also no longer need the variables for our object references, so go ahead and *remove* the following lines in our **GameController** script:

```
[Header("Object References")]
public Transform wall;
public Transform player;
public Transform orb;
public Transform goal;
```

Now that our level is no longer being created in the GameController, let's add the functionality back to our LevelEditor. Perform the following steps:

6. Add the following function:

```
void BuildLevel()
{

  //Go through each element inside our level variable
  for (int yPos = 0; yPos < level.Length; yPos++)
  {
    for (int xPos = 0; xPos < (level[yPos]).Length; xPos++)
    {
      CreateBlock(level[yPos][xPos], xPos, level.Length -
      yPos);
    }
  }
}
```

7. We haven't created the `CreateBlock` function, so right now, it'll show up as being red, but before we add it in, we need to create some variables:

```
int xMin = 0;
int xMax = 0;
int yMin = 0;
int yMax = 0;

public List<Transform> tiles;

GameObject dynamicParent;
```

8. At this point, the `List` type will show up in red. This is because it doesn't know what we're talking about. Add the following line to our `using` statements up at the top of the file:

```
using System.Collections.Generic; // Lists
```

Lists

We used arrays previously in this book, which are containers for multiple copies of an object. One of the problems with arrays is the fact that you have to know the size (or how many elements) of the array in advance, and you cannot add or subtract elements from the array.

The list type is basically a dynamically sized array, which is to say that we can add and remove elements from it at any point that we want. It also gives us access to some nice helper functions such as `IndexOf` (which will return to us the index of an element in a list, something that can be really useful when using the index operator `[]`).

 For more information on lists, check out `http://unity3d.com/learn/tutorials/modules/intermediate/scripting/lists-and-dictionaries`.

1. Now we need to actually create our `CreateBlock` function, as follows:

```
public void CreateBlock(int value, int xPos, int yPos)
{
    Transform toCreate = null;

    // We need to know the size of our level to save later
    if(xPos < xMin)
    {
        xMin = xPos;
    }
    if(xPos > xMax)
```

```
    {
      xMax = xPos;
    }

    if(yPos < yMin)
    {
      yMin = yPos;
    }
    if(yPos > yMax)
    {
      yMax = yPos;
    }

    //If value is set to 0, we don't want to spawn anything
    if(value != 0)
    {
      toCreate = tiles[value-1];
    }

    if(toCreate != null)
    {
      //Create the object we want to create
      Transform newObject = Instantiate(toCreate, new
      Vector3(xPos, yPos,  0), Quaternion.identity) as
      Transform;

      //Give the new object the same name as ours
      newObject.name = toCreate.name;

      if(toCreate.name == "Goal")
      {
        // We want to have a reference to the particle system
        // for later
        GameController._instance.GoalPS =
        newObject.gameObject.GetComponent<ParticleSystem>();

        // Move the particle system so it'll face up
        newObject.transform.Rotate(-90,0,0);
      }

      // Set the object's parent to the DynamicObjects
      // variable so it doesn't clutter our Hierarchy
      newObject.parent = dynamicParent.transform;
    }
  }
```

2. Finally, we need to initialize all of these variables in our `Start` function, as follows:

```
public void Start()
{
    // Get the DynamicObjects object so we can make it our
    // newly created objects' parent
    dynamicParent = GameObject.Find("Dynamic Objects");
    BuildLevel();

    enabled = false;
}
```

As we used previously, the `GameObject.Find` function looks within our scene to find an object with the name Dynamic Objects. If it does not find the object, it will return `null`. It's always a good idea to make sure that the value is not `null`, or you may be wondering why something in your code doesn't work when it's a spelling error or something of that sort. It's important to note that case is important and that DynamicObjects and dynamicObjects are different! If anything is different, it will not work:

```
if(dynamicParent == null)
{
    print("Object not found! Check spelling!");
}
```

This function should be used only on seldom occasions, as it can be quite slow. For more information on `GameObject.Find`, check out `http://docs.unity3d.com/ScriptReference/GameObject.Find.html`.

Next, go back to **Inspector** and attach the `LevelEditor` script to the **GameController** object by dragging the script file on top of it. Afterward, open up the **Tiles** variable and change **Size** to 4. Then, go to the `Prefabs` folder and drag `Wall`, `Player`, `Collectible`, and `Goal` to the **Element 0**, **Element 1**, **Element 2**, and **Element 3** variables, respectively.

3. Finally, save your scene and play the game! Take a look at the following screenshot:

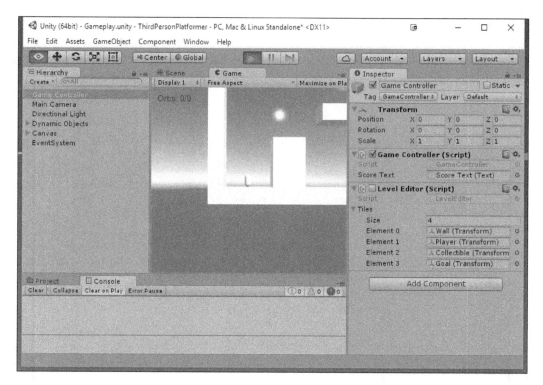

You'll note that now, the class creates our level and then turns itself off—a great start for our level editor!

Level editor – adding/removing walls at runtime

Now that our level editor will be able to load in this data, we now want to have a way to actually modify what we see onscreen. To do this, we'll need to create a GUI interface and functionality for our level editor.

1. The first thing we need to do is add a variable to keep track of what item we want to spawn:

```
// The object we are currently looking to spawn
private Transform toCreate;
```

2. Now, we need to initialize this variable inside our Start function:

```
toCreate = tiles[0];
```

3. Next, we need to update our Update function and then explain how it's working, as follows:

```
void Update()
{
    // Left click - Create object
    if (Input.GetMouseButton(0) &&
    GUIUtility.hotControl == 0)
    {
        Vector3 mousePos = Input.mousePosition;

/*
Set the position in the z axis to the
opposite of the camera's so that the position is on the world so
ScreenToWorldPoint will give us valid
values.
*/
        mousePos.z = Camera.main.transform.position.z *
        -1;

        Vector3 pos =
        Camera.main.ScreenToWorldPoint(mousePos);

        // Deal with the mouse being not exactly on a
        // block
        int posX = Mathf.FloorToInt(pos.x + .5f);
        int posY = Mathf.FloorToInt(pos.y + .5f);

        Collider[] hitColliders =
        Physics.OverlapSphere(pos, 0.45f);
        int i = 0;
        while (i < hitColliders.Length)
        {
            if (toCreate.name !=
            hitColliders[i].gameObject.name)
            {
                DestroyImmediate(hitColliders[i].gameObject);
            }
            else
            {
                // Already exists, no need to create
                // another
```

```
            return;
        }
        i++;
    }

    CreateBlock(tiles.IndexOf(toCreate) + 1, posX,
    posY);

}

// Right clicking - Delete object
if (Input.GetMouseButton(1) &&
GUIUtility.hotControl == 0)
{
    Ray ray =
    Camera.main.ScreenPointToRay
    (Input.mousePosition);

    RaycastHit hit = new RaycastHit();

    Physics.Raycast(ray, out hit, 100);

    // If we hit something other than the player
    // we want to destroy it!
    if ((hit.collider != null) &&
    (hit.collider.name != "Player"))
    {
        Destroy(hit.collider.gameObject);
    }
}
}
```

You'll note that we used something named `hotControl` when we were checking for input. The reason we did this was that whenever a player holds down a mouse button, it becomes "**hot**." No other controls are allowed to respond to mouse events while some control is "**hot**."

Once the user releases their mouse, hotControl gets set to 0 to indicate that other controls can respond to user input, which will be useful when we implement our GUI system, as we don't want to draw something when we're clicking on our mouse button.

> For more information on GUIUtility.hotControl, check out http://docs.unity3d.com/ScriptReference/ GUIUtility-hotControl.html.

A lot of the stuff contained in this code is from reusing a lot of the aspects you learned earlier in the book, back when we did our platformer game. Yet, now we are using the same functions to work with the mouse position in the world and converting it to world space.

We use the ScreenToWorldPoint function to convert our mouse position from screenspace into world space with the Z position of the point being the units away from the camera we want the position to be. Because our world is at 0, we want the Z to be negative whatever the camera's Z position is.

> For more information on ScreenToWorldPoint check out http://docs.unity3d.com/ScriptReference/ Camera.ScreenToWorldPoint.html.

We use this information to get the position we want to place the block at. Once we have this, we can just call Instantiate and create something, but we also need to make sure that we only have one object per tile, so we will use a raycast to determine if that area already has a block, and if it does, we will destroy it:

4. Now that we have all this set, let's save the file and then exit back to the Unity editor and play the game.

5. If you select the **GameController** object, you'll note that the checkbox next to the **LevelEditor** component is unchecked. This is because we disabled it in the `Start` function. We will enable it again in code later, but just for demonstration purposes, click on the checkbox to activate it once again. Then, in the **Game** tab, click on the screen and *right-click* on areas in the level. Take a look at the following screenshot:

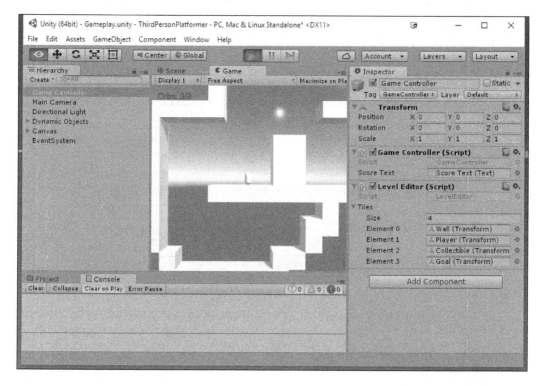

You'll note that now we can draw walls anywhere within our scene and delete anything aside from our player!

Level editor – toggling editor, GUI, and selecting additional tiles

Now that we have the basic functionality in, it wouldn't be that enjoyable if all we could do was added and remove walls. We also want to be able to spawn collectibles and change the player's starting location. Let's work on that next:

1. Back in `MonoDevelop` in the `LevelEditor` class, we're going to want to first add in an `OnGUI` function to display the types of things we can create:

```
void OnGUI()
{
  GUILayout.BeginArea(new Rect(Screen.width - 110, 20, 100,
  800));
  foreach(Transform item in tiles)
  {
    if (GUILayout.Button (item.name))
    {
      toCreate = item;

    }
  }
  GUILayout.EndArea();
}
```

2. The `OnGUI` function is called for rendering and handling GUI events using IMGUI which is a code-driven GUI system. While it was the way to create GUIs before Unity 4.6, it currently is primarily used by programmers for tools development and custom inspectors for scripts or new editors to extend Unity itself.

The anatomy of a IMGUI control

The most important concept to grasp first is the `GUILayout.Button` function. This is what we refer to as a **GUI control**, and there are many others that we will be using in the future. So, to clear up any confusion, let's talk about how all of these work now.

Creating any `GUILayout` control consists of the following:

```
ControlType(Content)
```

The parts of the preceding line of code are explained in the following sections:

ControlType

The ControlType function is a function that exists in Unity's GUI and GUILayout class, and is the name of the element that you want to create in the world. In the preceding code, we used GUILayout.Button, but there are many more.

Content

The argument for the control is the actual content that we want to display with the ControlType we are using. Right now, we're just passing in a string to display, but we can also display images and other content as well, including other controls. We will talk about other pieces of content that we can add in later.

GUI.Button

One of the most common UI elements is the Button control. This function is used to render a clickable object. If you look at the code we just wrote, you'll note that the button is cased inside of an if statement. This is because if the button is clicked on, then the function will return true when the button is released. If this is true, we will set toCreate to whatever object has that name.

GUILayout

By default, the GUILayout class will just put the buttons up at the top-left side, but we may also want our objects to be grouped together So, I specify an area that I want the menu to be in using the BeginArea function. Anything I place before I call the EndArea function will be inside that area, and GUILayout will attempt to place it in a pleasing way for me.

If you want to have precise control on where and how things are drawn, you can make use of the GUI class. However, if you do not want to manually specify a position and are okay with Unity automatically modifying the size and position of controls, you can use the GUILayout class that adds a parameter for a position.

> [For more information on IMGUI check out http://docs.unity3d. com/Manual/GUIScriptingGuide.html.]

1. Next, inside our GameController class, add the following code to our Update function (create the function as well if it doesn't exist in your current implementation, such as the example code):

```
void Update()
{
```

```
if(Input.GetKeyDown("f2"))
{
  this.gameObject.GetComponent<LevelEditor>().enabled =
  true;
}
}
```

Now, if we move back to the game and press the *F2* key, you'll see that a menu pops up, which we can then select items from. This works fine for the walls and the collectibles, but there's a bit of an issue with the player and the collectibles. Take a look at the following screenshot:

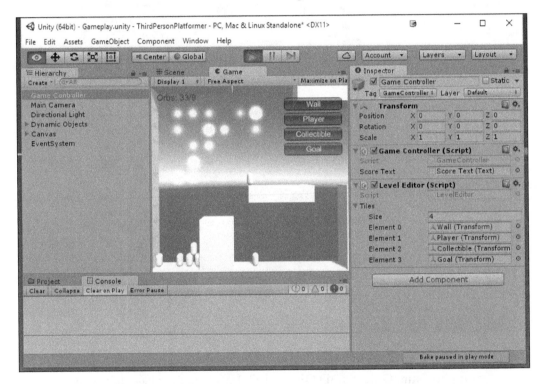

As you can see, we are spawning more players that all respond to player input, and the number of collectibles on our screen are not reflected properly in our text. We will solve both of these issues now. We will first create a new object named `PlayerSpawner`, which will act as the place where the player will start when the game starts, and make it such that we can only have one of them.

2. In **Project Browser**, select **Create | New Material**. Rename it to PlayerSpawn by clicking on the name of the material in the project browser, typing in the new name and then pressing *Enter*.

3. With the PlayerSpawn object selected, set the **Rendering Mode** to **Transparent** so that we can make the material semitransparent. Then, change the **Main Color** property to a red color with a low alpha value.

If all goes well, it should look like the following screenshot:

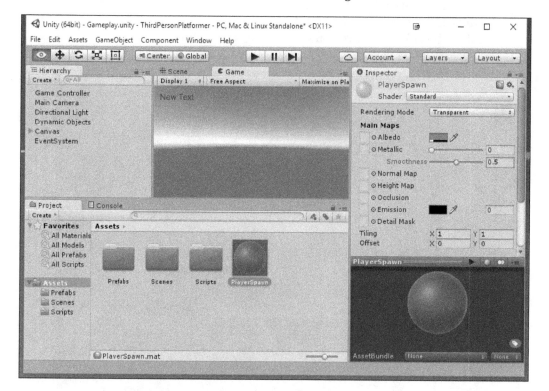

4. Now, let's create a cube to act as the visual representation of our level by going to **GameObject | 3D Object | Cube**. Once the object is created, give it a name, PlayerSpawn. Switch to the **Scene** view if you haven't so that you can see the newly created object.

5. Under the **Mesh Renderer** component, set the **Materials | Element 0** property to our newly created `PlayerSpawn` material. Take a look at the following screenshot:

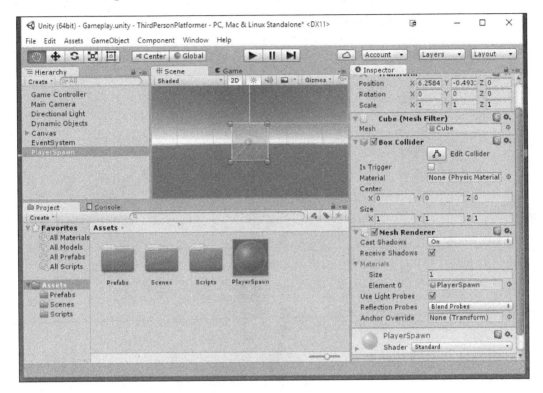

6. Next, go to the `Scripts` folder and create a new C# script named `PlayerStart`. Once that's finished, open your IDE and use the following code for the file:

```
using UnityEngine;
using System.Collections;

public class PlayerStart : MonoBehaviour
{
    //A reference to our player prefab
    public Transform player;

    //Have we spawned yet?
    public static bool spawned = false;

    public static PlayerStart _instance;

    // Use this for initialization
```

```
void Start ()
{
  // If another PlayerStart exists, this will replace it
  if(_instance != null)
    Destroy(_instance.gameObject);

  _instance = this;

  // Have we spawned yet? If not, spawn the player
  if(!spawned)
  {
    SpawnPlayer();
    spawned = true;
  }
}

void SpawnPlayer()
{
  Transform newObject = Instantiate(player,
                          this.transform.position,
                          Quaternion.identity) as
                          Transform;

  newObject.name = "Player";
}

}
```

7. Back in the editor, attach our new component to the **PlayerStart** object in **Hierarchy**. Then, back in **Inspector**, set the **Player** variable to our `Player` prefab.

8. Finally, in the **Box Collider** component, check the **Is Trigger** property.

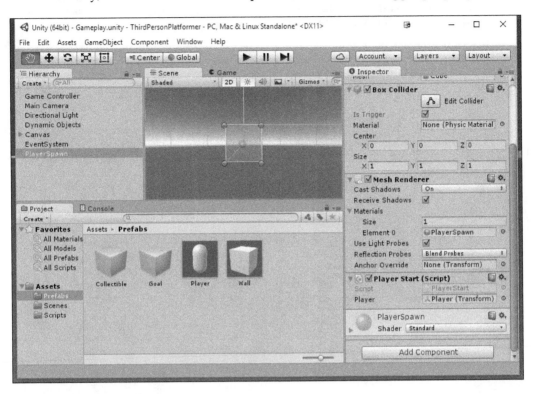

9. Now, drag the `PlayerStart` object from **Hierarchy** to the `Prefabs` folder to make it a prefab. Then, delete the object from **Hierarchy**.

10. Next, select the `GameController` object and assign the `PlayerStart` prefab where you used to see the player in **Tiles | Element 1**. Save your scene and play the game. Take a look at the following screenshot:

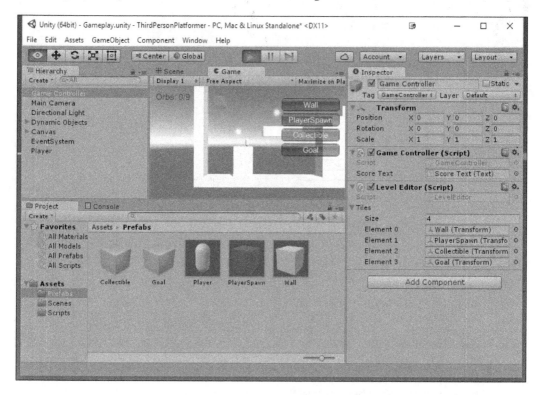

We can now select the **PlayerStart** object from the button and place it wherever we want, and there will always just be one. Also, once we have levels saving/loading, the code will properly spawn the player wherever the **PlayerStart** object is placed!

11. Now, to update the number of orbs we have in the level, we need to open **GameController** and add in a new function, as follows:

```
public void UpdateOrbTotals(bool reset = false)
{
    if (reset)
    orbsCollected = 0;

    GameObject[] orbs;
```

```
orbs = GameObject.FindGameObjectsWithTag("Orb");

orbsTotal = orbs.Length;

scoreText.text = "Orbs: " + orbsCollected + "/" +
orbsTotal;
    }
```

12. Now that we have this function written, we need to call it every time we do something to modify our level. Go to the `LevelEditor` class and add the following line to the end of our `Start` function:

```
GameController._instance.UpdateOrbTotals(true);
```

13. Then, inside the `Update` function, we'll need to add the following lines in bold:

```
void Update()
{
    // Left click - Create object
    if (Input.GetMouseButton(0) &&
    GUIUtility.hotControl == 0)
    {
        Vector3 mousePos = Input.mousePosition;

/*
Set the position in the z axis to the
opposite of the camera's so that the position is on the
world so ScreenToWorldPoint will give us valid
values.
*/
        mousePos.z = Camera.main.transform.position.z *
        -1;

        Vector3 pos =
        Camera.main.ScreenToWorldPoint(mousePos);

        // Deal with the mouse being not exactly on a
        // block
        int posX = Mathf.FloorToInt(pos.x + .5f);
        int posY = Mathf.FloorToInt(pos.y + .5f);

        Collider[] hitColliders =
        Physics.OverlapSphere(pos, 0.45f);
        int i = 0;
        while (i < hitColliders.Length)
        {
```

```
                    if (toCreate.name !=
                    hitColliders[i].gameObject.name)
                    {
                        DestroyImmediate(hitColliders[i]
                        .gameObject);
                    }
                    else
                    {
                        // Already exists, no need to create
                        // another
                        return;
                    }
                    i++;
                }


            CreateBlock(tiles.IndexOf(toCreate) + 1, posX,
            posY);

            GameController._instance.UpdateOrbTotals();
        }


        // Right clicking - Delete object
        if (Input.GetMouseButton(1) &&
        GUIUtility.hotControl == 0)
        {
            Ray ray =
            Camera.main.ScreenPointToRay
            (Input.mousePosition);

            RaycastHit hit = new RaycastHit();

            Physics.Raycast(ray, out hit, 100);

            // If we hit something other than the player, we
            // want to destroy it!
            if ((hit.collider != null) &&
            (hit.collider.name != "Player"))
            {
                Destroy(hit.collider.gameObject);
            }

            GameController._instance.UpdateOrbTotals();
        }


    }
```

14. Save the file, save your project, and start the game. Press *F2* to open our menu and then draw. Take a look at the following screenshot:

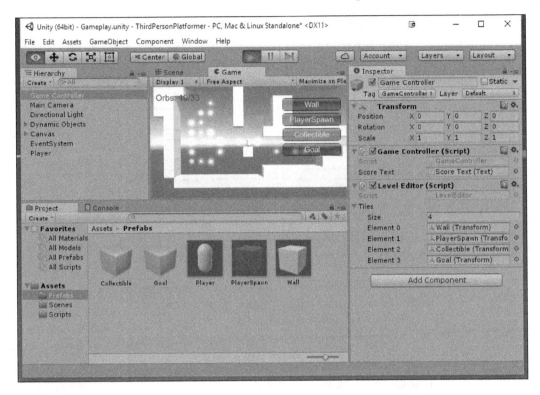

As you can see, we're now able to draw over the other object and place everything that we want for our level!

Level editor – saving/loading levels to file

Now that we have the groundwork all placed and ready, let's get to the real meat of the level editor: saving and loading! Perform the following steps:

1. Open our `LevelEditor` class in your IDE. The first step will be to include some additional functionality at the beginning of our file:

```
//You must include these namespaces
//to use BinaryFormatter
using System;
using System.Runtime.Serialization.Formatters.Binary;
using System.IO;
```

2. The first thing we'll want to add is a variable, as follows:

```
private string levelName = "Level1";
```

3. Now, we'll need to add the following code to the OnGUI function:

```
GUILayout.BeginArea(new Rect(10, 20, 100, 100));
levelName = GUILayout.TextField(levelName);
if (GUILayout.Button ("Save"))
{
  SaveLevel();
}
if (GUILayout.Button ("Load"))
{
  //If we have a file with the name typed in, load it!
  if(File.Exists(Application.persistentDataPath + "/" +
  levelName + ".lvl"))
  {
    LoadLevelFile(levelName);
    PlayerStart.spawned = false;

    // We need to wait one frame before UpdateOrbTotals
    // will work (Orbs need to have Tag assigned)
    StartCoroutine(LoadedUpdate());
  }
  else
  {
    levelName = "Error";
  }
}
if (GUILayout.Button ("Quit"))
{
  enabled = false;
}
GUILayout.EndArea();
```

4. We are missing some of these functions, so let's start with SaveLevel, as follows:

```
void SaveLevel()
{
  List<string> newLevel = new List<string>();

  for(int i = yMin; i <= yMax; i++)
  {
    string newRow = "";
```

```
for(int j = xMin; j <= xMax; j++)
{
  Vector3 pos = new Vector3(j, i, 0);
  Ray ray = Camera.main.ScreenPointToRay(pos);
  RaycastHit hit = new RaycastHit();

  Physics.Raycast(ray, out hit, 100);

  // Will check if there is something hitting us within
  // a distance of .1
  Collider[] hitColliders = Physics.OverlapSphere(pos,
  0.1f);

  if(hitColliders.Length > 0)
  {
    // Do we have a tile with the same name as this
    // object?
    for(int k = 0; k < tiles.Count; k++)
    {
      // If so, let's save that to the string
      if(tiles[k].name ==
      hitColliders[0].gameObject.name)
      {
        newRow += (k+1).ToString() + ",";
      }
    }
  }
  else
  {
    newRow += "0,";
  }
}
newRow += "\n";
newLevel.Add(newRow);
}
// Reverse the rows to make the final version rightside
// up
newLevel.Reverse();

string levelComplete = "";

foreach(string level in newLevel)
{
```

```
            levelComplete += level;
        }
        // This is the data we're going to be saving
        print(levelComplete);

        //Save to a file
        BinaryFormatter bFormatter = new BinaryFormatter();
        FileStream file =
        File.Create(Application.persistentDataPath + "/"+
        levelName + ".lvl");
        bFormatter.Serialize (file, levelComplete);
        file.Close ();

    }
```

To do this, we will go through the map, see what tiles are at a certain place, and add them to a string for each column using a list to store each of the rows. Then, we put them all together into a single string, which we could just store in `PlayerPrefs`.

However, instead of using the `PlayerPrefs` class as we did before, we will store our data in an actual file using the `FileStream` class.

FileStreams

To determine where to save our file, we will use the `Application.persistentDataPath` variable. This value will point to something differently, depending on what platform you're working with. For instance, on a Windows 8 computer, it will save to `C:\Users\YOUR_USER_NAME\AppData\LocalLow\COMPANY_NAME\PROJECT_NAME`. For more information, check out `http://docs.unity3d.com/ScriptReference/Application-persistentDataPath.html`.

For more information on `FileStreams`, check out the Microsoft Developers Network's page on it at `http://msdn.microsoft.com/en-us/library/system.io.filestream(v=vs.110).aspx`.

BinaryFormatter

We don't want the file to be easy to read, so we'll use the `BinaryFormatter` class, which will convert our object into a byte array and be a stream of bytes, which will be much harder for potential hackers to read.

For more information on the `BinaryFormatter` class, check out the Microsoft Developers Network's page on it at `http://msdn.microsoft.com/en-us/library/system.runtime.serialization.formatters.binary.binaryformatter(v=vs.110).aspx`.

1. Now we need to add in the following functions to load the file that we'll be creating from the save functionality:

```
void LoadLevelFile(string level)
{
  // Destroy everything inside our currently level that's
  // created dynamically
  foreach(Transform child in dynamicParent.transform) {
    Destroy(child.gameObject);
  }

  BinaryFormatter bFormatter = new BinaryFormatter();
  FileStream file =
  File.OpenRead(Application.persistentDataPath + "/"+ level
  + ".lvl");

  // Convert the file from a byte array into a string
  string levelData = bFormatter.Deserialize(file) as
  string;

  // We're done working with the file so we can close it
  file.Close ();

  LoadLevelFromString(levelData);

  // Set our text object to the current level.
  levelName = level;
}

  public void LoadLevelFromString(string content)
  {
    // Split our string by the new lines (enter)
    List <string> lines = new List <string> (content.Split
('\n'));
    // Place each block in order in the correct x and y
    // position
    for(int i = 0; i < lines.Count; i++)
    {
      string[] blockIDs = lines[i].Split (',');
```

```
      for(int j = 0; j < blockIDs.Length - 1; j++)
      {
        CreateBlock(int.Parse(blockIDs[j]), j, lines.Count
        - i);
      }
    }
  }
```

2. Finally, we need to add in `LoadedUpdate` so that `Orbs` will be updated after they've been created, as follows:

```
IEnumerator LoadedUpdate()
{
  //returning 0 will make it wait 1 frame
  yield return 0;

  GameController._instance.UpdateOrbTotals(true);
}
```

3. **Save** the file and exit the editor. Save the project and play the game! Take a look at the following screenshot:

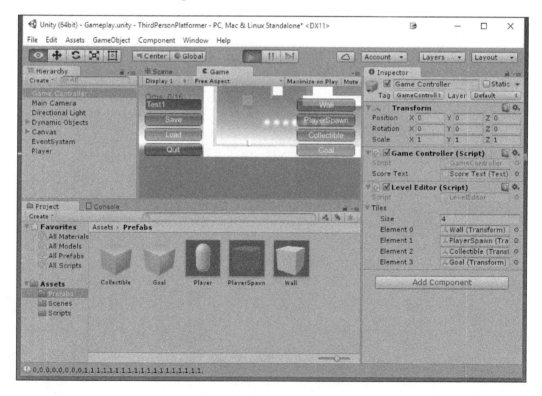

As you can see, when we play the game you'll see a new menu appear on the left-hand side? We can now give a name to all of our files that we want, type in their name, hit **Save** to save it to a file, and **Load** to load the data for the level if it exists! Finally, we can click on **Quit** to exit out of the editor whenever we want.

Take a look at the following screenshot:

As you can see here, the files are saved in our `Application.persistentDataPath` location (print it out to know exactly where it is)!

Summary

We now have an in-game level editor and explored some of the various ways in which it's possible to save data inside Unity! This knowledge, plus exposure to the list class and IMGUI, should leave you ready to add additional functionality, such as this, to all of your future projects!

Challenges

For those of you who want to do more with this project, there are still plenty of things you can do, especially after finishing the rest of this book. Here are some ideas to get your mind thinking:

- In the same way that we can only create one `PlayerStart`, change it so that we can only place one goal! In that same line of thinking, have the player start to be invisible when we are playing the game!

- In our first-person "shooter" game, save the player's **Position** and **Rotation** so that whenever you quit and resume the game, you start off where you were!

- Now that we have the new level editor working, change the system so that we start the game loading a level from a file instead of from the provided array!

- You may notice that at some places, collectibles are placed on top of one another. Now, this doesn't really hurt levels loaded, as when you save the level, it will only place one of them. However, should you want to fix this, you can just change the collider from a sphere collider to a box collider, as in the corners, it's not detecting that it's colliding.

- There are other additional ways to save files, such as using XML. For an example of this check out the Unity Wiki at `http://wiki.unity3d.com/index.php?title=Saving_and_Loading_Data:_XmlSerializer`.

11
Finishing Touches

We've come a long way, and now we have a series of completed projects! But, taking the time to get these projects out into the world is just as important. Playing the game in the editor is nice and all, but actually getting the game as its own standalone version has a special feel to it that you can't duplicate in the editor.

And once you get the game published, you can just give someone a `.zip` file with your game, but you spent quality time on your project and want to give it the respect that it deserves.

People note the polish that you put into your game and the little things, such as an installer, can help to get players into the mood of your project early on and see your game as a professional title.

Project overview

In this chapter, you are going to learn all about exporting our game from Unity and then creating an installer so that we can give it to all of our friends, family, and prospective customers!

Your objectives

This project will be split into a number of tasks. It will be a simple step-by-step process from beginning to end. Here is the outline of our tasks:

- Setting up the build settings
- Customizing your exported project via the player settings
- Building an installer for Windows

Prerequisites

In this chapter, we will be using one of the projects that we created in the previous chapters, specifically the `Twinstick Shooter` project that we worked on in *Chapter 1, 2D Twin-Stick Shooter*, and *Chapter 2, Creating GUIs*. You may continue with your previous projects or pick up a copy along with the assets for this chapter from the example code provided for this book on Packt Publishing's website at `https://www.packtpub.com/books/content/support`.

In addition, the complete project and source files are located there for you to check whether you have any questions or need clarification.

Setting up the build settings

There are many times during development that you may want to see what your game looks like if you build it outside of the editor. It can give you a sense of accomplishment; I know, I felt that way the first time I pushed a build to a console devkit. Whether it's for PC, Mac, Linux, web player, mobile, or console, we all have to go through the same menu, the **Build Settings** menu. We perform the following steps:

1. We are going to first open our `Twinstick Shooter` project that we created back in *Chapter 1, 2D Twin-Stick Shooter*, *Chapter 2, Creating GUIs*. Open up your main menu scene (in the example code, it is saved as `Main_Menu`). Take a look at the following screenshot:

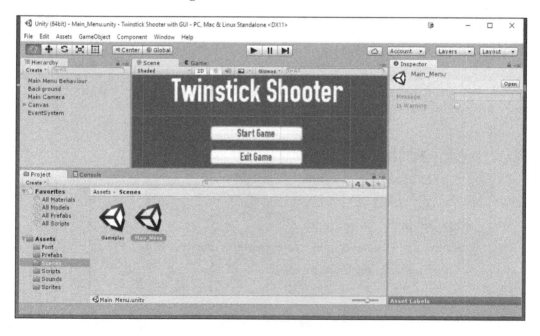

2. To access our **Build Settings** menu, we will need to navigate to **File | Build Settings** from the top menu (or press *Ctrl + Shift + B*). Take a look at the following screenshot:

Build Settings	x

Scenes In Build

☑ Scenes/Main_Menu.unity   0
☑ Scenes/Gameplay.unity   1

`Add Open Scenes`

Platform

   Web Player   PC, Mac & Linux Standalone

   PC, Mac & Linux Standalone ◀   Target Platform   `Windows` ⬍
                                Architecture   `x86` ⬍
   iOS   Development Build   ☐
                                  Autoconnect Profiler   ☐
   Android   Script Debugging   ☐

   BlackBerry

   Tizen

   Xbox 360

`Switch Platform`   `Player Settings...`   `Build`   `Build And Run`

3. If you have been following thoroughly from *Chapter 2, Creating GUIs*, you should see two icons in the **Scenes In Build** section. If you have not, click on the **Add Open Scenes** button for each level.

Another way to add levels to your build is to just drag and drop them from the project browser. It's also important to note that you can also drag them around to order them however you want. The level that is at index 0 will be the one that the game starts with.

4. Once you're ready, select a platform from the bottom-left corner menu. The Unity logo shows which one you're currently compiling for. We're going to compile for Windows now, so if it is currently not set to **PC, Mac, and Linux Standalone**, select that, and click on the **Switch Platform** button if needed.

5. Once you have all this set up, click on the **Build** button. Once this is done, it will ask you for a name and a location to put the game in. I'm going to name it `TwinstickShooter` and put it in an `Export` folder located in the same directory as the `Assets` and `Library` folder. Afterward, hit **Save**. Take a look at the following screenshot:

6. You may need to wait a bit, but as soon as it finishes, it will open up the folder with your new game. Take a look at the following screenshot:

When building for Windows, you should get something like the preceding screenshot. We have the executable, but we also have a data folder that contains all the assets for our application (right now called TwinstickShooter_Data). You must include the data folder with your game, or it will not run. This is a slight pain, but later on in this chapter, we will create an installer so that we can put it on a computer without any hassle.

If you build for Mac, it will bundle the app and data all together, so once you export it, all you need to give people is the application.

 If you are interested in submitting your Mac game to the Mac App Store, there is a nice tutorial about doing just that at http://www.conlanrios.com/2013/12/signing-unity-game-for-mac-app-store.html.

If you *double-click* on the .exe file to run the game, you'll be brought to the following startup menu, as shown in the following screenshot:

Twinstick Shooter Configuration		⬓	✕

Graphics	Input

Screen resolution	1024 x 768 ⌄	☑ Windowed
Graphics quality	Fantastic ⌄	
Select monitor	Display 2 ⌄	

	Play!	Quit

This will allow players to customize their **Screen Resolution** values as well as other options, such as what buttons to use for input. I personally feel that this menu makes projects look more unprofessional, so I'll be teaching you how to remove this as well.

Anyway, once we click on the **Play!** button, we'll be taken to the proper game screen, as shown in the following screenshot:

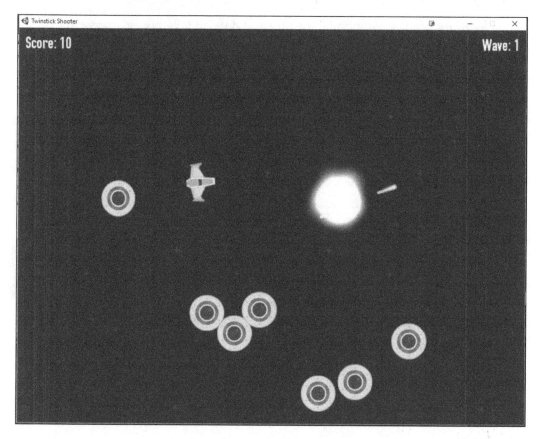

And it's working great. We can work at any resolution that we choose, and all the menus are functioning as well!

 For more information on publishing and specific things to look out for, check out the following link: `http://docs.unity3d.com/Manual/PublishingBuilds.html`

Customizing your exported project via the player settings

Now that we know what happens by default, let's take some time to customize the project to make it look as nice as possible. The **PlayerSettings** section is where we can define different parameters for each platform that we want to put the game onto. We perform the following steps:

1. To open the player settings, you can either click on the **Player Settings...** button from the **Build Settings** menu or navigate to **Edit | Project Settings | Player**. Take a look at the following screenshot:

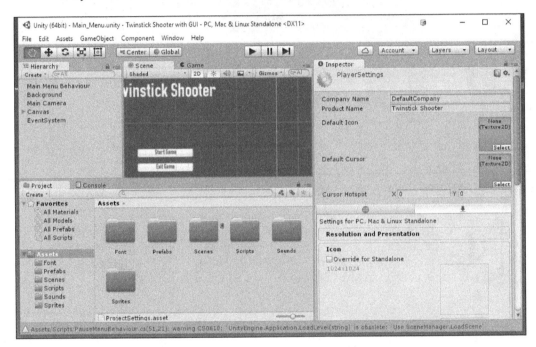

The player settings are actually shown in the **Inspector** tab. There are some key properties at the top, which are cross-platform, which means that they will apply to all platforms (or rather, that they will be the defaults that you can later override).

2. Now, in the `Example Code` folder, you'll find a `cursor_hand` image. Drag and drop that image to the **Assets/Sprites** location of the project browser. Once there, select the image, and in the **Inspector** tab, change the **Texture Type** value to `Cursor`.

3. Then, in the **PlayerSettings** section, drag and drop the **cursor_hand** image into the **Default Cursor** property and the **playerShip** image into the **Default Icon** property. Take a look at the following screenshot:

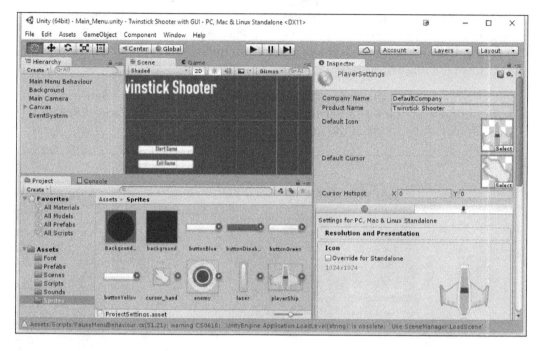

 If you want your game to have multiple cursors or change cursors at runtime, the Cursor.SetCursor function will be quite helpful. For more information on this, check out http://docs.unity3d.com/ScriptReference/Cursor.SetCursor.html.

4. On your computer, in the `Example Code` folder, move the `ConfigBanner` image into the `Sprites` folder. Then, under **PlayerSettings**, click on the **Splash Image** section to open the **Config Dialog Banner** property, which you should set to our newly imported image:

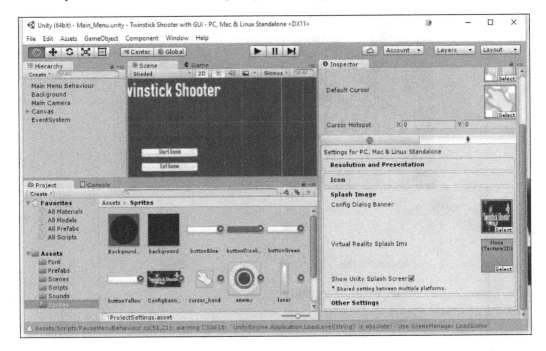

> If you want to create a config dialog banner of your own, the maximum image size is 432 x 163 pixels. The image will not be scaled up to fit the screen selector. Instead, it will be centered and cropped.

5. Next, you'll need to decide whether you want to display the display resolution dialog or not. If you want to keep it, skip this step. Otherwise, open up the **Resolution and Presentation** section, and under **Standalone Player Options**, set the **Display Resolution Dialog** value to `Disabled`.

6. Having finished this, navigate to **File | Save Project** and build the game once more, overwriting the previously created one. Depending on your choice, you'll see the menu shown in the following screenshot:

Twinstick Shooter Configuration

Twinstick Shooter

Graphics Input

Screen resolution	1024 x 768	☑ Windowed
Graphics quality	Fantastic	
Select monitor	Display 2	

Play!   Quit

Or just jump straight into the game.

The game already looks much better and more polished than earlier! There are a number of other things that you can do, such as restrict the kind of aspect ratios your game runs or resolutions, or force windowed, or full screen. I leave it to you to play around and get your project as nice as possible before moving onward!

> For more information on the properties for all the different platforms that are available, check out http://docs.unity3d.com/Manual/class-PlayerSettings.html.

Building an installer for Windows

Just as I mentioned previously, having a separate `Data` folder with our `.exe` file is somewhat of a pain. Rather than give people a `.zip` file and hope that they extract it all and then keep everything in the same folder, I will make the process automatic and give the person an opportunity to have it installed just like a professional game. With that in mind, I'm going to go over a free way to create a Windows installer, as follows:

1. The first thing we need to do is get our setup program. For our demonstration, I will be using Jordan Russell's Inno Setup software. Go to `http://jrsoftware.org/isinfo.php` and *click* on the **Download Inno Setup** link. Take a look at the following screenshot:

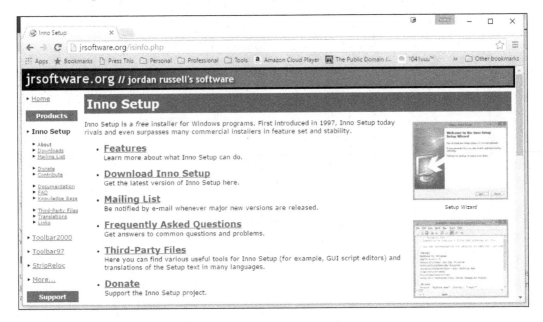

2. From there, click on the **Stable Release** button and select the **isetup-5.5.8.exe** file. Once it's finished, *double-click* on the executable to open it, clicking on the **Run** button. If it shows a security warning message, click on **Yes** to allow the changes to take place. Take a look at the following screenshot:

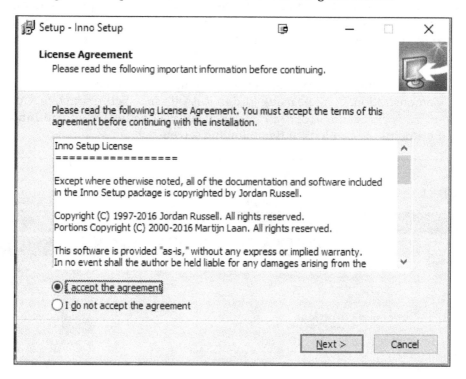

3. From there, run through the installation, making sure to uncheck the **Install Inno Setup Preprocessor** option since we won't be using it. Upon finishing this task, make sure that **Launch Inno Setup** is checked and then click on the **Finish** button.

4. When you open the program, it will look somewhat like the following screenshot:

5. From there, choose **Create a new script file using the Script Wizard** and then click on **OK**.

6. From there, click on the **Next** button, and you'll come to the **Application Information** section. Fill in your information and then click on **Next**. Take a look at the following screenshot:

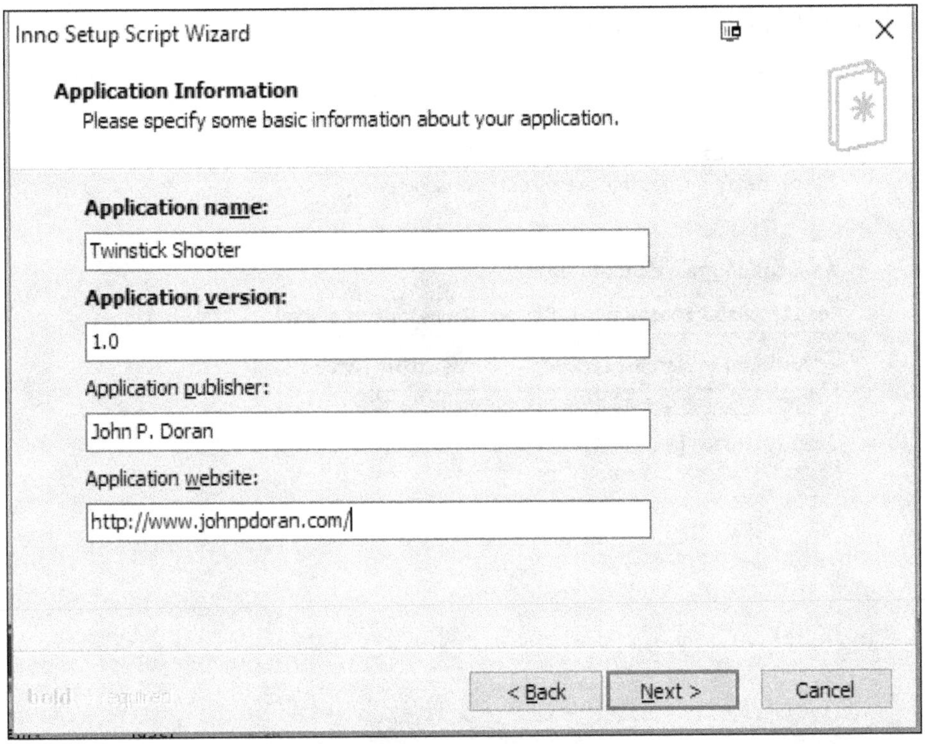

7. Next, you'll come to some information about the application folder. In general, you will not want to change this information, so I will click on **Next**.

8. From here, we'll be brought to the **Application Files** section where we need to specify the files we want to install. Under the **Application main executable file:** section, click on **Browse** to go to the location of your `Export` folder where the `.exe` file is present, select it, and click on **Open**. Take a look at the following screenshot:

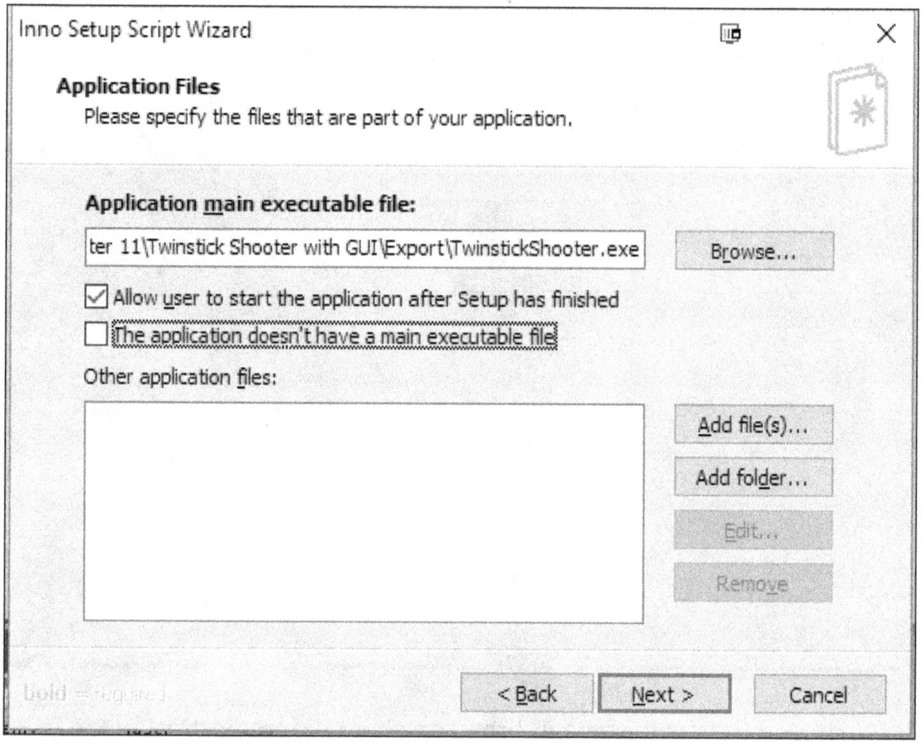

9. Now, we need to add in the data folder. Click on the **Add Folder...** button, select the data folder, and click on **OK**. Take a look at the following screenshot:

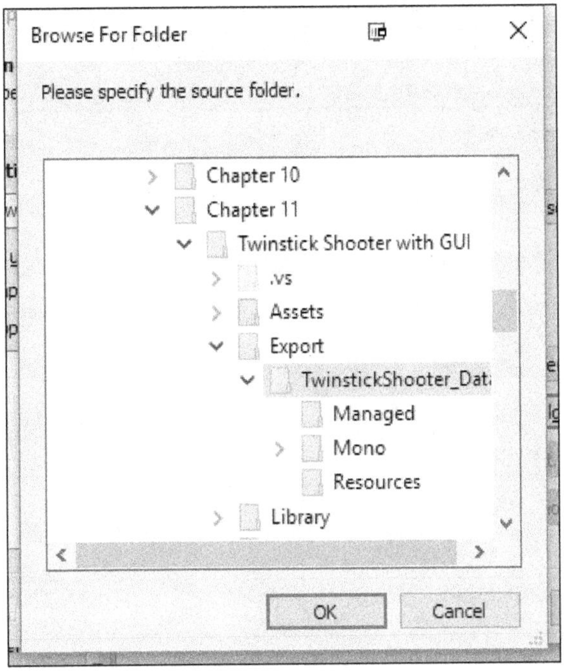

10. It will then ask if files in subfolders should be included as well. Select **Yes**. Then, select the folder in the **Other Applications file** section and click on the **Edit** button. From there, set the **Destination subfolder** property to the same name as your data folder and click on **OK**. Take a look at the following screenshot:

11. Finally, click on the **Add Files** option, select the two `player_win_x86` files, and select **Open** for them as well, then click on **Next**.

12. In the next menu, check whichever options you want and then click on **Next**.

13. Now, you'll have an option to include a license file, such as EULA or whatever your publisher may require, and any personal stuff you want to tell your users before or after installation. The program accepts `.txt` and `.rtf` files. Once you're ready, click on the **Next** button.

14. Next, they'll allow you to specify what languages you want the installation to work for. I'll just go for English, but you can add more. Afterward, click on **Next**.

15. Finally, we need to set where we want the setup to be placed as well as the icon for it or a password. I created a new folder on my desktop named `TwinstickSetup` and used it. Then, click on **Next**, as shown in the following screenshot:

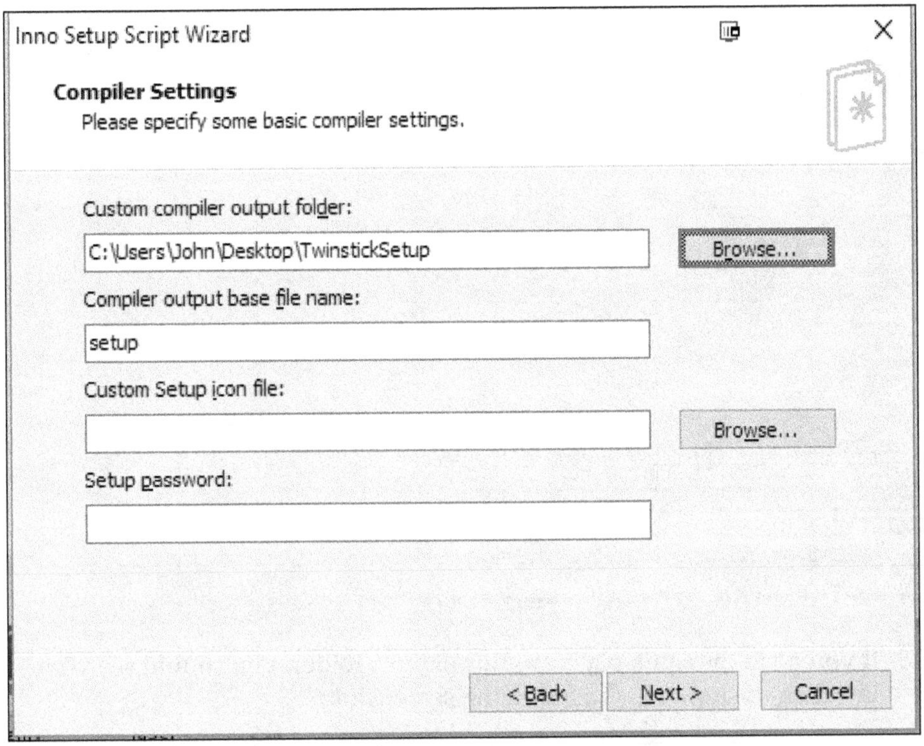

> [✎ If you want to include a custom icon but don't have a `.ico` file, you can use the `http://www.icoconverter.com/` link.]

16. Next, you'll be brought to the successfully completed script wizard screen. After this, click on **Finish**. Take a look at the following screenshot:

17. Now, it will ask you if you want to compile the script. Select **Yes**. It'll also ask you if you want to save your script. You'll also want to say **Yes**, and I saved it to the same folder as my exporting folder. It'll take a minute or two, but as soon as you see **Finished** in the console window, it should be ready. Take a look at the following screenshot:

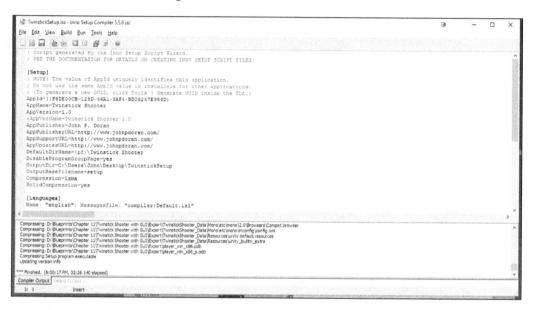

18. If you go to the same place as your Export folder, you should see your installer, as shown in the following screenshot:

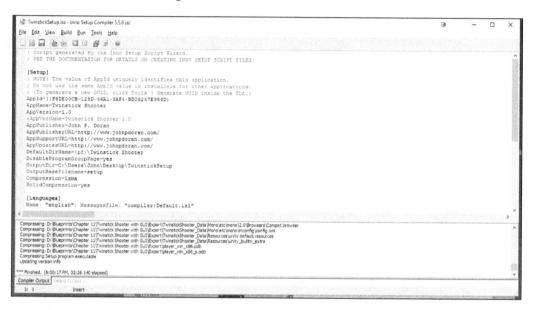

19. If you run it, it'll look somewhat like the following screenshot:

And with that, we now have a working installer for our game!

Summary

Our game has now been compiled with the possibility of running on multiple platforms (including the Web), and you have learned how to create an installer for Windows! This information will serve you quite well when you create projects of your own to get them out to as many people as possible!

Challenges

For those of you who want to do more with this project, there are still plenty of things you can do. Here are some ideas to get your mind thinking:

- There are still a number of things you can do with Inno Setup. You may wish to do more things, such as change the image on the right-hand side of the installer welcome screen. For more information on this, check out the documentation for Inno Setup at `http://jrsoftware.org/ishelp/`.

- Now that you know how to export to PC, Mac, and Linux, you can try exporting your game to Android as well! You'll need to have the Android SDK and a few other things to take into consideration, but it's not too bad at all. For more information on doing Android development, check out `http://docs.unity3d.com/Manual/android-GettingStarted.html`.

- You may also be interested in getting your game onto iOS. For information on iOS, check out `http://docs.unity3d.com/Manual/iphone-GettingStarted.html`.

Index

CPSIA information can be obtained
at www.ICGtesting.com
Printed in the USA
FSHW022056310821
84277FS

9 781785 883118